LETTERS ON

DEMONOLOGY
AND
WITCHCRAFT

LETTERS ON
DEMONOLOGY
AND
WITCHCRAFT

By Sir Walter Scott

With a new Introduction and Notes by
RAYMOND LAMONT BROWN

New York: THE CITADEL PRESS

Introduction: by RAYMOND LAMONT BROWN

The works of Sir Walter Scott are so steeped in references to witchcraft and demonology, that it is not surprising he wrote a book entirely concerning the subject. He was invited to contribute some stories, which were to be published by John Murray as part of a series. This series of books, which appeared between 1829-1847, ultimately formed an eighty volume set known as *Murray's Family Library*. At five shillings per copy, the books were designed to secure for the public a wide selection of good literature, during a time of effort to redress social and economic evils, which were to culminate in the Reform Bill of 1832.

Letters on Demonology and Witchcraft is a work of consequence on the supernatural, and no less important still, as it tells us, indirectly, much about Sir Walter Scott the man. Here are revealed hints of the many facets of Scott's life and labours; he tackled the research for the book with the practicability, sober calculation and the diligent labour he had inherited from his father and the law, enriched throughout by the obsession for legends and folk-lore inspired by his mother.

The proclivities of Walter Scott as a boy towards the oral tradition of his beloved Borderland, are seen in the *Demonology*. As he lived for several years with his grandparents (he was sent to them as a baby, from Edinburgh, after suffering from an attack of infantile paralysis), he quickly acquired an " older " outlook and from their lips heard the lisp of Border ballads which remained with him all his life.

Walter Scott was as in love with the supernatural as he was with the triple peaks of Eildon and the old Border keeps, peopled, the old folks said, with a motley of ghostly figures of a bygone age. Born in 1771, Scott was too young to have witnessed such trials as that of Elspeth Ross, the last person tried by the Scottish Court of Judiciary in 1709 on the general charge of being a notorious witch, but he noted fact after fact as he came across them of the four thousand four hundred or so witches who died at the stake in Scotland.

The law against witchcraft in Scotland included certain distinctive features and witches, although most of them were in fact too poor to take advantage of the privilege, were permitted to retain Counsel. High on the hills of Tweeddale, Scott held mock Courts defending imaginary witches to his heart's content, and when tired of that listened to the ewe-milkers and cow-baillies tell the stories of Scottish demons and " whigmaleeries "; his encyclopaedic memory storing every fact to be mirrored again some fifty years later in his *Demonology*.

Although a Jacobite in sentiment, Scott was controlled by a direct realist and even rational outlook, and his treatment of the supernatural in the *Demonology* shows that he was of the Age of Hume. In religion, Letter VIII reveals that the Anglican ritual appealed to Scott more than the memories he held of the Kirk of his youth.

For all the pressures of decay and self-inflicted hard work, the *Demonology* contains passages as worthy as those of his heyday. Even today this largely unregarded work is worth the time and trouble of the general reader to seek out for enjoyment, no less than as a mirror of the true Walter Scott.

NOTES

Page 10, line 18:
Robert Pitcairn, *Criminal Trials in Scotland from AD 1488 to 1624,* Maitland Club, Edinburgh, 1883.

Page 11:
While taking an, in the main, non-partisan attitude toward the discussion of Demonology, Sir Walter Scott was a superstitious man. As late as 1814, a woman called Bessie Millie, of Stromness, S.W. mainland of Orkney, sold winds ("Winds by the Devil's help to Sea-men "); Sir Walter bought one and recorded the fact in his diary.

Page 11, lines 21-22:
Non omnis moriar—I shall not wholly die.

Page 17, line 2:
Platonists; those who adhered to the philosophy of Plato, 427-347 BC, the great Athenian philosopher. He founded a school at Athens under the name of the Academy, where he taught philosophy and mathematics. His great work is the *Dialogues* which includes the *Republic,* the longest and most celebrated prose piece of them all. Joseph Addison, 1672-1719, pointed out:

> "It was an opinion of the Platonists that the souls of men, having contracted in the body great stains and pollutions of vice and ignorance, there were several purgations and cleansings necessary to be passed through both here and hereafter, in order to refine and purify them."

Page 17, line 22:
Castor and Pollux, the Dioscuri, the twin Heroes. According to Homer they were sons of Leda, daughter of Thestius, and King Tyndareus of Sparta. Neptune (Poseidon) gave them power over wind and wave, and thus they were worshipped as protectors of sailors. Regarded as inventors of the war-dance, they were the patrons of bards, and presided at the Spartan games. In art they are usually represented as mounted on magnificent white

horses, carrying spears and star-mounted helmets. The worship of the Dioscuri spread from Sparta.

Page 18, line 16:
Historia verdadera de la Conquista de la Nueva España, written by Bernal Diaz, a native of Medina del Campo, in Old Castile. Born in 1514, he began his soldier's career under Cordova.

Page 18, line 18:
Hernando Cortez (or Cortes), 1488-1547, a Spanish adventurer. Captured and held Mexico for Spain for ten years.

Page 18, line 20:
Crónica de la Nueva España (this work appeared first at Medina in 1553, thence at Antwerp) was written by Francisco Lopez de Gomara, a native of Seville, chaplain to Cortez.

Page 18, line 21:
Saint Iago: See, W. H. Prescott's *History of the Conquest of Mexico* (Allen & Unwin, 1929) for his appearance in battle, page 392 and the notes on 136 and 420 of that book.

Page 18, line 29:
Francisco de Morla, one of Cortez's "select corps."

Page 20, line 26:
Lion of Percy; from the armorial bearings of the Percys, whose family were the Dukes of Northumberland.

Page 22, line 11:
Tale of a Tub, Johnathan Dean Swift, 1667-1745.

Page 22, line 36:
Blue Devils; a slang phrase for dejection. Also applied to *delirium tremens* from the apparitions which habitual drunkards are supposed to see.

Page 25, lines 3-6:
For a modern approach to the subject see: *Drugs and the Mind*, Robert S. de Ropp, Gollancz 1957.

Page 25, line 7:
See John Ferriar, 1761-1815, various writings such as "*Of Popular Illusions and more particularly of Modern Demonology.*"

Page 27, line 14:
Forres; the heath around the municipal burgh and market town of Forres on the river Findhorn, Scotland. This region is the scene of part of Shakespeare's *Macbeth*.

Page 31, line 18:
Alain René Le Sage, 1668-1747, dramatist of note and author of the famous stories *Gil Blas* and *Le Diable Boiteux.*

Page 32, line 30:
Beau Nash: Richard Nash, 1674-1762, was so fond of indulging in the gay life and fancy clothes that his friends suspected him of being a highwayman to eke out his meagre means.

Page 37, line 6:
Eidolon; a likeness, image or representation; a shade or spectre, or apparition (See; Poe's works).

Page 40, lines 21-22:
Milton, from *Comus*, 1.195, the Oxford edition gives:
". . . And airy tongues that syllable men's names
   On sands, and shores, and desert wildernesses."

Page 41, line 3:
Obi (or Obeah) women, those who practice a type of magical art or witchcraft among certain African tribes.

Page 42, line 4:
Types of "Wild Huntsman" are found in legend all over Central Europe, Denmark, Holland, Belgium and N.E. France; based on the idea that the dead ride the night wind and vent their spite on the living; i.e., it is not particularly Teutonic in origin.

Page 43, lines 32-33:
Quote from Titus Lucretius Carus: 99-55 BC:
Ut si forte manu, quam vis jam corporis, ipse Tute tibi partem ferias, aeque experiare.

As you might try for yourself now if you strike any part of your body with your hand.

(De Rerum Natura. II 440-441)

Page 44, line 32:

John (or Sir John) Barleycorn was a humorous personification of the spirit of barley, or malt liquor. Although the use of the name is lost in antiquity, Robert Burns used it as a pseudonym in his " Address of the Scottish Distillers to the Rt. Hon. William Pitt " which appeared in *The Gazetteer and New Daily Advertiser;* a complaint against the liquor tax.

Page 45, lines 2-4:

This refers to John Aubrey, F.R.S.'s citing of Propertius *(mansit odor; posses scire fuisse Deam—* rough translation, " she left, in the place where she had been, a sweet perfume, so that it might be known that a goddess passed that way ") when coming to the conclusion that a ghost which appeared near Chichester in the year 1670 was a good spirit: " . . . being demanded whether a good spirit, or a bad?, returned no answer, but disappeared with a curious and most melodious twang."

LETTER II

Page 50, lines 24-25:

Sir Thomas Overbury, 1581-1613, a poet and victim of Court intrigue.

Simon Forman, 1552-1611, astrologer and general charlatan, suspected of using witchcraft to further his ends:

> " This year (1579) I did profecie the truth of many thinges which afterwardes cam to passe, and the verie spirits were subjecte unto me; what I spake was done . . . (1581) I tok a house in Sarum on the dich by the skinner, and ther I dwelte practising physick and surgery . . . (1588) This yeare I began to practise necromancy, and to calle aungells and spirits . . . "

(vi)

Page 53, line 12 *passim*

Most believers in witchcraft during this period, sought justification for their beliefs in the Bible. The so-called Witch of Endor in I Samuel XXVIII, shows how Saul, wishing to destroy the Philistine army consulted a medium. Following, almost the lines of a modern séance, Saul supposedly heard the voice of Samuel through some ventriloquial expertise on the part of the medium. The Latin Vulgate calls such a woman a *pythonissa,* or *mulier pythonem habens,* and the Greek Septuagint translates the Hebrew *ôbh* as *heggastramythos* (ventriloquist). Such was the Witch of Endor.

Page 72, line 29:

The Rev. Cotton Mather, 1662-1728, investigated many cases of sorcery and was instrumental in bringing culprits to punishment, he reflected the prejudices of his age. See: *Magnalia Christi* (London 1702).

LETTER III

Page 77, line 1:

Zoroaster; This is the Greek form of the name of the *Circa* seventh century prophet Zarathustra. A monotheist, he believed in one good and holy god, Ahura Mazda. His teachings today survive amongst the Parsees of India.

Page 78, line 17:

Thomas Pennant, 1726-1798, traveller and naturalist. In 1771 published his *Tour of Scotland,* the success of this work led him to undertake a second Scottish journey beginning, May 18, 1772. Many thought Pennant's writings on Scotland to be superficial and inaccurate.

Page 78, line 18:

Beltane from Beal, or Bel, the sun, the sun god. The name of a kind of festival formerly observed in Ireland (21st of June) and Scotland (1st of May); sometimes by kindling fires on the hills to worship the sun; not only peculiar to the Celts. In Ireland it was thought that the door from fairyland to the mortal world was open, and that the supernatural beings come to steal away beautiful mortals as their brides.

Page 82, line 11:

Flaccus Quintus Horatius, 65-8 BC, Roman satirist and poet.

Page 82, line 16:

Pan, the Greek misshapen god with goat's feet, horns and tail; the god of shepherds and flocks; took joy in frightening lone travellers. Ceres, Roman counterpart of Demeter worshipped by the Greeks as a corn goddess.

Page 83, line 31:

Sabines: One of an ancient people from whom the founders of Rome took their daughters by force, ultimately the women acted as mediators when the Sabines sought revenge. In Italy the Sabines and Marsians were thought to have the highest proportion of witches among them.

Page 84, line 6 *passim*:

James Hepburn, 4th Earl of Bothwell, 1535-1575, married Mary Queen of Scots on May 15, 1567. The credulous considered May an unlucky month for marriage anyway, but thought that this particular day had been chosen by witches; so hated were the French faction around the luckless queen. Someone wrote these lines from Ovid on a plaque and pinned them to Mary's palace gates:

mense malas maio nubere vulgus ait
The people say
That wantons marry
In the month of May

Page 86, line 19:

Lucian, 120-200 AD, Greek orator, advocate, philosopher and satirist.

Apuleius (Lucius), born c. 123 AD, studied philosophy under Plato, was a Latin writer of note, a Roman rhetorician best known for his *Metamorphoses* and *The Golden Ass*.

Page 88, line 1:

Tacitus, Caius Cornelius 55-c. 120 AD, soldier and chronicler.

Page 89, lines 29-30 and note
Dextra mihi Deus, et telum, quod missile libro Nunc adsint;
May God, my right hand, and the weapon which I poise and throw, now help me!
De causis contemptae necis
Concerning the causes of despised death.

Page 99, line 31:
Tasso (Torquato) 1544-1595, Italian poet.

Page 101, note at foot of page:
Newstead was the site of the Roman fort of *Trimontium*.

Sir Walter is undoubtedly referring to the altar of Gaius Arrius Domitianus found in 1830 three feet below the surface, on a spot to the right of the junction of the Leader Water and the river Tweed.

Its inscription:

Deo Silvano pro salute sua et suorum C. Arrius Domitianus c(enturio) leg(ionis) XX V(aleriae) V(ictricis) v(otum) s(olvit) l(ibens) l(ubens) merito
To the God Silvanus, Gaius Arrius Domitianus, centurion of the 20th Legion, Valeria Victrix, has paid his vow willingly, gladly and deservedly for his own safety and that of his household.

Domitianus set up several altars in the area to the wild life around and to the goddess Diana in particular. Silvanus, god of the wilderness as well as of hunting, would be considered by the invaders as in possession of the deserted Flavian site when they re-occupied it in 139-40 AD.

Silvanus is usually represented with a sickle in his right hand and a bough in his left.

LETTER IV

Page 102, line 24 and note:

John Leyden, 1775-1811, physician and poet. Son of a shepherd from Roxburghshire, Leyden was well versed in the folk-lore and demonology of the Scottish Border. Scott received much help from Leyden in the compilation of Border lore and ballad; Leyden was a scholar, Scott was not. Scott contributed a "Memoir of Leyden" to the *Edinburgh Annual Register* of 1811.

Page 107, line 20:

Joseph Glanville, 1636-1680, theologian, wrote various treatise on witchcraft: *Some Philosophical considerations Touching The Being of Witches and Witchcraft* (London 1661 and 1667) and so on.

Page 108, line 23:

Alison Pearson (or, Allison Peirson); In 1588 this person, of Byre Hills, Fifeshire was burned at the stake for prescribing magic potions and having converse with the Queen of Elfhame; Pearson had recommended that the Bishop of St. Andrews cure his hypochondria with spiced claret and boiled capon. She was suspected, too, of having sexual intercourse with the devil.

Page 108, line 26:

William Maitland of Lethington, 1528?-1573, Secretary to Mary Queen of Scots, was a man of grace, scholarship, and courtly accomplishments, but a treacherous friend who would use any means to his ends; he was universally known as "Secretary Lethington."

Knight of Buccleugh: probably refers to Sir Walter Scott of Buccleugh and Branxholm 1490-1552.

Page 110, line 15:

William Dunbar, 1460?-1521?, generally accepted as the man representative of Scots poetry during the Golden Age of King James IV of Scotland. *The Flyting of Dunbar and Kennedie* mentioned in the note is one of Dunbar's wildest exuberances.

Page 111, line 34:

It should be remembered that the story of Thomas of Erceldoune is essentially that told also in German and

Italian legend. It is probable that the Celtic Thomas story was the original with Thomas becoming Tannhäuser in Germany, and the elves and fairies, Venus and her ladies as reflected in Italian legend.

Page 116, line 16:
Reginald Scot, 1538-1599, born of a Kentish family, attended Oxford University, but left without taking a degree to be a country gentleman; this life he combined with the governmental post of collector of subsidies, a year as an MP and manager of his cousin Sir Thomas's estate.

Twice married, Scot became interested in witchcraft around the mid-1580s and produced a book *Discovery of Witchcraft*, which was first published in 1584. Published at Scot's own responsibility (it was not registered in the Stationers' Register), because of his attack on the witchcraft delusion—he said, among other things, that sorcery had been a figment of the imagination of the Roman Catholic Inquisition—the book was described by King James I (and VI) as "damnable", and the monarch had all the copies of the book destroyed. The second edition did not appear until 1651.

LETTER V

Page 139, line 26:
Convicta et combusta—convicted and burnt. (Can be either feminine, or neuter plural).

Page 137, line 24:
Rosicrucians: A mystical sect reputedly founded by Christian Rosenkreux, 1378-1484.

LETTER VI

Page 146, line 5:

Richard Corbett, 1582-1635, poet and Bishop of Oxford and Norwich.

Page 149, lines 10-15:
A list of various demons; *bull-beggar,* a hobgoblin, or any object of terror; *satyr,* a sylvan deity represented as half-man, half-goat, with horns and tail of a goat, they were common attendants to Bacchus in classical mythology; *Kitt-with-the-candlestick,* an illuminatory demon, sometimes fireflies were mistaken for demons; *triton,* a sea demon, from Triton son of Poseidon and Amphitrite in classical mythology; *calcar,* a malevolent nipping devil; *incubus,* according to the religious texts, an angel who fell from heaven because of lust for women—this spirit is supposed to assume either male or female shape; *fire-drake* a fiery dragon, or serpent; *puckle,* of the goblin family.

Page 157, lines 5-6:
de existentia—Concerning existence.
de modo existendi—Concerning the way of existing.

Page 157, line 16:
Jean Bodin, author of *De La Démonomanie des Sorciers* (Paris 1580). Bodin had a great gift for analysing the legal and political structures of societies, but he was a mediocre physician and dubious theologian.

Page 157, line 18:
Wierus—a German physician Jean de Weir.

Page 157, line 28:
Martin del Rio, famous for his *Disquisitionum magicarum* (Louvain 1599).

Page 158, line 15:
Jan Baptista van Helmont, 1577-1644, a Belgian chemist who devoted himself to the study of gasses.

Philippus Aureolus Paracelsus, 1493-1541, a Swiss mystic and alchemist; he was the first to use laudanum in alchemy.

Page 160, line 2:
John Napier, 1550-1617, mathematician, inventor of logarithms.

LETTER VII

Page 161 line 27:
Surge tandem carnifex—Arise at last, O executioner/scoundrel.

Page 170, line 33:
Pierre de (Rosteguy, Sieur de) Lancre, 1553-1631, was the son of a rich winegrower, he studied law and in 1582 became a lawyer for the Parlement at Bordeaux. He is particularly valuable today for his eyewitness account of a witch hunt in his *Tableau de l'inconstance des mauvais anges et démons* (1612).

LETTER VIII

Page 186, line 4:
Vestigia nulla retrorsum—No footprints behind (See: Horace, *Epistles*. 1.1.75—story of the lion and the fox.)

Page 190, line 5:
Francis Hutchinson, 1660-1739 was Bishop of Down and Connor, Ireland. His first permanent vicarage was at Hoxne, Suffolk, where his attention was drawn to local witches; this led to his work on the history of witchcraft published in 1718; *An Historical Essay concerning Witchcraft*.

Page 191, lines 24-31:
Sir Walter Scott is here referring to the case of the Salmesbury (Lancashire) witches, Janet and Ellen Bierley, who in 1612 were charged with bewitching a child to death. 14 year old Grace Sowerbutts testified that the women exhumed a corpse and:—

" . . . having it there did boil some thereof in a pot, and some did boil on the coals, of both which the said Jannet *(sic)* and Ellen did eat . . . And afterwards the said Jannet and Ellen did see the bones of the said child in a pot, and with the fat that came out of the said bones, they said they would anoint themselves, that thereby they might sometimes change themselves into other shapes."

It was a general belief that to achieve transvection or metamorphosis, witches rubbed their bodies with ointment. (See: Samuel Harsnett—*A Declaration of Egregious Popish Impostures . . . under the pretense of Casting out Devils*, (London 1603, 1605).

Page 193, line 2:
Dr. Johnson in a *Letter to Boswell* p. 76, March 1781.

Page 193, line 34:
" Sir Samuel Cromwell "—here Sir Walter is referring to Sir *Henry* Cromwell, grandfather of Oliver Cromwell; Robert Throckmorton was a prominent squire of Warboys, Huntingdon, his daughter Jane in truth was a sufferer of hysteria and, no doubt, epileptic fits. Cromwell's appropriation of the Samuel's goods (as Lord of the Manor) was nothing but a grasping pretext. The " annual lecture " continued until 1812 although the tone changed to one of warning *against belief* in witchcrafts.

Page 199, line 17:
Liberavimus animas nostra—We have freed our souls.

Page 199, line 12:
One of the so called bewitched was Anne Thorne, a servant wench, who had fits and hallucinations. A doctor ordered that she wash her hands and face twice a day (a novelty in those days) and be watched by a " lusty young fellow." This is an interesting appendix to the Wenham Trial which throws a certain amount of light on possessed girls. The Trial of Jane Wenham in 1712 is important for it was the last trial for witchcraft in England. The jury at the Hereford Assizes returned a verdict of guilty, but Mr. Justice Powell (propably citing the case tried by Chief Justice Sir John Holt earlier) opposed the jury.

Page 205, line 19:
Star Chamber: A tribunal of State, instituted in 1487 (or possibly earlier) for the trying of offences against the government, unfettered by the ordinary rules of law; in effect it was a Privy Council given judicial functions. Charles I used the Court to punish opponents; the Chamber

was abolished in 1641 by a Bill.

Page 205, line 29-30:
Ad gravem hanc impietatem, connivent theologi plerique omnes. Almost all theologians connive at this grave impiety.

Page 211, line 24:
i.e., Samuel Butler, 1612-1680; *Hudibras,* 1664.

Page 215, line 32
Sadducismus Triumphatus—Sadducism Triumphant! The Sadducees' (2nd century BC) view of human conduct was that it was within the control of a man's own will. Their view of the future existence was that, as in Mosaic Law, a veil was drawn across it. (See: Stanley, A.P. *History of the Jewish Church,* Vol 3 p. 335).

Page 220, line 18:
Last case of lynching for witchcraft in England.

LETTER IX

Page 229, line 26:
Hector Boetius author of *Scotorum Historiae a prima gentis origine:* he referred to supernatural women as *parcas,* or *Nymphas aliques fatidicas.* Boetius appears to have died at Aberdeen around 1536 when he would be over seventy years of age.

George Buchanan, 1506-82, Scottish humanist who spent most of his life in France lecturing, and writing Latin poems and prose. Montaign, Mary Queen of Scots and King James VI were all his pupils at various times. The most important of his works were *De jure regni apud Scotos* and *Rerum Scoticarum historia.*

Page 230, line 8:
Earl of Mar accused 1479.

Page 230, line 20:
i.e., King James V; Lady Glammis (or Glamis) was burnt in 1537.

Page 231, line 11:
George Sinclair was a professor of philosophy at the

University of Glasgow; his work *Satan's Invisible World Discovered* (1685) " formed during the eighteen century a part of every cottage library in Scotland."

Page 231, line 23:
Isobel Gowdie's trial in 1662 ranks as one of the most significant in Scotland. The imaginative and freely given confessions (four in all) embrace the entire range of witchcraft, including rapid changes from human to animal forms.

Page 236, line 16:
Sir George MacKenzie, 1636-1691, King's Advocate during the period of the Covenanting persecution in Scotland.

Page 237, line 17:
ex certissima scientia—From most certain knowledge.

Page 240, line 10ff:
" Common pricker ": In various works on witchcraft the ignoble office of pricker is mentioned. The idea of " pricking " a witch was linked to the theory of Devil's marks (moles and birthmarks) indicating that the person was branded by Satan as his own.

Should a suspect witch have no apparent marks, she was " pricked " to find hidden areas. As the Devil's marks were reputed morbid, a pin stuck into them would produce no pain; the shaving of the body usually preceded pricking.

Some examinations were "rigged ", i.e., some of the instruments used for " pricking " had retractable blades and hollow shafts, so that when the blade was pressed against the accused, the blade retracted and they felt no pain. John Kincaid of Tranent is one of three famous Scottish " prickers ", the other two being John Balfour of Corhouse and John Dick.

Page 240, line 32:
Lord Fountainhall (Sir John Lauder) 1646-1722, member of parliament and historical writer. His diaries were considered worthy of permanent record and these (1680-1701) were annotated by Sir Walter Scott and published in 1822.

Page 242, line 6:

damnum minatum, et malum secutum—An injury threatened and an evil deed followed.

Page 261, line 11:

Torture of Witches: Torture for use in witch trials was intellectually justified. There was only one just God, the pious declared, and that God was continually assailed by the Devil in an attempt to set up a rival system. Anyone supporting the Devil then, was fighting this Christian God and must be stopped before spreading wrong ideas. As the crime of aiding the Devil (witchcraft) was not physical but spiritual, ordinary rules of law did not apply. Under Roman and Continental law, sorcery was regarded as a *crimen excepta,* so difficult to prove that normal legal procedures were superseded.

Now, as it was obvious that the Devil would not appear to implicate one of his own, it was necessary to obtain a confession on the part of the human for this supernatural intercourse; thus a witch had to be tortured until she, or, in the case of warlocks and magicians, he confessed guilt.

Killing of witches was an act of universal benefit argued the pious; stopping the Devil's subversion was a good thing for the world as a whole, and killing the witch would bring absolution and forgiveness.

Methods of torturing varied from century to century, from country to country, and from hangman to hangman.

However, a table of tortures was drawn up:
" Steps of torture in witchcraft trials "

I.   *Preparation:* To force a confession of guilt. Methods; stripping, threatening, binding, whipping, thumbscrews, the rack. All thought to produce " voluntary " confessions.

II. *Final:* Method (a) *strappado,* (b) *squassation.*

III. *Supplementary:* Cutting off hands and legs; tearing flesh with red hot irons.

IV. *Occasional:* Spiked Chair, Scalding Baths. (No limit).

(xvii)

V. *Occasional* (Class II): Reserved for really recalcitrant subjects. The wheel.

" Popular " tortures in the British Isles for witches, consisted of denying sleep, heated boots, whipping in the stocks and various limb tortures.

Page 275:
Procedure against witches in Scotland:
Initially the Privy Council would appoint a commission of eight local gentlemen (a man of good family or good social position, a man above the rank of yeoman, including noblemen) to investigate whether or not a case should be brought to Court. These commissions could order the death penalty without real trial. If the evidence was more involved (should the accused be " powerful " socially in some way or other) the commission ordered the sheriff to summon an assize (of no more than 45 local men). The commissioners acted as Judges. Sometimes the local ministers and elders initiated charges of witchcraft and applied direct to the Privy Council to direct the Civil Judges to pass sentence.

Costs of trial were paid by the accused who had the right to appoint a lawyer. A confession was not necessary before conviction or execution; a person's " reputation " as a witch was enough for an indictment.

The Burning of Witches:
All countries except England and New England executed witches at the stake. While witches were burnt alive in the fanatic Roman Catholic countries of Spain and Italy, in Germany, Scotland and France the refinement of strangling (or hanging) the witch before burning was instituted. Again the pious cited justification based on the theology of " holy " men; Augustine in his *Liber de Fide ad Petrum Diaconum* had written—. . . *omnes hereticos . . . qui extra Ecclesiam catholicam praesentem finiunt vitam, in ignem eternum ituros, qui paratus est daibolo et angelis eius.*

LETTER X

Page 278, line 20:

William Lilly, astrologer, epitomises the curious and inconsistent ideas towards the supernatural of his day. Alchemists and astrologers enjoyed an immunity from witchcraft persecutions; probably because the astrologers claimed to be in constant touch with the good fairies and angels; Lilly, himself, made definite assertions of the advice to mortals from fairies:

The *Fairies* love the Southern Side of Hills,
Mountains and Groves—Neatness and Cleanliness
In Apparel, a strict Diet, an upright Life,
Fervent Prayers unto God, conduct much to
The Assistance of those who are curious (in)
These Ways.

While Hopkins was persecuting witches for less, Lilly received an annuity from Parliament. By Lilly's time the vogue for alchemy had declined a little. See *Mr. William Lilly's History of His Life and Times from the Year 1602 to 1681* (2nd Edition 1715).

Page 279, line 33:

Until his death in 1640 (he was stoned to death by a mob at St. Paul's Cross, London), Lamb was personal physician to the Duke of Buckingham. Like the remarkable John Dee (1527-1608) " Queen Elizabeth's Merlin " he experimented in alchemy and esoteric magical practices.

The " maid-servant " mentioned by Sir Walter Scott was Mrs. Anne Bodenham, whom the gossips said had lived " scandalously " with her unmarried employer for many years; she was universally known as " Dr. Lamb's Darling!"

After the death of her master, Mrs. Bodenham, although uneducated, earned the name of a wise woman and her knowledge of herbs was much sought after; and of course the " magic trickes " Lamb had taught her. Moving to Fisherton Anger, in Wiltshire, she continued her " consultations " on the future, herbs and poisons, and became acquainted with the family of Richard Goddard.

Now, Mrs. Richard Goddard, probably a psycopath, fearing she was being poisoned by her daughters resorted to play them at their own game and bought, through a go-between Ann Styles, poison from Anne Bodenham. This connection led, after a time and through false evidence laid by Ann Styles, to a conviction for witchcraft and Anne Bodenham was executed (hanged) at Salisbury, Wiltshire, in 1653.

Page 283, line 26:

James Hogg, 1770-1835, " The Ettrick Shepherd ", contemporary and friend of Sir Walter Scott, was a genuine rural bard without schooling. Son of a shepherd, Hogg was of interesting stock, with witches on the paternal side; his maternal grandfather Will O'Phawhope was reputed to be the last man in the Borders to have conversed with the fairies.

Page 187, line 7:

Edward Hyde, 1st Earl of Clarendon, 1609-1674, wrote about this apparition in his *History of the Rebellion*. To which this interesting letter may be added:

APPARITION OF SIR GEORGE VILLIERS TO PARKER SERVANT TO THE FIRST DUKE OF BUCKINGHAM. BEING A LETTER FROM MR. DOUCH TO MR. GLANVIL.

Sir:

Since the writing to you last, a passage concerning an apparition of Sir George Villiers giving warning of his son's (the Duke of Buckingham's) murder, is come into my mind; which has been assured by a servant of the duke's to be a great truth, thus: Some few days before the duke's going to Portsmouth (where he was stabbed by Felton), the ghost of his father Sir George Villiers appeared to one Parker (formerly his own servant, but then servant to the duke), in his morning gown, charging Parker to tell his son that he should decline that employment and the design he was going upon, or else he would certainly be murdered. Parker promised the apparition to do it but neglected it. The duke making preparations for his expedition to Rochel, the apparition came again to Parker, taxing him very severely for his breach of promise, and requiring him not to delay the acquainting his son of the danger he was in: this Parker the next day told the duke that his father's ghost had appeared twice to him, and had commanded him to give that warning: the duke slighted and told him he was an old doting fool. That night the apparition came to Parker the third time, saying, "Parker, thou hast done well in warning my son of his danger, but though he will not yet believe thee, go to him once more, however, and tell him from me, by such a token (naming a private token), which nobody knows but only he and I, that if he will no decline this voyage such a knife as this (pulling a long knife out from under his gown) will be his death." This message Parker also delivered the next day to the duke, who, when he heard the private token believed that he had it from his father's ghost, yet said, that his honour was now at stake, and he could not go back from what he had undertaken, come life, come death . . .

(See: Jarvis, T.M. *Accredited Ghost Stories*, London 1823).

Page 288, line 36:
Actually the apparition seen by Sir John Sherbroke and General Wynard at Nova Scotia. This case is sometimes quoted in a refutation of the idea that ghosts can't cross water.

Page 311, line 36:
Anabaptist: one who holds with the baptism of adults.

Page 312, line 37:
Daniel Defoe, 1660-1731, political writer.

Page 318, line 6:
Dunvegan Castle: N.W. Isle of Skye, Inverness-shire, seat of the MacLeods.

LETTERS

ON

DEMONOLOGY

AND

WITCHCRAFT

BY

SIR WALTER SCOTT, Bart.

WITH AN INTRODUCTION BY HENRY MORLEY
LL.D., PROFESSOR OF ENGLISH LITERATURE AT
UNIVERSITY COLLEGE, LONDON

LONDON
GEORGE ROUTLEDGE AND SONS
BROADWAY, LUDGATE HILL
NEW YORK: 9 LAFAYETTE PLACE
1884

(Original title page)

INTRODUCTION.

SIR WALTER SCOTT'S "Letters on Demonology and Witch-craft" were his contribution to a series of books, published by John Murray, which appeared between the years 1829 and 1847, and formed a collection of eighty volumes known as "Murray's Family Library." The series was planned to secure a wide diffusion of good literature in cheap five-shilling volumes, and Scott's " Letters," written and published in 1830, formed one of the earlier books in the collection.

The Society for the Diffusion of Useful Knowledge had been founded in the autumn of 1826, and Charles Knight, who had then conceived a plan of a National Library, was entrusted, in July, 1827, with the superintendence of its publi-cations. Its first treatises appeared in sixpenny numbers, once a fortnight. Its "British Almanac" and "Companion to the Almanac" first appeared at the beginning of 1829. Charles Knight started also in that year his own "Library of Entertaining Knowledge." John Murray's "Family Library" was then begun, and in the spring of 1832—the year of the Reform Bill—the advance of civilization by the diffusion of good literature, through cheap journals as well as cheap books, was sought by the establishment of "Chambers's Edinburgh Journal" in the North, and in London of "The Penny Magazine."

In the autumn of that year, 1832, on the 21st of September, Sir Walter Scott died. The first warning of death had come to him in February, 1830, with a stroke of apoplexy. He had been visited by an old friend who brought him memoirs of her father, which he had promised to revise for the press. He seemed for half an hour to be bending over the papers at his desk, and reading them; then he rose, staggered into the drawing-room, and fell, remaining speechless until he had been bled. Dieted for weeks on pulse and water, he so far recovered that to friends outside his family but little change in him was visible. In that condition, in the month after his seizure, he was writing these Letters, and also a fourth series of the " Tales of a Grandfather." The slight softening of the brain found after death had then begun. But the old delight in anecdote and skill in story-telling that, at the beginning of his career, had caused a critic of his " Border Minstrelsy" to say that it contained the germs of a hundred romances, yet survived. It gave to Scott's " Letters on Demonology and Witchcraft" what is for us now a pathetic charm. Here and there some slight confusion of thought or style represents the flickering of a light that flashes yet with its old brilliancy. There is not yet the manifest suggestion of the loss of power that we find presently afterwards in " Count Robert of Paris" and " Castle Dangerous," published in 1831 as the Fourth Series of " Tales of My Landlord," with which he closed his life's work at the age of sixty.

Milton has said that he who would not be frustrate of his hope to write well in laudable things, ought himself to be a true poem. Scott's life was a true poem, of which the music entered into all he wrote. If in his earlier days the consciousness of an unlimited productive power tempted him to make haste to be rich, that he might work out, as founder of a family, an ideal of life touched by his own genius of romance, there was not in his desire for gain one touch of sordid greed, and his ideal of life only brought him closer home to all its duties. Sir Walter Scott's good sense, as Lord Cockburn said, was a more wonderful gift than his genius. When the mistake of a trade connection with James Ballantyne brought ruin to him in 1826, he repudiated bankruptcy, took on himself the burden of a debt of £130,000, and sacrificed his life to the successful endeavour to pay off all. What was left unpaid at his death was cleared afterwards by the success of his annotated edition of his novels. No tale of physical strife in the battlefield could be as heroic as the story·of the close of Scott's life, with five years of a death-struggle against adversity, animated by the truest sense of honour. When the ruin was impending he wrote in his diary, "If things go badly in London, the magic wand of the Unknown will be shivered in his grasp. The feast of fancy will be over with the feeling of independence. He shall no longer have the delight of waking in the morning with bright ideas in his mind, hasten to commit them to paper, and count them monthly, as the means of planting such scaurs and purchasing such wastes; replacing dreams of fiction by other prospective visions of walks by

> ' Fountain-heads, and pathless groves;
> Places which pale passion loves.'

This cannot be; but I may work substantial husbandry— *i.e.*, write history, and such concerns." It was under pressure of calamity like this that Sir Walter Scott was compelled to make himself known as the author of "Waverley." Closely upon this followed the death of his wife, his thirty years' companion. "I have been to her room," he wrote in May, 1826; "there was no voice in it— no stirring; the pressure of the coffin was visible on the bed, but it had been removed elsewhere; all was neat as she loved it, but all was calm—calm as death. I remembered the last sight of her: she raised herself in bed, and tried to turn her eyes after me, and said with a sort of smile, ' You have all such melancholy faces.' These were the last words I ever heard her utter, and I hurried away, for she did not seem quite conscious of what she said; when I returned, immediately departing, she was in a deep sleep. It is deeper now. This was but seven days since. They are arranging the chamber of death—that which was long the

apartment of connubial happiness, and of whose arrangement (better than in richer houses) she was so proud. They
are treading fast and thick. For weeks you could have
heard a footfall. Oh, my God !"

A few years yet of his own battle, while the shadows of
night and death were gathering about him, and they were
re-united. In these "Letters upon Demonology and
Witchcraft," addressed to his son-in-law, written under the
first grasp of death, the old kindliness and good sense, joined
to the old charm in story-telling, stand firm yet against
every assault ; and even in the decay that followed, when the
powers were broken of the mind that had breathed, and is
still breathing, its own health into the minds of tens of
thousands of his countrymen, nothing could break the fine
spirit of love and honour that was in him. When the end
was very near, and the son-in-law to whom these Letters
were addressed found him one morning entirely himself,
though in the last extreme of feebleness : his eye was clear
and calm—every trace of the wild fire of delirium was
extinguished : "Lockhart," he said, "I may have but a
minute to speak to you. My dear, be a good man—be
virtuous, be religious—be a good man. Nothing else will
give you any comfort when you come to lie here."

Another volume of this Library may give occasion to
recall Scott in the noontide of his strength, companion of

> " The blameless Muse who trains her sons
> For hope and calm enjoyment."

Here we remember only how from among dark clouds the
last light of his genius shone on the path of those who
were endeavouring to make the daily bread of intellectual
life—good books—common to all.

H. M.

February, 1884.

LETTERS

ON

DEMONOLOGY AND WITCHCRAFT

To J. G. LOCKHART, Esq.

———◆————

LETTER I.

Origin of the general Opinions respecting Demonology among Mankind
—The Belief in the Immortality of the Soul is the main inducement
to credit its occasional re-appearance—The Philosophical Objections to the Apparition of an Abstract Spirit little understood
by the Vulgar and Ignorant—The situations of excited Passion
incident to Humanity, which teach Men to wish or apprehend
Supernatural Apparitions—They are often presented by the Sleeping
Sense—Story of Somnambulism—The Influence of Credulity contagious, so that Individuals will trust the Evidence of others in
despite of their own Senses—Examples from the "Historia
Verdadera" of Bernal Dias del Castillo, and from the Works of
Patrick Walker—The apparent Evidence of Intercourse with the
Supernatural World is sometimes owing to a depraved State of the
bodily Organs—Difference between this Disorder and Insanity, in
which the Organs retain their tone, though that of the Mind is lost
—Rebellion of the Senses of a Lunatic against the current of his
Reveries—Narratives of a contrary Nature, in which the Evidence
of the Eyes overbore the Conviction of the Understanding—
Example of a London Man of Pleasure—Of Nicolai, the German
Bookseller and Philosopher—Of a Patient of Dr. Gregory—Of an
Eminent Scottish Lawyer, deceased—Of this same fallacious
Disorder are other instances, which have but sudden and momentary
endurance—Apparition of Maupertuis—Of a late illustrious modern
Poet—The Cases quoted chiefly relating to false Impressions on the

Visual Nerve, those upon the Ear next considered—Delusions of
the Touch chiefly experienced in Sleep—Delusions of the Taste—
And of the Smelling—Sum of the Argument.

You have asked of me, my dear friend, that I should assist
the "Family Library" with the history of a dark chapter in
human nature, which the increasing civilization of all well-
instructed countries has now almost blotted out, though the
subject attracted no ordinary degree of consideration in the
older times of their history.

Among much reading of my earlier days, it is no doubt
true that I travelled a good deal in the twilight regions of
superstitious disquisitions. Many hours have I lost—"I
would their debt were less !"—in examining old as well as
more recent narratives of this character, and even in looking
into some of the criminal trials so frequent in early days,
upon a subject which our fathers considered as a matter of
the last importance. And, of late years, the very curious
extracts published by Mr. Pitcairn, from the Criminal
Records of Scotland, are, besides their historical value,
of a nature so much calculated to illustrate the credulity of
our ancestors on such subjects, that, by perusing them, I
have been induced more recently to recall what I had read
and thought upon the subject at a former period.

As, however, my information is only miscellaneous, and I
make no pretensions, either to combat the systems of those
by whom I am anticipated in consideration of the subject,
or to erect any new one of my own, my purpose is, after a
general account of Demonology and Witchcraft, to confine
myself to narratives of remarkable cases, and to the observations which naturally and easily arise out of them ;—in
the confidence that such a plan is, at the present time of
day, more likely to suit the pages of a popular miscellany,
than an attempt to reduce the contents of many hundred
tomes, from the largest to the smallest size, into an abridge-
ment, which, however compressed, must remain greatly too
large for the reader's powers of patience.

A few general remarks on the nature of Demonology, and the original cause of the almost universal belief in communication betwixt mortals and beings of a power superior to themselves, and of a nature not to be comprehended by human organs, are a necessary introduction to the subject.

The general, or, it may be termed, the universal belief of the inhabitants of the earth, in the existence of spirits separated from the encumbrance and incapacities of the body, is grounded on the consciousness of the divinity that speaks in our bosoms, and demonstrates to all men, except the few who are hardened to the celestial voice, that there is within us a portion of the divine substance, which is not subject to the law of death and dissolution, but which, when the body is no longer fit for its abode, shall seek its own place, as a sentinel dismissed from his post. Unaided by revelation, it cannot be hoped that mere earthly reason should be able to form any rational or precise conjecture concerning the destination of the soul when parted from the body ; but the conviction that such an indestructible essence exists, the belief expressed by the poet in a different sense, *Non omnis moriar*, must infer the existence of many millions of spirits who have not been annihilated, though they have become invisible to mortals who still see, hear, and perceive, only by means of the imperfect organs of humanity. Probability may lead some of the most reflecting to anticipate a state of future rewards and punishments ; as those experienced in the education of the deaf and dumb find that their pupils, even while cut off from all instruction by ordinary means, have been able to form, out of their own unassisted conjectures, some ideas of the existence of a Deity, and of the distinction between the soul and body—a circumstance which proves how naturally these truths arise in the human mind. The principle that they do so arise, being taught or communicated, leads to further conclusions.

These spirits, in a state of separate existence, being

admitted to exist, are not, it may be supposed, indifferent to the affairs of mortality, perhaps not incapable of influencing them. It is true that, in a more advanced state of society, the philosopher may challenge the possibility of a separate appearance of a disembodied spirit, unless in the case of a direct miracle, to which, being a suspension of the laws of nature, directly wrought by the Maker of these laws, for some express purpose, no bound or restraint can possibly be assigned. But under this necessary limitation and exception, philosophers might plausibly argue that, when the soul is divorced from the body, it loses all those qualities which made it, when clothed with a mortal shape, obvious to the organs of its fellow-men. The abstract idea of a spirit certainly implies that it has neither substance, form, shape, voice, or anything which can render its presence visible or sensible to human faculties. But these sceptic doubts of philosophers on the possibility of the appearance of such separated spirits, do not arise till a certain degree of information has dawned upon a country, and even then only reach a very small proportion of reflecting and better-informed members of society. To the multitude, the indubitable fact, that so many millions of spirits exist around and even amongst us, seems sufficient to support the belief that they are, in certain instances at least, by some means or other, able to communicate with the world of humanity. The more numerous part of mankind cannot form in their mind the idea of the spirit of the deceased existing, without possessing or having the power to assume the appearance which their acquaintance bore during his life, and do not push their researches beyond this point.

Enthusiastic feelings of an impressive and solemn nature occur both in private and public life, which seem to add ocular testimony to an intercourse betwixt earth and the world beyond it. For example, the son who has been lately deprived of his father feels a sudden crisis approach, in which he is anxious to have recourse to his sagacious advice—or a bereaved husband earnestly desires again to behold the form of which the grave has deprived him for ever—or, to use a darker yet very common instance, the wretched man who has dipped his hand in his fellow-creature's blood, is haunted by the apprehension that the phantom of the slain stands by the bedside of his murderer. In all or any of these cases, who shall doubt that imagination, favoured by circumstances, has power to summon up to the organ of sight, spectres which only exist in the mind of those by whom their apparition seems to be witnessed?

If we add, that such a vision may take place in the course of one of those lively dreams in which the patient, except in respect to the single subject of one strong impression, is, or seems, sensible of the real particulars of the scene around him, a state of slumber which often occurs; if he is so far conscious, for example, as to know that he is lying on his own bed, and surrounded by his own familiar furniture at the time when the supposed apparition is manifested, it becomes almost in vain to argue with the visionary against the reality of his dream, since the spectre, though itself purely fanciful, is inserted amidst so many circumstances which he feels must be true beyond the reach of doubt or question. That which is undeniably certain becomes, in a manner, a warrant for the reality of the appearance to which doubt would have been otherwise attached. And if any event, such as the death of the person dreamt of, chances to take place, so as to correspond with the nature and the time of the apparition, the coincidence, though one which must be frequent, since our dreams usually refer to the accomplishment of that which haunts our minds when awake, and often presage the most probable events, seems perfect, and the chain of circumstances touching the evidence may not unreasonably be considered as complete. Such a concatenation, we repeat, must frequently take place, when it is considered of what stuff dreams are made—how naturally they turn upon those who occupy our mind while awake, and, when a soldier is exposed to death in battle, when a sailor is incurring the dangers of the sea, when a beloved wife or relative is attacked by disease, how readily our sleeping imagination rushes to the very point of alarm, which when waking it had shuddered to anticipate. The number of instances in which such lively dreams have been quoted, and both asserted and received as spiritual communications, is very great at all periods; in ignorant times, where the natural cause of dreaming is misapprehended and confused with an idea of mysticism, it is much greater. Yet, perhaps, considering the many thousands of dreams which must, night after night, pass through the imagination of individuals, the number of coincidences between the vision and real event are fewer and less remarkable than a fair calculation of chances would warrant us to expect. But in countries where such presaging dreams are subjects of attention, the number of those which seemed to be coupled with the corresponding issue, is large enough to spread a very general belief of a positive communication betwixt the living and the dead.

Somnambulism and other nocturnal deceptions frequently lend their aid to the formation of such *phantasmata* as are formed in this middle state, betwixt sleeping and waking. A most respectable person, whose active life had been spent as master and part owner of a large merchant vessel in the Lisbon trade, gave the writer an account of such an instance which came under his observation. He was lying in the Tagus, when he was put to great anxiety and alarm by the following incident and its consequences. One of his crew was murdered by a Portuguese assassin, and a report arose that the ghost of the slain man haunted the vessel. Sailors are generally superstitious, and those of my friend's vessel became unwilling to remain on board the ship; and it was probable they might desert rather then return to England with the ghost for a passenger. To prevent so great a calamity, the captain determined to examine the story to the bottom. He soon found that, though all pretended to have seen lights and heard noises, and so forth, the weight of the evidence lay upon the statement of one of his own mates, an Irishman and a Catholic, which might increase his tendency to superstition, but in other respects a veracious, honest, and sensible person, whom Captain —— had no reason to suspect would wilfully deceive him. He affirmed to Captain S—— with the deepest obtestations, that the spectre of the murdered man appeared to him almost nightly, took him from his place in the vessel, and, according to his own expression, worried his life out. He made these communications with a degree of horror which intimated the reality of his distress and apprehensions. The captain, without any argument at the time, privately resolved to watch the motions of the ghost-seer in the night; whether alone, or with a witness, I have forgotten. As the ship bell struck twelve, the sleeper started up, with a ghastly and disturbed countenance, and lighting a candle, proceeded to the galley or cook-room of the vessel. He sate down with his eyes open, staring before him as on some terrible object which he beheld with horror, yet from which he could not withhold his eyes. After a short space he arose, took up a tin can or decanter, filled it with water, muttering to himself all the while—mixed salt in the water, and sprinkled it about the galley. Finally, he sighed deeply, like one relieved from a heavy burden, and, returning to his hammock, slept soundly. In the next morning the haunted man told the usual precise story of his apparition, with the additional circumstances, that the ghost had led him to the galley, but that he had fortunately, he knew not how, obtained possession of some holy water, and succeeded in getting rid of his unwelcome visitor. The visionary was then informed of the real transactions of the night, with so many particulars as to satisfy him he had been the dupe of his imagination; he acquiesced in his commander's reasoning, and the dream, as often happens in these cases, returned no more after its imposture had been detected. In this case, we find the excited imagination acting upon the half-waking senses, which were intelligent enough for the purpose of making him sensible where he was, but not sufficiently so to judge truly of the objects before him.

But it is not only private life alone, or that tenor of thought which has been depressed into melancholy by gloomy anticipations respecting the future, which disposes the mind to mid-day fantasies, or to nightly apparitions—a state of eager anxiety, or excited exertion, is equally favourable to the indulgence of such supernatural communications. The anticipation of a dubious battle, with all the doubt and uncertainty of its event, and the conviction that it must involve his own fate and that of his country, was powerful enough to conjure up to the anxious eye of Brutus the spectre of his murdered friend Cæsar, respecting whose death he perhaps thought himself less justified than at the Ides of March, since, instead of having achieved the freedom of Rome, the event had only been the renewal of civil wars, and the issue might appear most likely to conclude in the total subjection of liberty. It is not miraculous that the masculine spirit of Marcus Brutus, surrounded by darkness and solitude, distracted probably by recollection of the kindness and favour of the great individual whom he had put to death to avenge the wrongs of his country, though by the slaughter of his own friend, should at length place before his eyes in person the appearance which termed itself his evil genius, and promised again to meet him at Philippi. Brutus' own intentions, and his knowledge of the military art, had probably long since assured him that the decision of the civil war must take place at or near that place; and, allowing that his own imagination supplied that part of his dialogue with the spectre, there is nothing else which might not be fashioned in a vivid dream or a waking reverie, approaching, in absorbing and engrossing character, the usual matter of which dreams consist. That Brutus, well acquainted with the opinions of the Platonists, should be disposed to receive without doubt the idea that he had seen a real apparition, and was not likely to scrutinize very minutely the supposed vision, may be naturally conceived ; and it is also natural to think, that although no one saw the figure but himself, his contemporaries were little disposed to examine the testimony of a man so eminent, by the strict rules of cross-examination and conflicting evidence, which they might have thought applicable to another person, and a less dignified occasion.

Even in the field of death, and amid the mortal tug of combat itself, strong belief has wrought the same wonder, which we have hitherto mentioned as occurring in solitude and amid darkness ; and those who were themselves on the verge of the world of spirits, or employed in dispatching others to these gloomy regions, conceived they beheld the apparitions of those beings whom their national mythology associated with such scenes. In such moments of undecided battle, amid the violence, hurry, and confusion of ideas incident to the situation, the ancients supposed that they saw their deities, Castor and Pollux, fighting in the van for their encouragement; the heathen Scandinavian beheld the Choosers of the slain ; and the Catholics were no less easily led to recognize the warlike Saint George or Saint James in the very front of the strife, showing them the way to conquest. Such apparitions being generally visible to a multitude, have in all times been supported by the greatest strength of testimony. When the common feeling of danger, and the animating burst of enthusiasm, act on the feelings of many men at once, their minds hold a natural correspondence with each other, as it is said is the case with stringed instruments tuned to the same pitch, of which, when one is played, the chords of the others are supposed to vibrate in unison with the tones produced. If an artful or enthusiastic individual exclaims, in the heat of action, that he perceives an apparition of the romantic kind which has been intimated, his companions catch at the idea with emulation, and most are willing to sacrifice the conviction of their own senses, rather than allow that they did not witness the same favourable emblem, from which all draw confidence and hope. One warrior catches the idea from another; all are alike eager to acknowledge the present miracle, and the battle is won before the mistake is discovered. In such cases, the number of persons present, which would otherwise lead to detection of the fallacy, becomes the means of strengthening it.

Of this disposition, to see as much of the supernatural as is seen by others around, or, in other words, to trust to the eyes of others rather than to our own, we may take the liberty to quote two remarkable instances.

The first is from the " Historia Verdadera" of Don Bernal Dias del Castillo, one of the companions of the celebrated Cortez in his Mexican conquest. After having given an account of a great victory over extreme odds, he mentions the report inserted in the contemporary Chronicle of Gomara, that Saint Iago had appeared on a white horse in van of the combat, and led on his beloved Spaniards to victory. It is very curious to observe the Castilian cavalier's internal conviction that the rumour arose out of a mistake, the cause of which he explains from his own observation; whilst, at the same time, he does not venture to disown the miracle. The honest Conquestador owns that he himself did not see this animating vision; nay, that he beheld an individual cavalier, named Francisco de Morla, mounted on a chestnut horse, and fighting strenuously in the very place where Saint James is said to have appeared. But instead of proceeding to draw the necessary inference, the devout Conquestador exclaims—" Sinner that I am, what am I that I should have beheld the blessed apostle !"

The other instance of the infectious character of superstition occurs in a Scottish book, and there can be little doubt that it refers, in its first origin, to some uncommon appearance of the aurora borealis, or the northern lights, which do not appear to have been seen in Scotland so frequently as to be accounted a common and familiar atmospherical phenomenon, until the beginning of the eighteenth century. The passage is striking and curious, for the narrator, Peter Walker, though an enthusiast, was a man of credit, and does not even affect to have seen the wonders, the reality of which he unscrupulously adopts on the testimony of others, to whose eyes he trusted rather than to his own. The conversion of the sceptical gentleman of whom he speaks is highly illustrative of popular credulity carried away into enthusiasm, or into imposture, by the evidence of those around, and at once shows the imperfection of such a general testimony, and the ease with which it is procured, since the general excitement of the moment impels even the more cold-blooded and judicious persons present to catch up the ideas and echo the exclamations of the majority, who, from the first, had considered the heavenly phenomenon as a supernatural weapon-schaw, held for the purpose of a sign and warning of civil wars to come.

"In the year 1686, in the months of June and July," says the honest chronicler, "many yet alive can witness that about the Crossford Boat, two miles beneath Lanark, especially at the Mains, on the water of Clyde, many people gathered together for several afternoons, where there were showers of bonnets, hats, guns, and swords, which covered the trees and the ground; companies of men in arms marching in order upon the waterside; companies meeting companies, going all through other, and then all falling to the ground and disappearing; other companies immediately appeared, marching the same way. I went there three afternoons together, and, as I observed, there were two-thirds of the people that were together saw, and a third that saw not; and, *though I could see nothing,* there was such a fright and trembling on those that did see, that was discernible to all from those that saw not. There was a gentleman standing next to me who spoke as too many gentlemen and others speak, who said, 'A pack of damned witches and warlocks that have the second sight ! the devil ha't do I see ;' and immediately there was a discernible change in his countenance. With as much fear and trembling as any woman I saw there, he called out, 'All you that do not see, say nothing ; for I persuade you it is matter of fact, and discernible to all that is not stone-blind.' And those who did see told what works (*i.e.*, locks) the guns had, and their length and wideness, and what handles the swords had, whether small or three-barr'd, or Highland guards, and the closing knots of the bonnets, black or blue ; and those who did see them there, whenever they went abroad, saw a bonnet and a sword drop in the way."*

This singular phenomenon, in which a multitude believed, although only two-thirds of them saw what must, if real, have been equally obvious to all, may be compared with the exploit of the humourist, who planted himself in an attitude of astonishment, with his eyes riveted on the well-known bronze lion that graces the front of Northumberland House in the Strand, and having attracted the attention of those who looked at him by muttering, " By heaven it wags ! it wags again !" contrived in a few minutes to blockade the whole street with an immense crowd, some conceiving that they had absolutely seen the lion of Percy wag his tail, others expecting to witness the same phenomenon.

On such occasions as we have hitherto mentioned, we have supposed that the ghost-seer has been in full possession of his ordinary powers of perception, unless in the case of dreamers, in whom they may have been obscured by temporary slumber, and the possibility of correcting vagaries of

---

* Walker's " Lives," Edinburgh, 1827, vol. i. p. xxxvi. It is evident that honest Peter believed in the apparition of this martial gear on the principle of Partridge's terror for the ghost of Hamlet—not that he was afraid himself, but because Garrick showed such evident marks of terror.

the imagination rendered more difficult by want of the ordinary appeal to the evidence of the bodily senses.   In other
respects their blood beat temperately, they possessed the
ordinary capacity of ascertaining the truth or discerning the
falsehood of external appearances by an appeal to the organ
of sight.   Unfortunately, however, as is now universally
known and admitted, there certainly exists more than one
disorder known to professional men of which one important
symptom is a disposition to see apparitions.

This frightful disorder is not properly insanity, although
it is somewhat allied to that most horrible of maladies, and
may, in many constitutions, be the means of bringing it on,
and although such hallucinations are proper to both.   The
difference I conceive to be that, in cases of insanity, the
mind of the patient is principally affected, while the senses,
or organic system, offer in vain to the lunatic their decided
testimony against the fantasy of a deranged imagination.
Perhaps the nature of this collision—between a disturbed
imagination and organs of sense possessed of their usual
accuracy—cannot be better described than in the embarrassment expressed by an insane patient confined in the Infirmary
of Edinburgh.   The poor man's malady had taken a gay
turn.   The house, in his idea, was his own, and he contrived to account for all that seemed inconsistent with his
imaginary right of property—there were many patients in it,
but that was owing to the benevolence of his nature, which
made him love to see the relief of distress.   He went little,
or rather never abroad—but then his habits were of a
domestic and rather sedentary character.   He did not see
much company—but he daily received visits from the first
characters in the renowned medical school of this city, and
he could not therefore be much in want of society.   With
so many supposed comforts around him—with so many
visions of wealth and splendour—one thing alone disturbed
the peace of the poor optimist, and would indeed have confounded most *bons vivants*.   " He was curious," he said, "in

his table, choice in his selection of cooks, had every day a dinner of three regular courses and a dessert; and yet, somehow or other, everything he eat *tasted of porridge.*" This dilemma could be no great wonder to the friend to whom the poor patient communicated it, who knew the lunatic eat nothing but this simple aliment at any of his meals. The case was obvious. The disease lay in the extreme vivacity of the patient's imagination, deluded in other instances, yet not absolutely powerful enough to contend with the honest evidence of his stomach and palate, which, like Lord Peter's brethren in "The Tale of a Tub," were indignant at the attempt to impose boiled oatmeal upon them, instead of such a banquet as Ude would have displayed when peers were to partake of it. Here, therefore, is one instance of actual insanity, in which the sense of taste controlled and attempted to restrain the ideal hypothesis adopted by a deranged imagination. But the disorder to which I previously alluded is entirely of a bodily character, and consists principally in a disease of the visual organs, which present to the patient a set of spectres or appearances which have no actual existence. It is a disease of the same nature which renders many men incapable of distinguishing colours; only the patients go a step further, and pervert the external form of objects. In their case, therefore, contrary to that of the maniac, it is not the mind, or rather the imagination, which imposes upon and overpowers the evidence of the senses, but the sense of seeing (or hearing) which betrays its duty and conveys false ideas to a sane intellect.

More than one learned physician, who have given their attestations to the existence of this most distressing complaint, have agreed that it actually occurs, and is occasioned by different causes. The most frequent source of the malady is in the dissipated and intemperate habits of those who, by a continued series of intoxication, become subject to what is popularly called the Blue Devils, instances of which mental disorder may be known to most who have lived for any period of their lives in society where hard drinking was a common vice. The joyous visions suggested by intoxication when the habit is first acquired, in time disappear, and are supplied by frightful impressions and scenes, which destroy the tranquillity of the unhappy debauchee. Apparitions of the most unpleasant appearance are his companions in solitude, and intrude even upon his hours of society : and when by an alteration of habits, the mind is cleared of these frightful ideas, it requires but the slightest renewal of the association to bring back the full tide of misery upon the repentant libertine.

Of this the following instance was told to the author by a gentleman connected with the sufferer. A young man of fortune, who had led what is called so gay a life as considerably to injure both his health and fortune, was at length obliged to consult the physician upon the means of restoring, at least, the former. One of his principal complaints was the frequent presence of a set of apparitions, resembling a band of figures dressed in green, who performed in his drawing-room a singular dance, to which he was compelled to bear witness, though he knew, to his great annoyance, that the whole *corps de ballet* existed only in his own imagination. His physician immediately informed him that he had lived upon town too long and too fast not to require an exchange to a more healthy and natural course of life. He therefore prescribed a gentle course of medicine, but earnestly recommended to his patient to retire to his own house in the country, observe a temperate diet and early hours, practising regular exercise, on the same principle avoiding fatigue, and assured him that by doing so he might bid adieu to black spirits and white, blue, green, and grey, with all their trumpery. The patient observed the advice, and prospered. His physician, after the interval of a month, received a grateful letter from him, acknowledging the success of his regimen. The greens goblins had disappeared, and with them the unpleasant train of emotions to which their visits had given rise, and the patient had ordered his town-house to be disfurnished and sold, while the furniture was to be sent down to his residence in the country, where he was determined in future to spend his life, without exposing himself to the temptations of town. One would have supposed this a well-devised scheme for health. But, alas! no sooner had the furniture of the London drawing-room been placed in order in the gallery of the old manor-house, than the former delusion returned in full force : the green *figurantés*, whom the patient's depraved imagination had so long associated with these moveables, came capering and frisking to accompany them, exclaiming with great glee, as if the sufferer should have been rejoiced to see them, " Here we all are—here we all are !" The visionary, if I recollect right, was so much shocked at their appearance, that he retired abroad, in despair that any part of Britain could shelter him from the daily persecution of this domestic ballet.

There is reason to believe that such cases are numerous, and that they may perhaps arise not only from the debility of stomach brought on by excess in wine or spirits, which derangement often sensibly affects the eyes and sense of sight, but also because the mind becomes habitually predominated over by a train of fantastic visions, the consequence of frequent intoxication ; and is thus, like a dislocated joint, apt again to go wrong, even when a different cause occasions the derangement.

It is easy to be supposed that habitual excitement by means of any other intoxicating drug, as opium, or its various substitutes, must expose those who practise the dangerous custom to the same inconvenience. Very frequent use of the nitrous oxide which affects the senses so strongly, and produces a short but singular state of ecstasy, would probably be found to occasion this species of disorder. But there are many other causes which medical men

find attended with the same symptom, of embodying before
the eyes of a patient imaginary illusions which are visible
to no one else. This persecution of spectral deceptions is
also found to exist when no excesses of the patient can be
alleged as the cause, owing, doubtless, to a deranged state
of the blood or nervous system.

The learned and acute Dr. Ferriar of Manchester was the
first who brought before the English public the leading case,
as it may be called, in this department, namely, that of
Mons. Nicolai, the celebrated bookseller of Berlin. This
gentleman was not a man merely of books, but of letters,
and had the moral courage to lay before the Philosophical
Society of Berlin an account of his own sufferings, from
having been, by disease, subjected to a series of spectral
illusions. The leading circumstances of this case may be
stated very shortly, as it has been repeatedly before the
public, and is insisted on by Dr. Ferriar, Dr. Hibbert, and
others who have assumed Demonology as a subject.
Nicolai traces his illness remotely to a series of disagreeable incidents which had happened to him in the beginning
of the year 1791. The depression of spirits which was
occasioned by these unpleasant occurrences, was aided by
the consequences of neglecting a course of periodical bleed-
ing which he had been accustomed to observe. This state
of health brought on the disposition to see *phantasmata*, who
visited, or it may be more properly said frequented, the
apartments of the learned bookseller, presenting crowds of
persons who moved and acted before him, nay, even spoke
to and addressed him. These phantoms afforded nothing
unpleasant to the imagination of the visionary either in
sight or expression, and the patient was possessed of too
much firmness to be otherwise affected by their presence
than with a species of curiosity, as he remained convinced
from the beginning to the end of the disorder, that these
singular effects were merely symptoms of the state of his
health, and did not in any other respect regard them as

a subject of apprehension. After a certain time, and some use of medicine, the phantoms became less distinct in their outline, less vivid in their colouring, faded, as it were, on the eye of the patient, and at length totally disappeared.

The case of Nicolai has unquestionably been that of many whose love of science has not been able to overcome their natural reluctance to communicate to the public the particulars attending the visitation of a disease so peculiar. That such illnesses have been experienced, and have ended fatally, there can be no doubt ; though it is by no means to be inferred, that the symptom of importance to our present discussion has, on all occasions, been produced from the same identical cause.

Dr. Hibbert, who has most ingeniously, as well as philosophically, handled this subject, has treated it also in a medical point of view, with science to which we make no pretence, and a precision of detail to which our superficial investigation affords us no room for extending ourselves.

The visitation of spectral phenomena is described by this learned gentleman as incidental to sundry complaints ; and he mentions, in particular, that the symptom occurs not only in plethora, as in the case of the learned Prussian we have just mentioned, but is a frequent hectic symptom—often an associate of febrile and inflammatory disorders—frequently accompanying inflammation of the brain—a concomitant also of highly excited nervous irritability—equally connected with hypochondria—and finally united in some cases with gout, and in others with the effects of excitation produced by several gases. In all these cases there seems to be a morbid degree of sensibility, with which this symptom is ready to ally itself, and which, though inaccurate as a medical definition, may be held sufficiently descriptive of one character of the various kinds of disorder with which this painful symptom may be found allied.

A very singular and interesting illustration of such combinations as Dr. Hibbert has recorded of the spectral illusion with an actual disorder, and that of a dangerous kind, was frequently related in society by the late learned and accomplished Dr. Gregory of Edinburgh, and sometimes, I believe, quoted by him in his lectures. The narrative, to the author's best recollection, was as follows :—A patient of Dr. Gregory, a person, it is understood, of some rank, having requested the doctor's advice, made the following extraordinary statement of his complaint. " I am in the habit," he said, " of dining at five, and exactly as the hour of six arrives I am subjected to the following painful visitation. The door of the room, even when I have been weak enough to bolt it, which I have sometimes done, flies wide open ; an old hag, like one of those who haunted the heath of Forres, enters with a frowning and incensed countenance, comes straight up to me with every demonstration of spite and indignation which could characterize her who haunted the merchant Abudah in the Oriental tale ; she rushes upon me, says something, but so hastily that I cannot discover the purport, and then strikes me a severe blow with her staff. I fall from my chair in a swoon, which is of longer or shorter endurance. To the recurrence of this apparition I am daily subjected. And such is my new and singular complaint." The doctor immediately asked whether his patient had invited any one to sit with him when he expected such a visitation. He was answered in the negative. The nature of the complaint, he said, was so singular, it was so likely to be imputed to fancy, or even to mental derangement, that he had shrunk from communicating the circumstance to any one. " Then," said the doctor, " with your permission, I will dine with you to-day, *tête-à-tête*, and we will see if your malignant old woman will venture to join our company." The patient accepted the proposal with hope and gratitude, for he had expected ridicule rather than sympathy. They met at dinner, and Dr. Gregory, who suspected some nervous disorder, exerted his powers of conversation, well known to be of the most varied and

brilliant character, to keep the attention of his host engaged, and prevent him from thinking on the approach of
the fated hour, to which he was accustomed to look forward
with so much terror. He succeeded in his purpose better
than he had hoped. The hour of six came almost un-
noticed, and it was hoped might pass away without any
evil consequence; but it was scarce a moment struck when
the owner of the house exclaimed, in an alarmed voice,
" The hag comes again !" and dropped back in his chair in
a swoon, in the way he had himself described. The
physician caused him to be let blood, and satisfied himself
that the periodical shocks of which his patient complained
arose from a tendency to apoplexy.

The phantom with the crutch was only a species of
machinery, such as that with which fancy is found to supply
the disorder called *Ephialtes*, or nightmare, or indeed any
other external impression upon our organs in sleep, which
the patient's morbid imagination may introduce into the
dream preceding the swoon. In the nightmare an oppression and suffocation is felt, and our fancy instantly
conjures up a spectre to lie on our bosom. In like manner
it may be remarked, that any sudden noise which the
slumberer hears, without being actually awakened by it—
any casual touch of his person occurring in the same
manner—becomes instantly adopted in his dream, and
accommodated to the tenor of the current train of thought,
whatever that may happen to be ; and nothing is more remarkable than the rapidity with which imagination supplies
a complete explanation of the interruption, according to the
previous train of ideas expressed in the dream, even when
scarce a moment of time is allowed for that purpose. In
dreaming, for example, of a duel, the external sound
becomes, in the twinkling of an eye, the discharge of the
combatants' pistols ;—is an orator haranguing in his sleep,
the sound becomes the applause of his supposed audience ;
—is the dreamer wandering among supposed ruins, the

noise is that of the fall of some part of the mass. In short, an explanatory system is adopted during sleep with such extreme rapidity, that supposing the intruding alarm to have been the first call of some person to awaken the slumberer, the explanation, though requiring some process of argument or deduction, is usually formed and perfect before the second effort of the speaker has restored the dreamer to the waking world and its realities. So rapid and intuitive is the succession of ideas in sleep, as to remind us of the vision of the prophet Mahommed, in which he saw the whole wonders of heaven and hell, though the jar of water which fell when his ecstasy commenced, had not spilled its contents when he returned to ordinary existence.

A second, and equally remarkable instance, was communicated to the author by the medical man under whose observation it fell, but who was, of course, desirous to keep private the name of the hero of so singular a history. Of the friend by whom the facts were attested I can only say, that if I found myself at liberty to name him, the rank which he holds in his profession, as well as his attainments in science and philosophy, form an undisputed claim to the most implicit credit.

It was the fortune of this gentleman to be called in to attend the illness of a person now long deceased, who in his lifetime stood, as I understand, high in a particular department of the law, which often placed the property of others at his discretion and control, and whose conduct, therefore, being open to public observation, he had for many years borne the character of a man of unusual steadiness, good sense, and integrity. He was, at the time of my friend's visits, confined principally to his sick-room, sometimes to bed, yet occasionally attending to business, and exerting his mind, apparently with all its usual strength and energy, to the conduct of important affairs intrusted to him; nor did there, to a superficial observer, appear anything in his conduct, while so engaged, that could argue vacillation of intellect, or depression of mind. His outward symptoms of malady argued no acute or alarming disease. But slowness of pulse, absence of appetite, difficulty of digestion, and constant depression of spirits, seemed to draw their origin from some hidden cause, which the patient was determined to conceal. The deep gloom of the unfortunate gentleman—the embarrassment, which he conld not conceal from his friendly physician—the briefness and obvious constraint with which he answered the interrogations of his medical adviser, induced my friend to take other methods for prosecuting his inquiries. He applied to the sufferer's family, to learn, if possible, the source of that secret grief which was gnawing the heart and sucking the life-blood of his unfortunate patient. The persons applied to, after conversing together previously, denied all knowledge of any cause for the burden which obviously affected their relative. So far as they knew—and they thought they could hardly be deceived—his worldly affairs were prosperous; no family loss had occurred which could be followed with such persevering distress ; no entanglements of affection could be supposed to apply to his age, and no sensation of severe remorse could be consistent with his character. The medical gentleman had finally recourse to serious argument with the invalid himself, and urged to him the folly of devoting himself to a lingering and melancholy death, rather than tell the subject of affliction which was thus wasting him. He specially pressed upon him the injury which he was doing to his own character, by suffering it to be inferred that the secret cause of his dejection and its consequences was something too scandalous or flagitious to be made known, bequeathing in this manner to his family a suspected and dishonoured name, and leaving a memory with which might be associated the idea of guilt, which the criminal had died without confessing. The patient, more moved by this species of appeal than by any which had yet been urged, expressed his desire to speak out frankly to

Dr. ——. Every one else was removed, and the door of the sick-room made secure, when he began his confession in the following manner :—

"You cannot, my dear friend, be more conscious than I, that I am in the course of dying under the oppression of the fatal disease which consumes my vital powers ; but neither can you understand the nature of my complaint, and manner in which it acts upon me, nor, if you did, I fear, could your zeal and skill avail to rid me of it."—"It is possible," said the physician, "that my skill may not equal my wish of serving you; yet medical science has many resources, of which those unacquainted with its powers never can form an estimate. But until you plainly tell me your symptoms of complaint, it is impossible for either of us to say what may or may not be in my power, or within that of medicine."—"I may answer you," replied the patient, "that my case is not a singular one, since we read of it in the famous novel of Le Sage. You remember, doubtless, the disease of which the Duke d'Olivarez is there stated to have died ?"—"Of the idea," answered the medical gentleman, "that he was haunted by an apparition, to the actual existence of which he gave no credit, but died, nevertheless, because he was overcome and heart-broken by its imaginary presence."—"I, my dearest doctor," said the sick man, "am in that very case ; and so painful and abhorrent is the presence of the persecuting vision, that my reason is totally inadequate to combat the effects of my morbid imagination, and I am sensible I am dying, a wasted victim to an imaginary disease." The medical gentleman listened with anxiety to his patient's statement, and for the present judiciously avoiding any contradiction of the sick man's preconceived fancy, contented himself with more minute inquiry into the nature of the apparition with which he conceived himself haunted, and into the history of the mode by which so singular a disease had made itself master of his imagination, secured, as it seemed, by strong powers of the understanding, against an attack so irregular. The sick person replied by stating that its advances were gradual, and at first not of a terrible or even disagreeable character. To illustrate this, he gave the following account of the progress of his disease :—

" My visions," he said, " commenced two or three years since, when I found myself from time to time embarrassed by the presence of a large cat, which came and disappeared I could not exactly tell how, till the truth was finally forced upon me, and I was compelled to regard it as no domestic household cat, but as a bubble of the elements, which had no existence save in my deranged visual organs or depraved imagination. Still I had not that positive objection to the animal entertained by a late gallant Highland chieftain, who has been seen to change to all the colours of his own plaid if a cat by accident happened to be in the room with him, even though he did not see it. On the contrary, I am rather a friend to cats, and endured with so much equanimity the presence of my imaginary attendant, that it had become almost indifferent to me ; when, within the course of a few months, it gave place to, or was succeeded by, a spectre of a more important sort, or which at least had a more imposing appearance. This was no other than the apparition of a gentleman-usher, dressed as if to wait upon a Lord Lieutenant of Ireland, a Lord High Commissioner of the Kirk, or any other who bears on his brow the rank and stamp of delegated sovereignty.

" This personage, arrayed in a court dress, with bag and sword, tamboured waistcoat, and chapeau-bras, glided beside me like the ghost of Beau Nash ; and, whether in my own house or in another, ascended the stairs before me, as if to announce me in the drawing-room, and at sometimes appeared to mingle with the company, though it was sufficiently evident that they were not aware of his presence, and that I alone was sensible of the visionary honours which this imaginary being seemed desirous to render me. This freak of the fancy did not produce much impression on me, though it led me to entertain doubts on the nature of my disorder and alarm for the effect it might produce on my intellects. But that modification of my disease also had its appointed duration. After a few months the phantom of the gentleman-usher was seen no more, but was succeeded by one horrible to the sight and distressing to the imagination, being no other than the image of death itself—the apparition of a *skeleton.* Alone or in company," said the unfortunate invalid, " the presence of this last phantom never quits me. I in vain tell myself a hundred times over that it is no reality, but merely an image summoned up by the morbid acuteness of my own excited imagination and deranged organs of sight. But what avail such reflections, while the emblem at once and presage of mortality is before my eyes, and while I feel myself, though in fancy only, the companion of a phantom representing a ghastly inhabitant of the grave, even while I yet breathe on the earth? Science, philosophy, even religion, has no cure for such a disorder ; and I feel too surely that I shall die the victim to so melancholy a disease, although I have no belief whatever in the reality of the phantom which it places before me."

The physician was distressed to perceive, from these details, how strongly this visionary apparition was fixed in the imagination of his patient. He ingeniously urged the sick man, who was then in bed, with questions concerning the circumstances of the phantom's appearance, trusting he might lead him, as a sensible man, into such contradictions and inconsistencies as might bring his common-sense, which seemed to be unimpaired, so strongly into the field as might combat successfully the fantastic disorder which produced such fatal effects. " This skeleton, then," said the doctor, " seems to you to be always present to your eyes?" " It is my fate, unhappily," answered the invalid, " always to see it." " Then I understand," continued the physician, "it is now present to your imagination?" " To my imagination it certainly is so," replied the sick man. "And in what part of the chamber do you now conceive the apparition to appear?" the physician inquired. "Immediately at the foot of my bed. When the curtains are left a little open," answered the invalid, "the skeleton, to my thinking, is placed between them, and fills the vacant space." "You say you are sensible of the delusion," said his friend; "have you firmness to convince yourself of the truth of this? Can you take courage enough to rise and place yourself in the spot so seeming to be occupied, and convince yourself of the illusion?" The poor man sighed, and shook his head negatively. "Well," said the doctor, "we will try the experiment otherwise." Accordingly, he rose from his chair by the bedside, and placing himself between the two half-drawn curtains at the foot of the bed, indicated as the place occupied by the apparition, asked if the spectre was still visible? "Not entirely so," replied the patient, "because ycur person is betwixt him and me ; but I observe his skull peering above your shoulder."

It is alleged the man of science started on the instant, despite philosophy, on receiving an answer ascertaining, with such minuteness, that the ideal spectre was close to his own person. He resorted to other means of investigation and cure, but with equally indifferent success. The patient sunk into deeper and deeper dejection, and died in the same distress of mind in which he had spent the latter months of his life; and his case remains a melancholy instance of the power of imagination to kill the body, even when its fantastic terrors cannot overcome the intellect, of the unfortunate persons who suffer under them. The patient, in the present case, sunk under his malady; and the circumstances of his singular disorder remaining concealed, he did not, by his death and last illness, lose any of his well-merited reputation for prudence and sagacity which had attended him during the whole course of his life.

Having added these two remarkable instances to the

general train of similar facts quoted by Ferriar, Hibbert, and other writers who have more recently considered the subject, there can, we think, be little doubt of the proposition, that the external organs may, from various causes, become so much deranged as to make false representations to the mind; and that, in such cases, men, in the literal sense, really *see* the empty and false forms and *hear* the ideal sounds which, in a more primitive state of society, are naturally enough referred to the action of demons or disembodied spirits. In such unhappy cases the patient is intellectually in the condition of a general whose spies have been bribed by the enemy, and who must engage himself in the difficult and delicate task of examining and correcting, by his own powers of argument, the probability of the reports which are too inconsistent to be trusted to.

But there is a corollary to this proposition, which is worthy of notice. The same species of organic derangement which, as a continued habit of his deranged vision, presented the subject of our last tale with the successive apparitions of his cat, his gentleman-usher, and the fatal skeleton, may occupy, for a brief or almost momentary space, the vision of men who are otherwise perfectly clear-sighted. Transitory deceptions are thus presented to the organs which, when they occur to men of strength of mind and of education, give way to scrutiny, and their character being once investigated, the true takes the place of the unreal representation. But in ignorant times those instances in which any object is misrepresented, whether through the action of the senses, or of the imagination, or the combined influence of both, for however short a space of time, may be admitted as direct evidence of a supernatural apparition; a proof the more difficult to be disputed if the phantom has been personally witnessed by a man of sense and estimation, who, perhaps satisfied in the general as to the actual existence of apparitions, has not taken time or trouble to correct his first impressions. This species of deception is so frequent that one of the greatest poets of the present time answered a lady who asked him if he believed in ghosts :—" No, madam ; I have seen too many myself." I may mention one or two instances of the kind, to which no doubt can be attached.

The first shall be the apparition of Maupertuis to a brother professor in the Royal Society of Berlin.

This extraordinary circumstance appeared in the Trans-actions of the Society, but is thus stated by M. Thiebault in his " Recollections of Frederick the Great and the Court of Berlin." It is necessary to premise that M. Gleditsch, to whom the circumstance happened, was a botanist of eminence, holding the professorship of natural philosophy at Berlin, and respected as a man of an habitually serious, simple, and tranquil character.

A short time after the death of Maupertuis,* M. Gleditsch being obliged to traverse the hall in which the Academy held its sittings, having some arrangements to make in the cabinet of natural history, which was under his charge, and being willing to complete them on the Thursday before the meeting, he perceived, on entering the hall, the apparition of M. de Maupertuis, upright and stationary, in the first angle on his left hand, having his eyes fixed on him. This was about three o'clock, afternoon. The professor of natural philosophy was too well acquainted with physical science to suppose that his late president, who had died at Bâle, in the family of Messrs. Bernoullie, could have found his way back to Berlin in person. He regarded the apparition in no other light than as a phantom produced by some derangement of his own proper organs. M. Gleditsch went to his own business, without stopping longer than to ascertain exactly the appearance of that object. But he related the vision to his brethren, and assured them that it was as defined and perfect as the actual person of Maupertuis could have pre-

---

* Long the president of the Berlin Academy, and much favoured by Frederick II., till he was overwhelmed by the ridicule of Voltaire. He retired, in a species of disgrace, to his native country of Switzerland, and died there shortly afterwards.

sented. When it is recollected that Maupertuis died at a distance from Berlin, once the scene of his triumphs—overwhelmed by the petulant ridicule of Voltaire, and out of favour with Frederick, with whom to be ridiculous was to be worthless—we can hardly wonder at the imagination even of a man of physical science calling up his Eidolon in the hall of his former greatness.

The sober-minded professor did not, however, push his investigation to the point to which it was carried by a gallant soldier, from whose mouth a particular friend of the author received the following circumstances of a similar story.

Captain C—— was a native of Britain, but bred in the Irish Brigade. He was a man of the most dauntless courage, which he displayed in some uncommonly desperate adventures during the first years of the French Revolution, being repeatedly employed by the royal family in very dangerous commissions. After the King's death he came over to England, and it was then the following circumstance took place.

Captain C—— was a Catholic, and, in his hour of adversity at least, sincerely attached to the duties of his religion. His confessor was a clergyman who was residing as chaplain to a man of rank in the west of England, about four miles from the place where Captain C—— lived. On riding over one morning to see this gentleman, his penitent had the misfortune to find him very ill from a dangerous complaint. He retired in great distress and apprehension of his friend's life, and the feeling brought back upon him many other painful and disagreeable recollections. These occupied him till the hour of retiring to bed, when, to his great astonishment, he saw in the room the figure of the absent confessor. He addressed it, but received no answer—the eyes alone were impressed by the appearance. Determined to push the matter to the end, Captain C—— advanced on the phantom, which appeared to retreat gradually before him. In this manner he followed it round the bed, when it seemed to sink down on an elbow-chair, and remain there in a sitting posture. To ascertain positively the nature of the apparition, the soldier himself sate down on the same chair, ascertaining thus, beyond question, that the whole was illusion ; yet he owned that, had his friend died about the same time, he would not well have known what name to give to his vision. But as the confessor recovered, and, in Dr. Johnson's phrase, "nothing came of it," the incident was only remarkable as showing that men of the strongest nerves are not exempted from such delusions.

Another illusion of the same nature we have the best reason for vouching as a fact, though, for certain reasons, we do not give the names of the parties. Not long after the death of a late illustrious poet, who had filled, while living, a great station in the eye of the public, a literary friend, to whom the deceased had been well known, was engaged, during the darkening twilight of an autumn evening, in perusing one of the publications which professed to detail the habits and opinions of the distinguished individual who was now no more. As the reader had enjoyed the intimacy of the deceased to a considerable degree, he was deeply interested in the publication, which contained some particulars relating to himself and other friends. A visitor was sitting in the apartment, who was also engaged in reading. Their sitting-room opened into an entrance-hall, rather fantastically fitted up with articles of armour, skins of wild animals, and the like. It was when laying down his book, and passing into this hall, through which the moon was beginning to shine, that the individual of whom I speak saw, right before him, and in a standing posture, the exact representation of his departed friend, whose recollection had been so strongly brought to his imagination. He stopped for a single moment, so as to notice the wonderful accuracy with which fancy had impressed upon the bodily eye the peculiarities of dress and posture of the illustrious poet. Sensible, however, of the delusion, he felt no sentiment save that of wonder at the extraordinary accuracy of the resemblance, and stepped onwards towards the figure, which resolved itself, as he approached, into the various materials of which it was composed. These were merely a screen, occupied by great-coats, shawls, plaids, and such other articles as usually are found in a country entrance-hall. The spectator returned to the spot from which he had seen the illusion, and endeavoured, with all his power, to recall the image which had been so singularly vivid. But this was beyond his capacity ; and the person who had witnessed the apparition, or, more properly, whose excited state had been the means of raising it, had only to return into the apartment, and tell his young friend under what a striking hallucination he had for a moment laboured.

There is every reason to believe that instances of this kind are frequent among persons of a certain temperament, and when such occur in an early period of society, they are almost certain to be considered as real supernatural appearances. They differ from those of Nicolai, and others formerly noticed, as being of short duration, and constituting no habitual or constitutional derangement of the system. The apparition of Maupertuis to Monsieur Gleditsch, that of the Catholic clergyman to Captain C——, that of a late poet to his friend, are of the latter character. They bear to the former the analogy, as we may say, which a sudden and temporary fever-fit has to a serious feverish illness. But, even for this very reason, it is more difficult to bring such momentary impressions back to their real sphere of optical illusions, since they accord much better with our idea of glimpses of the future world than those in which the vision is continued or repeated for hours, days, and months, affording opportunities of discovering, from other circumstances, that the symptom originates in deranged health.

Before concluding these observations upon the deceptions of the senses, we must remark that the eye is the organ most essential to the purpose of realizing to our mind the appearance of external objects, and that when the visual organ becomes depraved for a greater or less time, and to a farther or more limited extent, its misrepresentation of the objects of sight is peculiarly apt to terminate in such hallucinations as those we have been detailing. Yet the other senses or organs, in their turn, and to the extent of their power, are as ready, in their various departments, as the sight itself, to retain false or doubtful impressions, which mislead, instead of informing, the party to whom they are addressed.

Thus, in regard to the ear, the next organ in importance to the eye, we are repeatedly deceived by such sounds as are imperfectly gathered up and erroneously apprehended. From the false impressions received from this organ also arise consequences similar to those derived from erroneous reports made by the organs of sight. A whole class of superstitious observances arise, and are grounded upon inaccurate and imperfect hearing. To the excited and imperfect state of the ear we owe the existence of what Milton sublimely calls—

> The airy tongues that syllable men's names,
> On shores, in desert sands, and wildernesses.

These also appear such natural causes of alarm, that we do not sympathize more readily with Robinson Crusoe's apprehensions when he witnesses the print of the savage's foot in the sand, than in those which arise from his being waked from sleep by some one calling his name in the solitary island, where there existed no man but the shipwrecked mariner himself. Amidst the train of superstitions deduced from the imperfections of the ear, we may quote that visionary summons which the natives of the Hebrides acknowledged as one sure sign of approaching fate. The voice of some absent, or probably some deceased, relative was, in such cases, heard as repeating the party's name. Sometimes the aerial summoner intimated his own death, and at others it was no uncommon circumstance that the person who fancied himself so called, died in consequence;—for the same reason that the negro pines to death who is laid under the ban of an Obi woman, or the Cambro-Briton, whose name is put into the famous cursing well, with the usual ceremonies, devoting him to the infernal gods, wastes away and dies, as one doomed to do so. It may be remarked also, that Dr. Johnson retained a deep impression that, while he was opening the door of his college chambers, he heard the voice of his mother, then at many miles' distance, call him by his name; and it appears he was rather disappointed that no event of consequence followed a summons sounding so decidedly supernatural. It is unnecessary to dwell on this sort of auricular deception, of which most men's recollection will supply instances. The following may be stated as one serving to show by what slender accidents the human ear may be imposed upon. The author was walking, about two years since, in a wild and solitary scene with a young friend, who laboured under the infirmity of a severe deafness, when he heard what he conceived to be the cry of a distant pack of hounds, sounding intermittently. As the season was summer, this, on a moment's reflection, satisfied the hearer that it could not be the clamour of an actual chase, and yet his ears repeatedly brought back the supposed cry. He called upon his own dogs, of which two or three were with the walking party. They came in quietly, and obviously had no accession to the sounds which had caught the author's attention, so that he could not help saying to his companion, " I am doubly sorry for your infirmity at this moment, for I could otherwise have let you hear the cry of the Wild Huntsman." As the young gentleman used a hearing tube, he turned when spoken to, and, in doing so, the cause of the phenomenon became apparent. The supposed distant sound was in fact a nigh one, being the singing of the wind in the instrument which the young gentleman was obliged to use, but which, from various circumstances, had never occurred to his elder friend as likely to produce the sounds he had heard.

It is scarce necessary to add, that the highly imaginative superstition of the Wild Huntsman in Germany seems to have had its origin in strong fancy, operating upon the auricular deceptions, respecting the numerous sounds likely to occur in the dark recesses of pathless forests. The same clew may be found to the kindred Scottish belief, so finely embodied by the nameless author of " Albania :"—

> " There, since of old the haughty Thanes of Ross
> Were wont, with clans and ready vassals thronged,
> To wake the bounding stag, or guilty wolf ;
> There oft is heard at midnight or at noon,
> Beginning faint, but rising still more loud,
> And louder, voice of hunters, and of hounds,
> And horns hoarse-winded, blowing far and keen.
> Forthwith the hubbub multiplies, the air
> Labours with louder shouts and rifer din
> Of close pursuit, the broken cry of deer
> Mangled by throttling dogs, the shouts of men,
> And hoofs, thick-beating on the hollow hill :
> Sudden the grazing heifer in the vale
> Starts at the tumult, and the herdsman's ears
> Tingle with inward dread.   Aghast he eyes
> The upland ridge, and every mountain round,
> But not one trace of living wight discerns,
> Nor knows, o'erawed and trembling as he stands,
> To what or whom he owes his idle fear—
> To ghost, to witch, to fairy, or to fiend,
> But wonders, and no end of wondering finds."*

It must also be remembered, that to the auricular deceptions practised by the means of ventriloquism or otherwise,

---

* The poem of "Albania" is, in its original folio edition, so extremely scarce that I have only seen a copy belonging to the amiable and ingenious Dr. Beattie, besides the one which I myself possess, printed in the earlier part of last century.   It was reprinted by my late friend Dr. Leyden in a small volume entitled "Scottish Descriptive Poems."   "Albania" contains the above, and many other poetical passages of the highest merit.

may be traced many of the most successful impostures which credulity has received as supernatural communications.

The sense of touch seems less liable to perversion than either that of sight or smell, nor are there many cases in which it can become accessary to such false intelligence as the eye and ear, collecting their objects from a greater distance and by less accurate enquiry, are but too ready to convey. Yet there is one circumstance in which the sense of touch as well as others is very apt to betray its possessor into inaccuracy, in respect to the circumstances which it impresses on its owner. The case occurs during sleep, when the dreamer touches with his hand some other part of his own person. He is clearly, in this case, both the actor and patient, both the proprietor of the member touching, and of that which is touched ; while, to increase the complication, the hand is both toucher of the limb on which it rests, and receives an impression of touch from it ; and the same is the case with the limb, which at one and the same time receives an impression from the hand, and conveys to the mind a report respecting the size, substance, and the like, of the member touching. Now, as during sleep the patient is unconscious that both limbs are his own identical property, his mind is apt to be much disturbed by the complication of sensations arising from two parts of his person being at once acted upon, and from their reciprocal action ; and false impressions are thus received, which, accurately enquired into, would afford a clew to many puzzling phenomena in the theory of dreams. This peculiarity of the organ of touch, as also that it is confined to no particular organ, but is diffused over the whole person of the man, is noticed by Lucretius :—

> "Ut si forte manu. quam vis jam corporis, ipse
> Tute tibi partem ferias, æque experiare."

A remarkable instance of such an illusion was told me by a late nobleman. He had fallen asleep, with some uneasy feelings arising from indigestion. They operated in their usual course of visionary terrors. At length they were all summed up in the apprehension that the phantom of a dead man held the sleeper by the wrist, and endeavoured to drag him out of bed. He awaked in horror, and still felt the cold dead grasp of a corpse's hand on his right wrist. It was a minute before he discovered that his own left hand was in a state of numbness, and with it he had accidentally encircled his right arm.

The taste and the smell, like the touch, convey more direct intelligence than the eye and the ear, and are less likely than those senses to aid in misleading the imagination. We have seen the palate, in the case of the porridge-fed lunatic, enter its protest against the acquiescence of eyes, ears, and touch, in the gay visions which gilded the patient's confinement. The palate, however, is subject to imposition as well as the other senses. The best and most acute *bon vivant* loses his power of discriminating betwixt different kinds of wine, if he is prevented from assisting his palate by the aid of his eyes,—that is, if the glasses of each are administered indiscriminately while he is blindfolded. Nay, we are authorized to believe that individuals have died in consequence of having supposed themselves to have taken poison, when, in reality, the draught they had swallowed as such was of an innoxious or restorative quality. The delusions of the stomach can seldom bear upon our present subject, and are not otherwise connected with supernatural appearances, than as a good dinner and its accompaniments are essential in fitting out a daring Tam of Shanter, who is fittest to encounter them when the poet's observation is not unlikely to apply—

> " Inspiring bauld John Barleycorn,
> What dangers thou canst make us scorn !
> Wi' tippenny we fear nae evil,
> Wi' usquebae we'll face the devil.
> The swats sae ream'd in Tammie's noddle,
> Fair play, he caredna deils a bodle !"

Neither has the sense of smell, in its ordinary state, much connexion with our present subject. Mr. Aubrey tells us, indeed, of an apparition which disappeared with a curious perfume as well as a most melodious twang; and popular belief ascribes to the presence of infernal spirits a strong relish of the sulphureous element of which they are inhabitants. Such accompaniments, therefore, are usually united with other materials for imposture. If, as a general opinion assures us, which is not positively discountenanced by Dr. Hibbert, by the inhalation of certain gases or poisonous herbs, necromancers can dispose a person to believe he sees phantoms, it is likely that the nostrils are made to inhale such suffumigation as well as the mouth.*

I have now arrived, by a devious path, at the conclusion of this letter, the object of which is to show from what attributes of our nature, whether mental or corporeal, arises that predisposition to believe in supernatural occurrences. It is, I think, conclusive that mankind, from a very early period, have their minds prepared for such events by the consciousness of the existence of a spiritual world, inferring in the general proposition the undeniable truth that each man, from the monarch to the beggar, who has once acted his part on the stage, continues to exist, and may again, even in a disembodied state, if such is the pleasure of Heaven, for aught that we know to the contrary, be permitted or ordained to mingle amongst those who yet remain in the body. The abstract possibility of apparitions must be admitted by every one who believes in a Deity, and His superintending omnipotence. But imagination is apt to

---

* Most ancient authors, who pretend to treat of the wonders of natural magic, give receipts for calling up phantoms. The lighting lamps fed by peculiar kinds of medicated oil, and the use of suffumigations of strong and deleterious herbs, are the means recommended. From these authorities, perhaps, a professor of legerdemain assured Dr. Alderson of Hull, that he could compose a preparation of antimony, sulphur, and other drugs, which, when burnt in a confined room, would have the effect of causing the patient to suppose he saw phantoms.— See "Hibbert on Apparitions," p. 120.

intrude its explanations and inferences founded on inadequate evidence. Sometimes our violent and inordinate passions, originating in sorrow for our friends, remorse for our crimes, our eagerness of patriotism, or our deep sense of devotion—these or other violent excitements of a moral character, in the visions of night, or the rapt ecstasy of the day, persuade us that we witness, with our eyes and ears, an actual instance of that supernatural communication, the possibility of which cannot be denied. At other times the corporeal organs impose upon the mind, while the eye and the ear, diseased, deranged, or misled, convey false impressions to the patient. Very often both the mental delusion and the physical deception exist at the same time, and men's belief of the phenomena presented to them, however erroneously, by the senses, is the firmer and more readily granted, that the physical impression corresponded with the mental excitement.

So many causes acting thus upon each other in various degrees, or sometimes separately, it must happen early in the infancy of every society that there should occur many apparently well-authenticated instances of supernatural intercourse, satisfactory enough to authenticate peculiar examples of the general proposition which is impressed upon us by belief of the immortality of the soul. These examples of undeniable apparitions (for they are apprehended to be incontrovertible), fall like the seed of the husbandman into fertile and prepared soil, and are usually followed by a plentiful crop of superstitious figments, which derive their sources from circumstances and enactments in sacred and profane history, hastily adopted, and perverted from their genuine reading. This shall be the subject of my next letter.

LETTER II.

Consequences of the Fall on the Communication between Man and the Spiritual World—Effects of the Flood—Wizards of Pharaoh—Text in Exodus against Witches—The word *Witch* is by some said to mean merely Poisoner—Or if in the Holy Text it also means a Divineress, she must, at any rate, have been a Character very different to be identified with it—The original, *Chasaph*, said to mean a person who dealt in Poisons, often a Traffic of those who dealt with familiar Spirits—But different from the European Witch of the Middle Ages—Thus a Witch is not accessary to the Temptation of Job—The Witch of the Hebrews probably did not rank higher than a Divining Woman—Yet it was a Crime deserving the Doom of Death, since it inferred the disowning of Jehovah's Supremacy—Other Texts of Scripture, in like manner, refer to something corresponding more with a Fortune-teller or Divining Woman than what is now called a Witch—Example of the Witch of Endor—Account of her Meeting with Saul—Supposed by some a mere Impostor—By others, a Sorceress powerful enough to raise the Spirit of the Prophet by her own Art—Difficulties attending both Positions—A middle Course adopted, supposing that, as in the Case of Balak, the Almighty had, by Exertion of His Will, substituted Samuel, or a good Spirit in his Character, for the Deception which the Witch intended to produce—Resumption of the Argument, showing that the Witch of Endor signified something very different from the modern Ideas of Witchcraft—The Witches mentioned in the New Testament are not less different from modern Ideas than those of the Books of Moses, nor do they appear to have possessed the Power ascribed to Magicians—Articles of Faith which we may gather from Scripture on this point—That there might be certain Powers permitted by the Almighty to Inferior, and even Evil Spirits, is possible; and in some sense the Gods of the Heathens might be accounted Demons—More frequently, and in a general sense, they were but logs of wood, without sense or power of any kind, and their worship founded on imposture—Opinion that the Oracles were silenced at the Nativity adopted by Milton—Cases of Demoniacs—The Incarnate Possessions probably ceased at the same time as the intervention of Miracles—Opinion of the Catholics—Result, that witchcraft, as the Word is interpreted in the Middle Ages, neither occurs under the Mosaic or Gospel Dispensation—It arose in the Ignorant Period, when the Christians considered the Gods of the Mahommedan or Heathen Nations as Fiends, and their Priests as Conjurers or Wizards—Instance as to the Saracens, and among the Northern Europeans yet unconverted—The Gods of Mexico and Peru explained on the same system—Also the Powahs of North America—Opinion of Mather—Gibb, a supposed Warlock, persecuted by the other Dissenters—Conclusion.

WHAT degree of communication might have existed between the human race and the inhabitants of the other world had our first parents kept the commands of the Creator, can only be subject of unavailing speculation. We do not, perhaps, presume too much when we suppose, with Milton, that one necessary consequence of eating the "fruit of that forbidden tree" was removing to a wider distance from celestial essences the beings who, although originally but a little lower than the angels, had, by their own crime, forfeited the gift of immortality, and degraded themselves into an inferior rank of creation.

Some communication between the spiritual world, by the union of those termed in Scripture "sons of God" and the daughters of Adam, still continued after the Fall, though their inter-alliance was not approved of by the Ruler of mankind. We are given to understand—darkly, indeed, but with as much certainty as we can be entitled to require—that the mixture between the two species of created beings was sinful on the part of both, and displeasing to the Almighty. It is probable, also, that the extreme longevity of the antediluvian mortals prevented their feeling sufficiently that they had brought themselves under the banner of Azrael, the angel of death, and removed to too great a distance the period between their crime and its punishment. The date of the avenging Flood gave birth to a race whose life was gradually shortened, and who, being admitted to slighter and rarer intimacy with beings who possessed a higher rank in creation, assumed, as of course, a lower position in the scale. Accordingly, after this period we hear no more of those

unnatural alliances which preceded the Flood, and are given
to understand that mankind, dispersing into different parts
of the *world, separated from each other, and began, in
various places, and under separate auspices, to pursue the
work of replenishing the world, which had been imposed
upon them as an end of their creation. In the meantime,
while the Deity was pleased to continue his manifestations to
those who were destined to be the fathers of his elect people,
we are made to understand that wicked men—it may be by
the assistance of fallen angels—were enabled to assert rank
with, and attempt to match, the prophets of the God of
Israel. The matter must remain uncertain whether it was by
sorcery or legerdemain that the wizards of Pharaoh, King
of Egypt, contended with Moses, in the face of the prince
and people, changed their rods into serpents, and imitated
several of the plagues denounced against the devoted kingdom. Those powers of the Magi, however, whether obtained
by supernatural communications, or arising from knowledge
of legerdemain and its kindred accomplishments, were
openly exhibited ; and who can doubt that—though we may
be left in some darkness both respecting the extent of their
skill and the source from which it was drawn—we are told
all which it can be important for us to know? We arrive
here at the period when the Almighty chose to take upon
himself directly to legislate for his chosen people, without
having obtained any accurate knowledge whether the crime
of witchcraft, or the intercourse between the spiritual world
and embodied beings, for evil purposes, either existed after
the Flood, or was visited with any open marks of Divine
displeasure.

But in the law of Moses, dictated by the Divinity himself, was announced a text, which, as interpreted literally,
having been inserted into the criminal code of all Christian
nations, has occasioned much cruelty and bloodshed, eith'er
from its tenor being misunderstood, or that, being exclusively calculated for the Israelites, it made part of the judi-

cial Mosaic dispensation, and was abrogated, like the greater part of that law, by the more benign and clement dispensation of the Gospel.

The text alluded to is that verse of the twenty-second chapter of Exodus bearing, "men shall not suffer a witch to live." Many learned men have affirmed that in this remarkable passage the Hebrew word CHASAPH means nothing more than poisoner, although, like the word *veneficus*, by which it is rendered in the Latin version of the Septuagint, other learned men contend that it hath the meaning of a witch also, and may be understood as denoting a person who pretended to hurt his or her neighbours in life, limb, or goods, either by noxious potions, by charms, or similar mystical means. In this particular the witches of Scripture had probably some resemblance to those of ancient Europe, who, although their skill and power might be safely despised, as long as they confined themselves to their charms and spells, were very apt to eke out their capacity of mischief by the use of actual poison, so that the epithet of sorceress and poisoner were almost synonymous. This is known to have been the case in many of those darker iniquities which bear as their characteristic something connected with hidden and prohibited arts. Such was the statement in the indictment of those concerned in the famous murder of Sir Thomas Overbury, when the arts of Forman and other sorcerers having been found insufficient to touch the victim's life, practice by poison was at length successfully resorted to ; and numerous similar instances might be quoted. But supposing that the Hebrew witch proceeded only by charms, invocations, or such means as might be innoxious, save for the assistance of demons or familiars, the connexion between the conjurer and the demon must have been of a very different character under the law of Moses, from that which was conceived in latter days to constitute witchcraft. There was no contract of subjection to a diabolic power, no infernal stamp or sign of such a fatal league, no revellings of Satan and his nags, and no infliction of disease or misfortune upon good men. At least there is not a word in Scripture authorizing us to believe that such a system existed. On the contrary, we are told (how far literally, how far metaphorically, it is not for us to determine) that, when the Enemy of mankind desired to probe the virtue of Job to the bottom, he applied for permission to the Supreme Governor of the world, who granted him liberty to try his faithful servant with a storm of disasters, for the more brilliant exhibition of the faith which he reposed in his Maker. In all this, had the scene occurred after the manner of the like events in latter days, witchcraft, sorceries, and charms would have been introduced, and the Devil, instead of his own permitted agency, would have employed his servant the witch as the necessary instrument of the Man of Uzz's afflictions. In like manner, Satan desired to have Peter, that he might sift him like wheat. But neither is there here the agency of any sorcerer or witch. Luke xxii. 31.

Supposing the powers of the witch to be limited, in the time of Moses, to enquiries at some pretended deity or real evil spirit concerning future events, in what respect, may it be said, did such a crime deserve the severe punishment of death? To answer this question, we must reflect that the object of the Mosaic dispensation being to preserve the knowledge of the True Deity within the breasts of a selected and separated people, the God of Jacob necessarily showed himself a jealous God to all who, straying from the path of direct worship of Jehovah, had recourse to other deities, whether idols or evil spirits, the gods of the neighbouring heathen. The swerving from their allegiance to the true Divinity, to the extent of praying to senseless stocks and stones, which could return them no answer, was, by the Jewish law, an act of rebellion to their own Lord God, and as such most fit to be punished capitally. Thus the pro- phets of Baal were deservedly put to death, not on account of any success which they might obtain by their intercessions and invocations (which, though enhanced with all their vehemence, to the extent of cutting and wounding themselves, proved so utterly unavailing as to incur the ridicule of the prophet), but because they were guilty of apostasy from the real Deity, while they worshipped, and encouraged others to worship, the false divinity Baal. The Hebrew witch, therefore, or she who communicated, or attempted to communicate, with an evil spirit, was justly punished with death, though her communication with the spiritual world might either not exist at all, or be of a nature much less intimate than has been ascribed to the witches of later days; nor does the existence of this law, against the witches of the Old Testament sanction, in any respect, the severity of similar enactments subsequent to the Christian revelation, against a different class of persons, accused of a very different species of crime.

In another passage, the practices of those persons termed witches in the Holy Scriptures are again alluded to; and again it is made manifest that the sorcery or witchcraft of the Old Testament resolves itself into a trafficking with idols, and asking counsel of false deities ; in other words, into idolatry, which, notwithstanding repeated prohibitions, examples, and judgments, was still the prevailing crime of the Israelites. The passage alluded to is in Deuteronomy xviii. 10, 11—"There shall not be found among you any one that maketh his son or his daughter to pass through the fire, or that useth divination, or an observer of times, or an enchanter, or a witch, or a charmer, or a consulter with familiar spirits, or a wizard, or a necromancer." Similar denunciations occur in the nineteenth and twentieth chapters of Leviticus. In like manner, it is a charge against Manasses (2 Chronicles xxxviii.) that he caused his children to pass through the fire, observed times, used enchantments and witchcraft, and dealt with familiar spirits and with wizards. These passages seem to concur with the former, in classing witchcraft among other desertions of the prophets of the Deity, in order to obtain responses by the superstitious practices of the pagan nations around them. To understand the texts otherwise seems to confound the modern system of witchcraft, with all its unnatural and improbable outrages on common sense, with the crime of the person who, in classical days, consulted the oracle of Apollo —a capital offence in a Jew, but surely a venial sin in an ignorant and deluded pagan.

To illustrate the nature of the Hebrew witch and her prohibited criminal traffic, those who have written on this subject have naturally dwelt upon the interview between Saul and the Witch of Endor, the only detailed and particular account of such a transaction which is to be found in the Bible ; a fact, by the way, which proves that the crime of witchcraft (capitally punished as it was when discovered) was not frequent among the chosen people, who enjoyed such peculiar manifestations of the Almighty's presence. The Scriptures seem only to have conveyed to us the general fact (being what is chiefly edifying) of the interview between the witch and the King of Israel. They inform us that Saul, disheartened and discouraged by the general defection of his subjects, and the consciousness of his own unworthy and ungrateful disobedience, despairing of obtaining an answer from the offended Deity, who had previously communicated with him through his prophets, at length resolved, in his desperation, to go to a divining woman, by which course he involved himself in the crime of the person whom he thus consulted, against whom the law denounced death—a sentence which had been often executed by Saul himself on similar offenders. Scripture proceeds to give us the general information that the king directed the witch to call up the Spirit of Samuel, and that the female exclaimed that gods had arisen out of the earth—that Saul, more particularly requiring a description of the apparition (whom, consequently, he did not himself see), she described it as the figure of an old man with a mantle. In this figure the king acknowledges the resemblance of Samuel, and sinking on his face, hears from the apparition, speaking in the character of the prophet, the melancholy prediction of his own defeat and death.

In this description, though all is told which is necessary to convey to us an awful moral lesson, yet we are left ignorant of the minutiæ attending the apparition, which perhaps we ought to accept as a sure sign that there was no utility in our being made acquainted with them. It is impossible, for instance, to know with certainty whether Saul was present when the woman used her conjuration, or whether he himself personally ever saw the appearance which the Pythoness described to him. It is left still more doubtful whether anything supernatural was actually evoked, or whether the Pythoness and her assistant meant to practise a mere deception, taking their chance to prophesy the defeat and death of the broken-spirited king as an event which the circumstances in which he was placed rendered highly probable, since he was surrounded by a superior army of Philistines, and his character as a soldier rendered it likely that he would not survive a defeat which must involve the loss of his kingdom. On the other hand, admitting that the apparition had really a supernatural character, it remains equally uncertain what was its nature or by what power it was compelled to an appearance, unpleasing, as it intimated, since the supposed spirit of Samuel asks wherefore he was disquieted in the grave. Was the power of the witch over the invisible world so great that, like the Erictho of the heathen poet, she could disturb the sleep of the just, and especially that of a prophet so important as Samuel ; and are we to suppose that he, upon whom the Spirit of the Lord was wont to descend, even while he was clothed with frail mortality, should be subject to be disquieted in his grave at the voice of a vile witch, and the command of an apostate prince ? Did the true Deity refuse Saul the response of his prophets, and could a witch compel the actual spirit of Samuel to make answer notwithstanding ?

Embarrassed by such difficulties, another course of explanation has been resorted to, which, freed from some of the objections which attend the two extreme suppositions, is yet liable to others. It has been supposed that something took place upon this remarkable occasion similar to that which disturbed the preconcerted purpose of the prophet Balaam, and compelled him to exchange his premeditated curses for blessings. According to this hypothesis, the divining woman of Endor was preparing to practise upon Saul those tricks of legerdemain or jugglery by which she imposed upon meaner clients who resorted to her oracle. Or we may conceive that in those days, when the laws of Nature were frequently suspended by manifestations of the Divine Power, some degree of juggling might be permitted between mortals and the spirits of lesser note ; in which case we must suppose that the woman really expected or hoped to call up some supernatural appearance. But in either case, this second solution of the story supposes that the will of the Almighty substituted, on that memorable occasion, for the phantasmagoria intended by the witch, the spirit of Samuel in his earthly resemblance—or, if the reader may think this more likely, some good being, the messenger of the Divine pleasure, in the likeness of the departed prophet—and, to the surprise of the Pythoness herself, exchanged the juggling farce of sheer deceit or petty sorcery which she had intended to produce, for a deep tragedy, capable of appalling the heart of the hardened tyrant, and furnishing an awful lesson to future times.

This exposition has the advantage of explaining the surprise expressed by the witch at the unexpected consequences of her own invocation, while it removes the objection of supposing the spirit of Samuel subject to her influence. It does not apply so well to the complaint of Samuel that he was *disquieted*, since neither the prophet, nor any good

angel wearing his likeness, could be supposed to complain
of an apparition which took place in obedience to the direct
command of the Deity. If, however, the phrase is understood, not as a murmuring against the pleasure of Providence,
but as a reproach to the prophet's former friend Saul, that
his sins and discontents, which were the ultimate cause of
Samuel's appearance, had withdrawn the prophet for a
space from the enjoyment and repose of Heaven, to review
this miserable spot of mortality, guilt, grief, and misfortune,
the words may, according to that interpretation, wear no
stronger sense of complaint than might become the spirit of
a just man made perfect, or any benevolent angel by whom
he might be represented. It may be observed that in
Ecclesiasticus (xlvi. 19, 20), the opinion of Samuel's actual
appearance is adopted, since it is said of this man of God,
that *after death he prophesied, and showed the king his latter
end.*

Leaving the further discussion of this dark and difficult
question to those whose studies have qualified them to give
judgment on so obscure a subject, it so far appears clear
that the Witch of Endor, was not a being such as those
believed in by our ancestors, who could transform themselves and others into the appearance of the lower animals,
raise and allay tempests, frequent the company and join the
revels of evil spirits, and, by their counsel and assistance,
destroy human lives, and waste the fruits of the earth, or
perform feats of such magnitude as to a ter the face of
Nature. The Witch of Endor was a mere fortune-teller, to
whom, in despair of all aid or answer from the Almighty, the
unfortunate King of Israel had recourse in his despair, and
by whom, in some way or other, he obtained the awful
certainty of his own defeat and death. She was liable,
indeed, deservedly to the punishment of death for intruding
herself upon the task of the real prophets, by whom the will
of God was at that time regularly made known. But her
existence and her crimes can go no length to prove the

possibility that another class of witches, no otherwise resembling her than as called by the same name, either existed at a more recent period, or were liable to the same capital punishment, for a very different and much more doubtful class of offences, which, however odious, are nevertheless to be proved possible before they can be received as a criminal charge.

Whatever may be thought of other occasional expressions in the Old Testament, it cannot be said that, in any part of that sacred volume, a text occurs indicating the existence of a system of witchcraft, under the Jewish dispensation, in any respect similar to that against which the law-books of so many European nations have, till very lately, denounced punishment; far less under the Christian dispensation—a system under which the emancipation of the human race from the Levitical law was happily and miraculously perfected. This latter crime is supposed to infer a compact implying reverence and adoration on the part of the witch who comes under the fatal bond, and patronage, support, and assistance on the part of the diabolical patron. Indeed, in the four Gospels, the word, under any sense, does not occur; although, had the possibility of so enormous a sin been admitted, it was not likely to escape the warning censure of the Divine Person who came to take away the sins of the world. Saint Paul, indeed, mentions the sin of witchcraft, in a cursory manner, as superior in guilt to that of ingratitude; and in the offences of the flesh it is ranked immediately after idolatry, which juxtaposition inclines us to believe that the witchcraft mentioned by the Apostle must have been analogous to that of the Old Testament, and equivalent to resorting to the assistance of soothsayers, or similar forbidden arts, to acquire knowledge of futurity. Sorcerers are also joined with other criminals, in the Book of Revelations, as excluded from the city of God. And with these occasional notices, which indicate that there was a transgression so called, but leave us ignorant of its exact nature, the writers upon witchcraft attempt to wring out of the New Testament proofs of a crime in itself so disgustingly improbable. Neither do the exploits of Elymas, called the Sorcerer, or Simon, called Magus or the Magician, entitle them to rank above the class of impostors who assumed a character to which they had no real title, and put their own mystical and ridiculous pretensions to supernatural power in competition with those who had been conferred on purpose to diffuse the gospel, and facilitate its reception by the exhibition of genuine miracles. It is clear that, from his presumptuous and profane proposal to acquire, by purchase, a portion of those powers which were directly derived from inspiration, Simon Magus displayed a degree of profane and brutal ignorance inconsistent with his possessing even the intelligence of a skilful impostor; and it is plain that a leagued vassal of hell—should we pronounce him such— would have better known his own rank and condition, compared to that of the apostles, than to have made such a fruitless and unavailing proposal, by which he could only expose his own impudence and ignorance.

With this observation we may conclude our brief remarks upon *witchcraft*, as the word occurs in the Scripture; and it now only remains to mention the nature of the *demonology*, which, as gathered from the sacred volumes, every Christian believer is bound to receive as a thing declared and proved to be true.

And in the first place, no man can read the Bible, or call himself a Christian, without believing that, during the course of time comprehended by the Divine writers, the Deity, to confirm the faith of the Jews, and to overcome and confound the pride of the heathens, wrought in the land many great miracles, using either good spirits, the instruments of his pleasure, or fallen angels, the permitted agents of such evil as it was his will should be inflicted upon, or suffered by, the children of men. This proposition comprehends, of course, the acknowledgment of the truth of miracles during this early period, by which the ordinary laws of nature were occasionally suspended, and recognises the existence in the spiritual world of the two grand divisions of angels and devils, severally exercising their powers according to the commission or permission of the Ruler of the universe.

Secondly, wise men have thought and argued that the idols of the heathen were actually fiends, or, rather, that these enemies of mankind had power to assume the shape and appearance of those feeble deities, and to give a certain degree of countenance to the faith of the worshippers, by working seeming miracles, and returning, by their priests or their oracles, responses which "palter'd in a double sense" with the deluded persons who consulted them. Most of the fathers of the Christian Church have intimated such an opinion. This doctrine has the advantage of affording, to a certain extent, a confirmation of many miracles related in pagan or classical history, which are thus ascribed to the agency of evil spirits. It corresponds also with the texts of Scripture which declare that the gods of the heathen are all devils and evil spirits ; and the idols of Egypt are classed, as in Isaiah, chap. xix. ver. 2, with charmers, those who have familiar spirits, and with wizards. But whatever license it may be supposed was permitted to the evil spirits of that period—and although, undoubtedly, men owned the sway of deities who were, in fact, but personifications of certain evil passions of humanity, as, for example, in their sacrifices to Venus, to Bacchus, to Mars, &c., and therefore might be said, in one sense, to worship evil spirits—we cannot, in reason, suppose that every one, or the thousandth part of the innumerable idols worshipped among the heathen, was endowed with supernatural power ; it is clear that the greater number fell under the description applied to them in another passage of Scripture, in which the part of the tree burned in the fire for domestic purposes is treated as of the same power and estimation as that carved into an image, and pre-ferred for Gentile homage. This striking passage, in which

the impotence of the senseless block, and the brutish ignorance of the worshipper, whose object of adoration is the
work of his own hands, occurs in the 44th chapter of the
prophecies of Isaiah, verse 10 *et seq.* The precise words of
the text, as well as common sense, forbid us to believe that
the images so constructed by common artisans became the
habitation or resting-place of demons, or possessed any
manifestation of strength or power, whether through demoniacal influence or otherwise. The whole system of doubt,
delusion, and trick exhibited by the oracles, savours of the
mean juggling of impostors, rather than the audacious intervention of demons. Whatever degree of power the false
gods of heathendom, or devils in their name, might be permitted occasionally to exert, was unquestionably under the
general restraint and limitation of providence ; and though,
on the one hand, we cannot deny the possibility of such
permission being granted in cases unknown to us, it is certain, on the other, that the Scriptures mention no one spe-
cific instance of such influence expressly recommended to
our belief.

Thirdly, as the backsliders among the Jews repeatedly
fell off to the worship of the idols of the neighbouring
heathens, so they also resorted to the use of charms and
enchantments, founded on a superstitious perversion of
their own Levitical ritual, in which they endeavoured by
sortilege, by Teraphim, by observation of augury, or the
flight of birds, which they called *Nahas*, by the means
of Urim and Thummim, to find as it were a byroad to the
secrets of futurity. But for the same reason that withholds
us from delivering any opinion upon the degree to which the
devil and his angels might be allowed to countenance the
impositions of the heathen priesthood, it is impossible for
us conclusively to pronounce what effect might be permitted by supreme Providence to the ministry of such evil
spirits as presided over, and, so far as they had liberty,
directed, these sinful enquiries among the Jews themselves.

We are indeed assured from the sacred writings, that
the promise of the Deity to his chosen people, if they
conducted themselves agreeably to the law which he had
given, was, that the communication with the invisible world
would be enlarged, so that in the fulness of his time he
would pour out his spirit upon all flesh, when their sons and
daughters should prophesy, their old men see visions, and
their young men dream dreams. Such were the promises
delivered to the Israelites by Joel, Ezekiel, and other holy
seers, of which St. Peter, in the second chapter of the Acts
of the Apostles, hails the fulfilment in the mission of our
Saviour. And on the other hand, it is no less evident that
the Almighty, to punish the disobedience of the Jews,
abandoned them to their own fallacious desires, and suffered
them to be deceived by the lying oracles, to which, in
flagrant violation of his commands, they had recourse. Of
this the punishment arising from the Deity abandoning
Ahab to his own devices, and suffering him to be deceived
by a lying spirit, forms a striking instance.

Fourthly, and on the other hand, abstaining with reverence from accounting ourselves judges of the actions of
Omnipotence, we may safely conclude that it was not
his pleasure to employ in the execution of his judgments
the consequences of any such species of league or compact
betwixt devils and deluded mortals, as that denounced
in the laws of our own ancestors under the name of *witchcraft.* What has been translated by that word seems little
more than the art of a medicator of poisons, combined
with that of a Pythoness or false prophetess ; a crime,
however, of a capital nature, by the Levitical law, since, in
the first capacity, it implied great enmity to mankind, and
in the second, direct treason to the divine Legislator. The
book of Tobit contains, indeed, a passage resembling more
an incident in an Arabian tale or Gothic romance, than a
part of inspired writing. In this, the fumes produced
by broiling the liver of a certain fish are described as

having power to drive away an evil genius who guards the nuptial chamber of an Assyrian princess, and who has strangled seven bridegrooms in succession, as they approached the nuptial couch. But the romantic and fabulous strain of this legend has induced the fathers of all Protestant churches to deny it a place amongst the writings sanctioned by divine origin, and we may therefore be excused from entering into discussion on such imperfect evidence.

Lastly, in considering the incalculable change which took place upon the Advent of our Saviour and the announcement of his law, we may observe that, according to many wise and learned men, his mere appearance upon earth, without awaiting the fulfilment of his mission, operated as an act of banishment of such heathen deities as had hitherto been suffered to deliver oracles, and ape in some degree the attributes of the Deity. Milton has, in the " Paradise Lost," it may be upon conviction of its truth, embraced the theory which identifies the followers of Satan with the gods of the heathen ; and, in a tone of poetry almost unequalled, even in his own splendid writings, he thus describes, in one of his earlier pieces, the departure of these pretended deities on the eve of the blessed Nativity :—

> " The oracles are dumb,
>   No voice or hideous hum
> Runs through the arched roof in words deceiving ;
>   Apollo from his shrine
>   Can no more divine,
> With hollow shriek the steep of Delphos leaving ;
> No nightly trance or breathed spell
> Inspires the pale-eyed priests from the prophetic cell.
>
> " The lonely mountains o'er,
>   And the resounding shore,
> A voice of weeping heard and loud lament ;
>   From haunted spring and dale,
>   Edged with poplar pale,
> The parting Genius is with sighing sent ;

With flower-inwoven tresses torn,
The Nymphs in twilight shade of tangled thickets mourn.

"In consecrated earth,
    And on the holy hearth,
The Lars and Lemures moan with midnight plaint;
    In urns and altars round,
    A drear and dying sound
Affrights the Flamens at their service quaint;
And the chill marble seems to sweat,
While each peculiar Power foregoes his wonted seat.

"Peor and Baalim
    Forsake their temples dim,
With that twice-battered god of Palestine;
    And mooned Ashtaroth,
    Heaven's queen and mother both,
Now sits not girt with tapers' holy shine;
The Lybic Hammon shrinks his horn;
In vain the Tyrian maids their wounded Thammuz mourn.

"And sullen Moloch, fled,
    Hath left in shadows dread
His burning idol all of darkest hue;
    In vain with cymbals ring,
    They call the grisly king,
In dismal dance about the furnace blue;
The brutish gods of Nile as fast,
Isis and Orus, and the Dog Anubis, haste."

The quotation is a long one, but it is scarcely possible to
shorten what is so beautiful and interesting a description of
the heathen deities, whether in the classic personifications
of Greece, the horrible shapes worshipped by mere barbarians, or the hieroglyphical enormities of the Egyptian
Mythology. The idea of identifying the pagan deities,
especially the most distinguished of them, with the manifestation of demoniac power, and concluding that the
descent of our Saviour struck them with silence, so nobly
expressed in the poetry of Milton, is not certainly to be
lightly rejected. It has been asserted, in simple prose,
by authorities of no mean weight; nor does there

appear anything inconsistent in the faith of those who,
believing that, in the elder time, fiends and demons were
permitted an enlarged degree of power in uttering predictions, may also give credit to the proposition, that at the
Divine Advent that power was restrained, the oracles
silenced, and those demons who had aped the Divinity of
the place were driven from their abode on earth, honoured
as it was by a guest so awful.

It must be noticed, however, that this great event had not
the same effect on that peculiar class of fiends who were
permitted to vex mortals by the alienation of their minds,
and the abuse of their persons, in the case of what is called
Demoniacal possession.   In what exact sense we should
understand this word *possession* it is impossible to discover;
but we feel it impossible to doubt (notwithstanding learned
authorities to the contrary) that it was a dreadful disorder,
of a kind not merely natural; and may be pretty well assured
that it was suffered to continue after the Incarnation, because
the miracles effected by our Saviour and his apostles, in
curing those tormented in this way, afforded the most direct
proofs of his divine mission, even out of the very mouths of
those ejected fiends, the most malignant enemies of a power
to which they dared not refuse homage and obedience.
And here is an additional proof that witchcraft, in its
ordinary and popular sense, was unknown at that period;
although cases of possession are repeatedly mentioned in the
Gospels and Acts of the Apostles, yet in no one instance
do the devils ejected mention a witch or sorcerer, or plead
the commands of such a person, as the cause of occupying
or tormenting the victim;—whereas, in a great proportion of
those melancholy cases of witchcraft with which the records
of later times abound, the stress of the evidence is rested on
the declaration of the possessed, or the demon within him,
that some old man or woman in the neighbourhood had
compelled the fiend to be the instrument of evil.

It must also be admitted that in another most remarkable

respect, the power of the Enemy of mankind was rather enlarged than bridled or restrained, in consequence of the Saviour coming upon earth. It is indisputable that, in order that Jesus might have his share in every species of delusion and persecution which the fallen race of Adam is heir to, he personally suffered the temptation in the wilderness at the hand of Satan, whom, without resorting to his divine power, he drove, confuted, silenced, and shamed, from his presence. But it appears, that although Satan was allowed, upon this memorable occasion, to come on earth with great power, the permission was given expressly because his time was short.

The indulgence which was then granted to him in a case so unique and peculiar soon passed over and was utterly restrained. It is evident that, after the lapse of the period during which it pleased the Almighty to establish His own Church by miraculous displays of power, it could not consist with his kindness and wisdom to leave the enemy in the possession of the privilege of deluding men by imaginary miracles calculated for the perversion of that faith which real miracles were no longer present to support. There would, we presume to say, be a shocking inconsistency in supposing that false and deceitful prophecies and portents should be freely circulated by any demoniacal influence, deceiving men's bodily organs, abusing their minds, and perverting their faith, while the true religion was left by its great Author devoid of every supernatural sign and token which, in the time of its Founder and His immediate disciples, attested and celebrated their inappreciable mission. Such a permission on the part of the Supreme Being would be (to speak under the deepest reverence) an abandonment of His chosen people, ransomed at such a price, to the snares of an enemy from whom the worst evils were to be apprehended. Nor would it consist with the remarkable promise in holy writ, that "God will not suffer His people to be tempted above what they are able to bear." 1 Cor. x. 13. The Fathers of the Faith are not strictly agreed at what period the miraculous power was withdrawn from the Church; but few Protestants are disposed to bring it down beneath the accession of Constantine, when the Christian religion was fully established in supremacy. The Roman Catholics, indeed, boldly affirm that the power of miraculous interference with the course of Nature is still in being; but the enlightened even of this faith, though they dare not deny a fundamental tenet of their church, will hardly assent to any particular case, without nearly the same evidence which might conquer the incredulity of their neighbours the Protestants. It is alike inconsistent with the common sense of either that fiends should be permitted to work marvels which are no longer exhibited on the part of Heaven, or in behalf of religion.

It will be observed that we have not been anxious to decide upon the limits of probability on this question. It is not necessary for us to ascertain in what degree the power of Satan was at liberty to display itself during the Jewish dispensation, or down to what precise period in the history of the Christian Church cures of demoniacal possession or similar displays of miraculous power may have occurred. We have avoided controversy on that head, because it comprehends questions not more doubtful than unedifying. Little benefit could arise from attaining the exact knowledge of the manner in which the apostate Jews practised unlawful charms or auguries. After their conquest and dispersion they were remarked among the Romans for such superstitious practices; and the like, for what we know, may continue to linger among the benighted wanderers of their race at the present day. But all these things are extraneous to our enquiry, the purpose of which was to discover whether any real evidence could be derived from sacred history to prove the early existence of that branch of demonology which has been the object, in comparatively modern times, of criminal prosecution and capital punishment. We have already alluded to this as the contract of witchcraft, in which,

as the term was understood in the Middle Ages, the demon
and the witch or wizard combined their various powers of
doing harm to inflict calamities upon the person and property, the fortune and the fame, of innocent human beings,
imposing the most horrible diseases, aud death itself, as
marks of their slightest ill-will ; transforming their own persons and those of others at their pleasure ; raising tempests
to ravage the crops of their enemies, or carryiug them home
to their own garners ; annihilating or transferring to their
own dairies the produce of herds ; spreading pestilence
among cattle, infecting and blighting children ; and, in a
word, doing more evil than the heart of man might be
supposed capable of conceiving, by means far beyond mere
human power to accomplish. If it could be supposed that
such unnatural leagues existed, and that there were wretches
wicked enough, merely for the gratification of malignant spite
or the enjoyment of some beastly revelry, to become the
wretched slaves of infernal spirits, most just and equitable
would be those laws which cut them off from the midst of
every Christian commonwealth. But it is still more just and
equitable, before punishment be inflicted for any crime, to
prove that there is a possibility of that crime being committed. We have therefore advanced an important step in
our enquiry when we have ascertained that the *witch* of the
Old Testament was not capable of anything beyond the
administration of baleful drugs or the practising of paltry
imposture ; in other words, that she did not hold the character ascribed to a modern sorceress. We have thus removed out of the argument the startling objection that, in
denying the existence of witchcraft, we deny the possibility
of a crime which was declared capital in the Mosaic law,
and are left at full liberty to adopt the opinion, that the
more modern system of witchcraft was a part, and by no
means the least gross, of that mass of errors which appeared
among the members of the Christian Church when their
religion, becoming gradually corrupted by the devices of

men and the barbarism of those nations among whom it was spread showed, a light indeed, but one deeply tinged with the remains of that very pagan ignorance which its Divine Founder came to dispel.

We will, in a future part of this enquiry, endeavour to show that many of the particular articles of the popular belief respecting magic and witchcraft were derived from the opinions which the ancient heathens entertained as part of their religion. To recommend them, however, they had principles lying deep in the human mind and heart of all times; the tendency to belief in supernatural agencies is natural, and indeed seems connected with and deduced from the invaluable conviction of the certainty of a future state. Moreover, it is very possible that particular stories of this class may have seemed undeniable in the dark ages, though our better instructed period can explain them in a satisfactory manner by the excited temperament of specta-tors, or the influence of delusions produced by derangement of the intellect or imperfect reports of the external senses. They obtained, however, universal faith and credit; and the churchmen, either from craft or from ignorance, favoured the progress of a belief which certainly contributed in a most powerful manner to extend their own authority over the human mind.

To pass from the pagans of antiquity—the Mahomme-dans, though their profession of faith is exclusively unitarian, were accounted worshippers of evil spirits, who were sup-posed to aid them in their continual warfare against the Christians, or to protect and defend them in the Holy Land, where their abode gave so much scandal and offence to the devout. Romance, and even history, combined in repre-senting all who were out of the pale of the Church as the personal vassals of Satan, who played his deceptions openly amongst them; and Mahound, Termagaunt, and *Apollo* were, in the opinion of the Western Crusaders, only so many names of the arch-fiend and his principal angels.

The most enormous fictions spread abroad and believed through Christendom attested the fact, that there were open displays of supernatural aid afforded by the evil spirits to the Turks and Saracens; and fictitious reports were not less liberal in assigning to the Christians extraordinary means of defence through the direct protection of blessed saints and angels, or of holy men yet in the flesh, but already anticipating the privileges proper to a state of beatitude and glory, and possessing the power to work miracles.

To show the extreme grossness of these legends, we may give an example from the romance of " Richard Cœur de Lion," premising at the same time that, like other romances, it was written in what the author designed to be the style of true history, and was addressed to hearers and readers, not as a tale of fiction, but a real narrative of facts, so that the legend is a proof of what the age esteemed credible and were disposed to believe as much as if had been extracted from a graver chronicle.

The renowned Saladin, it is said, had dispatched an embassy to King Richard, with the present of a colt recommended as a gallant war-horse, challenging Cœur de Lion to meet him in single combat between the armies, for the purpose of deciding at once their pretensions to the land of Palestine, and the theological question whether the God of the Christians, or Jupiter, the deity of the Saracens, should be the future object of adoration by the subjects of both monarchs. Now, under this seemingly chivalrous defiance ⁚⁚ concealed a most unknightly stratagem, and which we ᴎ. ᴀt the same time call a very clumsy trick for the devil to be concerned in. A Saracen clerk had conjured two devils into a mare and her colt, with the instruction, that whenever the mare neighed, the foal, which was a brute of uncommon size, should kneel down to suck his dam. The enchanted foal was sent to King Richard in the belief that the foal, obeying the signal of its dam as usual, the

Soldan who mounted the mare might get an easy advantage over him.

But the English king was warned by an angel in a dream of the intended stratagem, and the colt was, by the celestial mandate, previously to the combat, conjured in the holy name to be obedient to his rider during the encounter. The fiend-horse intimated his submission by drooping his head, but his word was not entirely credited. His ears were stopped with wax. In this condition, Richard, armed at all points and with various marks of his religious faith displayed on his weapons, rode forth to meet Saladin, and the Soldan, confident of his stratagem, encountered him boldly. The mare neighed till she shook the ground for miles around; but the sucking devil, whom the wax prevented from hearing the summons, could not obey the signal. Saladin was dismounted, and narrowly escaped death, while his army were cut to pieces by the Christians. It is but an awkward tale of wonder where a demon is worsted by a trick which could hardly have cheated a common horse-jockey; but by such legends our ancestors were amused and interested, till their belief respecting the demons of the Holy Land seems to have been not very far different from that expressed in the title of Ben Jonson's play, "The Devil is an Ass."

One of the earliest maps ever published, which appeared at Rome in the sixteenth century, intimates a similar belief in the connexion of the heathen nations of the north of Europe with the demons of the spiritual world. In Esthonia, Lithuania, Courland, and such districts, the chart, for want, it may be supposed, of an accurate account of the country, exhibits rude cuts of the fur-clad natives paying homage at the shrines of demons, who make themselves visibly present to them; while at other places they are displayed as doing battle with the Teutonic knights, or other military associations formed for the conversion or expulsion of the heathens in these parts. Amid the pagans, armed with scimitars and dressed in caftans, the fiends are painted as assisting them, pourtrayed in all the modern horrors of the cloven foot, or, as the Germans term it, horse's foot, bat wings, saucer eyes, locks like serpents, and tail like a dragon. These attributes, it may be cursorily noticed, themselves intimate the connexion of modern demonology with the mythology of the ancients. The cloven foot is the attribute of Pan—to whose talents for inspiring terror we owe the word *panic*—the snaky tresses are borrowed from the shield of Minerva, and the dragon train alone seems to be connected with the Scriptural history.*

Other heathen nations, whose creeds could not have directly contributed to the system of demonology, because their manners and even their very existence was unknown when it was adopted, were nevertheless involved, so soon as Europeans became acquainted with them, in the same charge of witchcraft and worship of demons brought by the Christians of the Middle Ages against the heathens of northern Europe and the Mahommedans of the East. We learn from the information of a Portuguese voyager that even the native Christians (called those of St. Thomas), whom the discoverers found in India when they first arrived there, fell under suspicion of diabolical practices. It was almost in vain that the priests of one of their chapels produced to the Portuguese officers and soldiers a holy image, and called on them, as good Christians, to adore the Blessed Virgin. The sculptor had been so little acquainted with his art, and the hideous form which he had produced resembled an inhabitant of the infernal regions so much more than Our Lady of Grace, that one of the European officers, while, like his companions, he dropped on his

---

* The chart alluded to is one of the *jac-similes* of an ancient planisphere, engraved in bronze about the end of the 15th century, and called the Borgian Table, from its possessor, Cardinal Stephen Borgia, and preserved in his museum at Veletri.

knees, added the loud protest, that if the image represented the Devil, he paid his homage to the Holy Virgin.

In South America the Spaniards justified the unrelenting
cruelties exercised on the unhappy natives by reiterating,
in all their accounts of the countries which they discovered
and conquered, that the Indians, in their idol worship, were
favoured by the demons with a direct intercourse, and that
their priests inculcated doctrines and rites the foulest and
most abhorrent to Christian ears. The great snake-god of
Mexico, and other idols worshipped with human sacrifices
and bathed in the gore of their prisoners, gave but too much
probability to this accusation ; and if the images themselves
were not actually tenanted by evil spirits, the worship which
the Mexicans paid to them was founded upon such deadly
cruelty and dark superstition as might easily be believed to
have been breathed into mortals by the agency of hell.

Even in North America, the first settlers in New England
and other parts of that immense continent uniformly agreed
that they detected among the inhabitants traces of an intimate connexion with Satan. It is scarce necessary to remark that this opinion was founded exclusively upon the
tricks practised by the native powahs, or cunning men, to
raise themselves to influence among the chiefs, and to
obtain esteem with the people, which, possessed as they were
professionally of some skill in jugglery and the knowledge
of some medical herbs and secrets, the understanding of the
colonists was unable to trace to their real source—legerdemain and imposture. By the account, however, of the
Reverend Cotton Mather, in his *Magnalia*, book vi.,* he
does not ascribe to these Indian conjurers any skill greatly
superior to a maker of almanacks or common fortune-
teller. " They," says the Doctor, " universally acknowledged
and worshipped many gods, and therefore highly esteemed
and reverenced their priests, powahs, or wizards, who were
esteemed as having immediate converse with the gods. To

* " On Remarkable Mercies of Divine Providence."

them, therefore, they addressed themselves in all difficult cases : yet could not all that desired that dignity, as they esteemed it, obtain familiarity with the infernal spirits. Nor were all powahs alike successful in their addresses ; but they became such, either by immediate revelation, or in the use of certain rites and ceremonies, which tradition had left as conducing to that end. In so much, that parents, out of zeal, often dedicated their children to the gods, and educated them accordingly, observing a certain diet, debarring sleep, &c. : yet of the many designed, but few obtained their desire. Supposing that where the practice of witchcraft has been highly esteemed, there must be given the plainest demon-stration of mortals having familiarity with infernal spirits, I am willing to let my reader know, that, not many years since, here died one of the powahs, who never pretended to astrological knowledge, yet could precisely inform such who desired his assistance, from whence goods stolen from them were gone, and whither carried, with many things of the like nature ; nor was he ever known to endeavour to conceal his knowledge to be immediately *from a god subservient to him that the English worship.* This powah, being by an English-man worthy of credit (who lately informed me of the same), desired to advise him who had taken certain goods which had been stolen, having formerly been an eye-witness of his ability, the powah, after a little pausing, demanded why he requested that from him, since himself served another God ? that therefore he could not help him ; but added, ' *If you can believe that my god may help you, I will try what I can do ;* which diverted the man from further enquiry. I must a little digress, and tell my reader, that this powah's wife was accounted a godly woman, and lived in the practice and profession of the Christian religion, not only by the appro-bation, but encouragement of her husband. She constantly prayed in the family, and attended the public worship on the Lord's days. He declared that he could not blame her, for that she served a god that was above his ; but that as to himself, his god's continued kindness obliged him not to forsake his service." It appears, from the above and similar passages, that Dr. Cotton Mather, an honest and devout, but sufficiently credulous man, had mistaken the purpose of the tolerant powah. The latter only desired to elude the necessity of his practices being brought under the observant eye of an European, while he found an ingenious apology in the admitted superiority which he naturally conceded to the Deity of a people, advanced, as he might well conceive, so far above his own in power and attainments, as might reasonably infer a corresponding superiority in the nature and objects of their worship.

From another narrative we are entitled to infer that the European wizard was held superior to the native sorcerer of North America. Among the numberless extravagances of the Scottish Dissenters of the 17th century, now canonized in a lump by those who view them in the general light of enemies to Prelacy, was a certain ship-master, called, from his size, Meikle John Gibb. This man, a person called Jamie, and one or two other men, besides twenty or thirty females who adhered to them, went the wildest lengths of enthusiasm. Gibb headed a party, who followed him into the moorlands, and at the Ford Moss, between Airth and Stirling, burned their Bibles, as an act of solemn adherence to their new faith. They were apprehended in consequence, and committed to prison ; and the rest of the Dissenters, however differently they were affected by the persecution of Government, when it applied to themselves, were nevertheless much offended that these poor mad people were not brought to capital punishment for their blasphemous extravagances ; and imputed it as a fresh crime to the Duke of York that, though he could not be often accused of toleration, he considered the discipline of the house of correction as more likely to bring the unfortunate Gibbites to their senses than the more dignified severities of a public trial and the gallows. The Cameronians, however, did their best to correct this scandalous lenity. As Meikle John Gibb, who was their comrade in captivity, used to disturb their worship in jail by his maniac howling, two of them took turn about to hold him down by force, and silence him by a napkin thrust into his mouth. This mode of quieting the unlucky heretic, though sufficiently emphatic, being deemed ineffectual or inconvenient, George Jackson, a Cameronian, who afterwards suffered at the gallows, dashed the maniac with his feet and hands against the wall, and beat him so severely that the rest were afraid that he had killed him outright. After which specimen of fraternal chastisement, the lunatic, to avoid the repetition of the discipline, whenever the prisoners began worship, ran behind the door, and there, with his own napkin crammed into his mouth, sat howling like a chastised cur. But on being finally transported to America, John Gibb, we are assured, was much admired by the heathen for his familiar converse with the devil bodily, and offering sacrifices to him. "He died there," says Walker, "about the year 1720."* We must necessarily infer that the pretensions of the natives to supernatural communication could not be of a high class, since we find them honouring this poor madman as their superior; and, in general, that the magic, or powahing, of the North American Indians was not of a nature to be much apprehended by the British colonists, since the natives themselves gave honour and precedence to those Europeans who came among them with the character of possessing intercourse with the spirits whom they themselves professed to worship.

Notwithstanding this inferiority on the part of the powahs, it occurred to the settlers that the heathen Indians and Roman Catholic Frenchmen were particularly favoured by the demons, who sometimes adopted their appearance, and showed themselves in their likeness, to the great annoyance of the colonists. Thus, in the year 1692, a party of real or imaginary French and Indians exhibited themselves

* See Patrick Walker's "Biographia Presbyteriana," vol. ii. p. 23; also "God's Judgment upon Persecutors," and Wodrow's "History," upon the article John Gibb.

occasionally to the colonists of the town of Gloucester, in the county of Essex, New England, alarmed the country around very greatly, skirmished repeatedly with the English, and caused the raising of two regiments, and the dispatching a strong reinforcement to the assistance of the settlement. But as these visitants, by whom they were plagued more than a fortnight, though they exchanged fire with the settlers, never killed or scalped any one, the English became convinced that they were not real Indians and Frenchmen, but that the devil and his agents had assumed such an appearance, although seemingly not enabled effectually to support it, for the molestation of the colony.*

It appears, then, that the ideas of superstition which the more ignorant converts to the Christian faith borrowed from the wreck of the classic mythology, were so rooted in the minds of their successors, that these found corroboration of their faith in demonology in the practice of every pagan nation whose destiny it was to encounter them as enemies, and that as well within the limits of Europe as in every other part of the globe to which their arms were carried. In a word, it may be safely laid down, that the commonly received doctrine of demonology, presenting the same general outlines, though varied according to the fancy of particular nations, existed through all Europe. It seems to have been founded originally on feelings incident to the human heart, or diseases to which the human frame is liable—to have been largely augmented by what classic superstitions survived the ruins of paganism —and to have received new contributions from the opinions collected among the barbarous nations, whether of the east or of the west. It is now necessary to enter more minutely into the question, and endeavour to trace from what especial sources the people of the Middle Ages derived those notions which gradually assumed the shape of a regular system of demonology.

* "Magnalia," book vii. article xviii. The fact is also alleged in the "Life of Sir William Phipps."

LETTER III.

Creed of Zoroaster—Received partially into most Heathen Nations—
Instances among the Celtic Tribes of Scotland—Beltane Feast—
Gudeman's Croft—Such abuses admitted into Christianity after the
earlier Ages of the Church—Law of the Romans against Witchcraft
—Roman customs survive the fall of their Religion—Instances—
Demonology of the Northern Barbarians—Nicksas—Bhar-geist—
Correspondence between the Northern and Roman Witches—The
power of Fascination ascribed to the Sorceresses—Example from
the "Eyrbiggia Saga"—The Prophetesses of the Germans—The
Gods of Valhalla not highly regarded by their Worshippers—Often
defied by the Champions—Demons of the North—Story of Assueit
and Asmund—Act on of Ejectment against Spectres—Adventure of
a Champion with the Goddess Freya—Conversion of the Pagans of
Iceland to Christianity—Northern Superstitions mixed with those of
the Celts—Satyrs of the North—Highland Ourisk—Meming the
Satyr.

THE creed of Zoroaster, which naturally occurs to unassisted
reason as a mode of accounting for the mingled existence of
good and evil in the visible world—that belief which, in
one modification or another, supposes the co-existence of a
benevolent and malevolent principle, which contend together
without either being able decisively to prevail over his antagonist, leads the fear and awe deeply impressed on the
human mind to the worship as well of the author of evil, so
tremendous in all the effects of which credulity accounts him
the primary cause, as to that of his great opponent, who is
loved and adored as the father of all that is good and boun-
tiful.   Nay, such is the timid servility of human nature that
the worshippers will neglect the altars of the Author of good
rather than that of Arimanes, trusting with indifference to
the well-known mercy of the one, while they shrink from the
idea of irritating the vengeful jealousy of the awful father
of evil.

The Celtic tribes, by whom, under various denominations, Europe seems to have been originally peopled, possessed, in common with other savages, a natural tendency to the worship of the evil principle. They did not, perhaps, adore Arimanes under one sole name, or consider the malignant divinities as sufficiently powerful to undertake a direct struggle with the more benevolent gods ; yet they thought it worth while to propitiate them by various expiatory rites and prayers, that they, and the elementary tempests which they conceived to be under their direct command, might be merciful to suppliants who had acknowledged their power, and deprecated their vengeance.

Remains of these superstitions might be traced till past the middle of the last century, though fast becoming obsolete, or passing into mere popular customs of the country, which the peasantry observe without thinking of their origin. About 1769, when Mr. Pennant made his tour, the ceremony of the Baaltein, Beltane, or First of May, though varying in different districts of the Highlands, was yet in strict observance, and the cake, which was then baken with scrupulous attention to certain rites and forms, was divided into fragments, which were formally dedicated to birds or beasts of prey that they, or rather the being whose agents they were, might spare the flocks and herds.*

Another custom of similar origin lingered late among us. In many parishes of Scotland there was suffered to exist a certain portion of land, called *the gudeman's croft*, which was never ploughed or cultivated, but suffered to remain waste, like the TEMENOS of a pagan temple. Though it was not expressly avowed, no one doubted that " the goodman's croft" was set apart for some evil being ; in fact, that it was the portion of the arch-fiend himself, whom our ancestors distinguished by a name which, while it was generally under-

* See Pennant's " Scottish Tour," vol. i. p. 111. The traveller mentions that some festival of the same kind was in his time observed in Gloucestershire.

stood, could not, it was supposed, be offensive to the stern inhabitant of the regions of despair. This was so general a custom that the Church published an ordinance against it as an impious and blasphemous usage.

This singular custom sunk before the efforts of the clergy in the seventeenth century; but there must still be many alive who, in childhood, have been taught to look with wonder on knolls and patches of ground left uncultivated, because, whenever a ploughshare entered the soil, the elementary spirits were supposed to testify their displeasure by storm and thunder. Within our own memory, many such places, sanctified to barrenness by some favourite popular superstition, existed, both in Wales and Ireland, as well as in Scotland; but the high price of agricultural produce during the late war renders it doubtful if a veneration for greybearded superstition has suffered any one of them to remain undesecrated. For the same reason the mounts called Sith Bhruaith were respected, and it was deemed unlawful and dangerous to cut wood, dig earth and stones, or otherwise disturb them.*

Now, it may at first sight seem strange that the Christian religion should have permitted the existence of such gross and impious relics of heathenism, in a land where its doctrines had obtained universal credence. But this will not appear so wonderful when it is recollected that the original Christians under the heathen emperors were called to conversion by the voice of apostles and saints, invested for the purpose with miraculous powers, as well of language, for communicating their doctrine to the Gentiles, as of cures, for the purpose of authenticating their mission. These converts must have been in general such elect persons as were effectually called to make part of the infant church; and when hypocrites ventured, like Ananias and Sapphira, to intrude themselves into so select an association, they

---

* See "Essay on the Subterranean Commonwealth," by Mr. Robert Kirke. minister of Aberfoyle.

were liable, at the Divine pleasure, to be detected and punished. On the contrary, the nations who were converted after Christianity had become the religion of the empire were not brought within the pale upon such a principle of selection, as when the church consisted of a few individuals, who had, upon conviction, exchanged the errors of the pagan religion for the dangers and duties incurred by those who embraced a faith inferring the self-denial of its votaries, and at the same time exposing them to persecution. When the cross became triumphant, and its cause no longer required the direction of inspired men, or the evidence of miracles, to compel reluctant belief, it is evident that the converts who thronged into the fold must have, many of them, entered because Christianity was the prevailing faith — many because it was the church, the members of which rose most readily to promotion—many, finally, who, though content to resign the worship of pagan divinities, could not at once clear their minds of heathen ritual and heathen observances, which they inconsistently laboured to unite with the more simple and majestic faith that disdained such impure union. If this was the case, even in the Roman empire, where the converts to the Christian faith must have found, among the earlier members of the church, the readiest and the soundest instruction, how much more imperfectly could those foreign and barbarous tribes receive the necessary religious information from some zealous and enthusiastic preacher, who christened them by hundreds in one day? Still less could we imagine them to have acquired a knowledge of Christianity, in the genuine and perfect sense of the word, when, as was frequently the case, they only assumed the profession of the religion that had become the choice of some favoured chief, whose example they followed in mere love and loyalty, without, perhaps, attaching more consequence to a change of religion than to a change of garments. Such hasty converts, professing themselves Christians, but neither weaned from their old belief, nor instructed in their new one, entered the sanctuary without laying aside the superstitions with which their young minds had been imbued ; and accustomed to a plurality of deities, some of them who bestowed unusual thought on the matter, might be of opinion that, in adopting the God of the Christians, they had not renounced the service of every inferior power.

If, indeed, the laws of the empire could have been supposed to have had any influence over those fierce barbarians, who conceived that the empire itself lay before them as a spoil, they might have been told that Constantine, taking the offence of alleged magicians and sorcerers in the same light in which it was viewed in the law of Moses, had denounced death against any who used these unlawful enquiries into futurity. " Let the unlawful curiosity of prying into futurity," says the law, ": be silent in every one henceforth and for ever.* For, subjected to the avenging sword of the law, he shall be punished capitally who disobeys our commands in this matter."

If, however, we look more closely into this enactment, we shall be led to conclude that the civil law does not found upon the prohibitions and penalties in Scripture ; although it condemns the *ars mathematica* (for the most mystic and uncertain of all sciences, real or pretended, at that time held the title which now distinguishes the most exact) as a damnable art, and utterly interdicted, and declares that the practitioners therein should die by fire, as enemies of the human race—yet the reason of this severe treatment seems to be different from that acted upon in the Mosaical institutions. The weight of the crime among the Jews was placed on the blasphemy of the diviners, and their treason against the theocracy instituted by Jehovah. The Roman legislators were, on the other hand, moved chiefly by the danger arising to the person of the prince and the quiet of the state, so apt to be unsettled by every pretence or

* "Codex," lib. ix. tit. 18, cap. 1, 2, 3, 5, 6, 7, 8.

encouragement to innovation. The reigning emperors, therefore, were desirous to place a check upon the mathematics (as they termed the art of divination), much more for a political than a religious cause, since we observe, in the history of the empire, how often the dethronement or death of the sovereign was produced by conspiracies or mutinies which took their rise from pretended prophecies. In this mode of viewing the crime, the lawyers of the lower empire acted upon the example of those who had compiled the laws of the twelve tables.* The mistaken and misplaced devotion which Horace recommends to the rural nymph, Phidyle, would have been a crime of a deep dye in a Christian convert, and must have subjected him to excommunication, as one relapsed to the rites of paganism ; but he might indulge his superstition by supposing that though he must not worship Pan or Ceres as gods, he was at liberty to fear them in their new capacity of fiends. Some compromise between the fear and the ·conscience of the new converts, at a time when the church no longer consisted exclusively of saints, martyrs, and confessors, the disciples of inspired Apostles, led them, and even their priestly guides, subject like themselves to human passions and errors, to resort as a charm, if not as an act of worship, to those sacrifices, words, and ritual, by which the heathen, whom they had succeeded, pretended to arrest evil or procure benefits.

When such belief in a hostile principle and its imagina-

---

* By this more ancient code, the punishment of death was indeed denounced against those who destroyed crops, awakened storms, or brought over to their barns and garners the fruits of the earth ; but, by good fortune, it left the agriculturists of the period at liberty to use the means they thought most proper to render their fields fertile and plentiful. Pliny informs us that one Caius Furius Cresinus, a Roman of mean estate, raised larger crops from a small field than his neighbours could obtain from more ample possessions. He was brought before the judge upon a charge averring that he conjured the fruits of the earth, produced by his neighbours' farms, into his own possession. Cresinus appeared, and, having proved the return of his farm to be the produce of his own hard and unremitting labour, as well as superior skill, was dismissed with the highest honours.

tions was become general in the Roman empire, the ignorance of its conquerors, those wild nations, Franks, Goths,
Vandals, Huns, and similar classes of unrefined humanity,
made them prone to an error which there were few judicious
preachers to warn them against; and we ought rather
to wonder and admire the Divine clemency, which imparted
to so rude nations the light of the Gospel, and disposed
them to receive a religion so repugnant to their warlike
habits, than that they should, at the same time, have
adopted many gross superstitions, borrowed from the pagans,
or retained numbers of those which had made part of their
own national forms of heathenism.

Thus, though the thrones of Jupiter and the superior
deities of the heathen Pantheon were totally overthrown
and broken to pieces, fragments of their worship and many
of their rites survived the conversion to Christianity—nay,
are in existence even at this late and enlightened period,
although those by whom they are practised have not preserved the least memory of their original purpose. We may
hastily mention one or two customs of classical origin, in
addition to the Beltane and those already noticed, which
remain as examples that the manners of the Romans once
gave the tone to the greater part of the island of Britain,
and at least to the whole which was to the south of the wall
of Severus.

The following customs still linger in the south of Scotland,
and belong to this class : The bride, when she enters the
house of her husband, is lifted over the threshold, and to
step on it or over it voluntarily is reckoned a bad omen.
This custom was universal in Rome, where it was observed
as keeping in memory the rape of the Sabines, and that it
was by a show of violence towards the females that the
object of peopling the city was attained. On the same
occasion a sweet cake, baked for the purpose, is broken
above the head of the bride; which is also a rite of classic
antiquity.

In like manner, the Scottish, even of the better rank, avoid contracting marriage in the month of May, which genial season of flowers and breezes might, in other respects, appear so peculiarly favourable for that purpose. It was specially objected to the marriage of Mary with the profligate Earl of Bothwell, that the union was formed within this interdicted month. This prejudice was so rooted among the Scots that, in 1684, a set of enthusiasts, called Gibbites, proposed to renounce it, among a long list of stated festivals, fast-days, popish relics, not forgetting the profane names of the days of the week, names of the months, and all sorts of idle and silly practices which their tender consciences took an exception to. This objection to solemnize marriage in the merry month of May, however nt a season for courtship, is also borrowed from the Roman pagans, which, had these fanatics been aware of it, would have been an additional reason for their anathema against the practice. The ancients have given us as a maxim, that it is only bad women who marry in that month.*

The custom of saying God bless you, when a person in company sneezes, is, in like manner, derived from sternutation being considered as a crisis of the plague at Athens, and the hope that, when it was attained the patient had a chance of recovery.

But besides these, and many other customs which the various nations of Europe received from the classical times, and which it is not our object to investigate, they derived from thence a shoal of superstitious beliefs, which, blended and mingled with those which they brought with them out of their own country, fostered and formed the materials of a demonological creed which has descended down almost to our own times. Nixas, or Nicksa, a river or ocean god, worshipped on the shores of the Baltic, seems to have taken uncontested possession of the attributes of Neptune. Amid the twilight winters and overpowering tempests of these gloomy

* " Malæ nubent Maia."

regions, he had been not unnaturally chosen as the power most adverse to man, and the supernatural character with which he was invested has descended to our time under two different aspects. The Nixa of the Germans is one of those fascinating and lovely fays whom the ancients termed Naiads ; and unless her pride is insulted or her jealousy awakened by an inconstant lover, her temper is generally mild and her actions beneficent. The Old Nick known in England is an equally genuine descendant of the northern sea-god, and possesses a larger portion of his powers and terrors   The British sailor, who fears nothing else, confesses his terror for this terrible being, and believes him the author of almost all the various calamities to which the precarious life of a seaman is so continually exposed.

The Bhar-guest, or Bhar-geist, by which name it is gene-rally acknowledged through various country parts of England, and particularly in Yorkshire, also called a Dobie —a local spectre which haunts a particular spot under various forms—is a deity, as his name implies, of Teutonic descent; and if it be true, as the author has been informed, that some families bearing the name of Dobie carry a phantom or spectre, passant, in their armorial bearings,* it plainly implies that, however the word may have been selected for a proper name, its original derivation had not then been forgotten.

The classic mythology presented numerous points in which it readily coalesced with that of the Germans, Danes, and Northmen of a later period.   They recognized the power of Erictho, Canidia, and other sorceresses, whose spell could perplex the course of the elements, intercept the influence of the sun, and prevent his beneficial opera-

---

* A similar bearing has been ascribed, for the same reason, to those of the name of Fantome, who carried of old a goblin, or phantom, in a shroud sable passant, on a field azure.   Both bearings are founded on what is called canting heraldry, a species of art disowned by the writers on the science, yet universally made use of by those who practise the art of blazonry.

tion upon the fruits of the earth, call down the moon from her appointed sphere, and disturb the original and destined course of Nature by their words and charms and the power of the evil spirits whom they invoked. They were also professionally implicated in all such mystic and secret rites and ceremonies as were used to conciliate the favour of the infernal powers, whose dispositions were supposed as dark and wayward as their realms were gloomy and dismal. Such hags were frequent agents in the violation of un-buried bodies, and it was believed, by the vulgar at least, that it was dangerous to leave corpses unguarded lest they should be mangled by the witches, who took from them the most choice ingredients composing their charms. Above all, it must not be forgotten that these frightful sorceresses possessed the power of transforming themselves and others into animals, which are used in their degree of quadrupeds, or in whatever other laborious occupation belongs to the transformed state. The poets of the heathens, with authors of fiction, such as Lucian and Apuleius, ascribe all these powers to the witches of the pagan world, combining them with the art of poisoning, and of making magical philtres to seduce the affections of the young and beautiful ; and such were the characteristics which, in greater or less extent, the people of the Middle Ages ascribed to the witches of their day.

But in thus adopting the superstitions of the ancients, the conquerors of the Roman Empire combined them with similar articles of belief which they had brought with them from their original settlements in the North, where the existence of hags of the same character formed a great fea-ture in their Sagas and their Chronicles. It requires but a slight acquaintance with these compositions to enable the reader to recognize in the Galdrakinna of the Scalds the *Stryga* or witch-woman of more classical climates. In the northern ideas of witches there was no irreligion concerned with their lore. On the contrary, the possession of magical knowledge was an especial attribute of Odin himself; and to intrude themselves upon a deity, and compel him to instruct them in what they desired to know, was accounted not an act of impiety, but of gallantry and high courage, among those sons of the sword and the spear. Their matrons possessed a high reputation for magic, for prophetic powers, for creating illusions ; and, if not capable of transformations of the human body, they were at least able to impose such fascination on the sight of their enemies as to conceal for a period the objects of which they were in search.

There is a remarkable story in the Eyrbiggia Saga ("Historia Eyranorum"), giving the result of such a controversy between two of these gifted women, one of whom was determined on discovering and putting to death the son of the other, named Katla, who in a brawl had cut off the hand of the daughter-in-law of Geirada. A party detached to avenge this wrong, by putting Oddo to death, returned deceived by the skill of his mother. They had found only Katla, they said, spinning flax from a large distaff. "Fools," said Geirada, "that distaff was the man you sought." They returned, seized the distaff, and burnt it. But this second time, the witch disguised her son under the appearance of a tame kid. A third time he was a hog, which grovelled among the ashes. The party returned yet again; augmented as one of Katla's maidens, who kept watch, informed her mistress, by one in a blue mantle. "Alas !" said Katla, " it is the sorceress Geirada, against whom spells avail not." Accordingly, the hostile party, entering for the fourth time, seized on the object of their animosity, and put him to death. This species of witchcraft is well known in Scotland as the *glamour*, or *deceptio visus*, and was supposed to be a special attribute of the race of Gipsies.

Neither are those prophetesses to be forgotten, so much honoured among the German tribes, that, as we are assured

* Eyrbiggia Saga, in " Northern Antiquities."

by Tacitus, they rose to the highest rank in their councils, by their supposed supernatural knowledge, and even obtained a share in the direction of their armies. This peculiarity in the habits of the North was so general, that it was no unusual thing to see females, from respect to their supposed views into futurity, and the degree of divine inspiration which was vouchsafed to them, arise to the degree of HAXA, or chief priestess, from which comes the word *Hexe*, now universally used for a witch ; a circumstance which plainly shows that the mythological system of the ancient natives of the North had given to the modern language an appropriate word for distinguishing those females who had intercourse with the spiritual world.*

It is undeniable that these Pythonesses were held in high respect while the pagan religion lasted ; but for that very reason they became odious so soon as the tribe was converted to Christianity. They were, of course, if they pretended to retain their influence, either despised as impostors or feared as sorceresses ; and the more that, in particular instances, they became dreaded for their power, the more they were detested, under the conviction that they derived it from the enemy of man. The deities of the northern heathens underwent a similar metamorphosis, resembling that proposed by Drawcansir in the " Rehearsal," who threatens " to make a god subscribe himself a devil."

The warriors of the North received this new impression

---

* It may be worth while to notice that the word Haxa is still used in Scotland in its sense of a druidess, or chief priestess, to distinguish the places where such females exercised their ritual. There is a species of small intrenchment on the western descent of the Eildon hills, which Mr. Milne, in his account of the parish of Melrose, drawn up about eighty years ago, says, was denominated *Bourjo*, a word of unknown derivation, by which the place is still known. Here an universal and subsisting tradition bore that human sacrifices were of yore offered, while the people assisting could behold the ceremony from the elevation of the glacis which slopes inward. With this place of sacrifice communicated a path, still discernible, called the *Haxell-gate*, leading to a small glen or rarrow valley called the *Haxellcleuch*—both which words are probably derived from the Haxa or chief priestess of the pagans.

concerning the influence of their deities, and the source from which it was derived, with the more indifference, as their worship, when their mythology was most generally established, was never of a very reverential or devotional character. Their idea of their own merely human prowess was so high, that the champions made it their boast, as we have already hinted, they would not give way in fight even to the immortal gods themselves. Such, we learn from Cæsar, was the idea of the Germans concerning the Suevi, or Swabians, a tribe to whom the others yielded the palm of valour; and many individual stories are told in the Sagas concerning bold champions, who had fought, not only with the sorcerers, but with the demigods of the system, and come off unharmed, if not victorious, in the contest. Hother, for example, encountered the god Thor in battle, as Diomede, in the Iliad, engages with Mars, and with like success. Bartholsine* gives us repeated examples of the same kind. "Know this," said Kiartan to Olaus Trigguasen, "that I believe neither in idols nor demons. I have travelled through various strange countries, and have encountered many giants and monsters, and have never been conquered by them; I therefore put my sole trust in my own strength of body and courage of soul." Another yet more broad answer was made to St. Olaus, King of Norway, by Gaukater. "I am neither Pagan nor Christian. My comrades and I profess no other religion than a perfect confidence in our own strength and invincibility in battle." Such chieftains were of the sect of Mezentius—

> "Dextra mihi Deus, et telum, quod missile libro,
> Nunc adsint!"†

And we cannot wonder that champions of such a character, careless of their gods while yet acknowledged as such, readily regarded them as demons after their conversion to Christianity.

* "De causis contemptæ necis," lib. i. cap 6.
† "Æneid," lib. x. line 773.

To incur the highest extremity of danger became accounted a proof of that insuperable valour for which every Northman desired to be famed, and their annals afford numerous instances of encounters with ghosts, witches, furies, and fiends, whom the Kiempé, or champions, compelled to submit to their mere mortal strength, and yield to their service the weapons or other treasures which they guarded in their tombs.

The Norsemen were the more prone to these superstitions, because it was a favourite fancy of theirs that, in many instances, the change from life to death altered the temper of the human spirit from benignant to malevolent ; or perhaps, that when the soul left the body, its departure was occasionally supplied by a wicked demon, who took the opportunity to enter and occupy its late habitation.

Upon such a supposition the wild fiction that follows is probably grounded ; which, extravagant as it is, possesses something striking to the imagination. Saxo Grammaticus tells us of the fame of two Norse princes or chiefs, who had formed what was called a brotherhood in arms, implying not only the firmest friendship and constant support during all the adventures which they should undertake in life, but binding them by a solemn compact, that after the death of either, the survivor should descend alive into the sepulchre of his brother-in-arms, and consent to be buried alongst with him. The task of fulfilling this dreadful compact fell upon Asmund, his companion, Assueit, having been slain in battle. The tomb was formed after the ancient northern custom in what was called the age of hills, that is, when it was usual to bury persons of distinguished merit or rank on some conspicuous spot, which was crowned with a mound. With this purpose a deep narrow vault was constructed, to be the apartment of the future tomb over which the sepulchral heap was to be piled. Here they deposited arms, trophies, poured forth, perhaps, the blood of victims, introduced into the tomb the war-horses of the champions,

and when these rites had been duly paid, the body of
Assueit was placed in the dark and narrow house, while his
faithful brother-in-arms entered and sat down by the corpse,
without a word or look which testified regret or unwillingness
to fulfil his fearful engagement.   The soldiers who had witnessed this singular interment of the dead and living, rolled
a huge stone to the mouth of the tomb, and piled so much
earth and stones above the spot as made a mound visible
from a great distance, and then, with loud lamentation for
the loss of such undaunted leaders, they dispersed themselves
like a flock which has lost its shepherd.

Years passed away after years, and a century had elapsed
ere a noble Swedish rover, bound upon some high adventure
and supported by a gallant band of followers, arrived in the
valley which took its name from the tomb of the brethren-in-
arms.   The story was told to the strangers, whose leader determined on opening the sepulchre, partly because, as already
hinted, it was reckoned a heroic action to brave the anger of
departed heroes by violating their tombs ; partly to attain
the arms and swords of proof with which the deceased had
done their great actions.   He set his soldiers to work, and
soon removed the earth and stones from one side of the
mound, and laid bare the entrance.   But the stoutest of the
rovers started back when, instead of the silence of a tomb,
they heard within horrid cries, the clash of swords, the clang
of armour, and all the noise of a mortal combat between two
furious champions.   A young warrior was let down into the
profound tomb by a cord, which was drawn up shortly after,
in hopes of news from beneath.   But when the adventurer
descended, some one threw him from the cord, and took his
place in the noose.   When the rope was pulled up, the
soldiers, instead of their companion, beheld Asmund, the
survivor of the brethren-in-arms.   He rushed into the open
air, his sword drawn in his hand, his armour half torn from
his body, the left side of his face almost scratched off, as by
the talons of some wild beast.   He had no sooner appeared

in the light of day, than, with the improvisatory poetic talent,
which these champions often united with heroic strength and
bravery, he poured forth a string of verses containing the
history of his hundred years' conflict within the tomb.   It
seems that no sooner was the sepulchre closed than the corpse
of the slain Assueit arose from the ground, inspired by some
ravenous goule, and having first torn to pieces and devoured
the horses which had been entombed with them, threw himself upon the companion who had just given him such a sign
of devoted friendship, in order to treat him in the same
manner.   The hero, no way discountenanced by the horrors
of his situation, took to his arms, and defended himself man-
fully against Assueit, or rather against the evil demon who
tenanted that champion's body.   In this manner the living
brother waged a preternatural combat, which had endured
during a whole century, when Asmund, at last obtaining the
victory, prostrated his enemy, and by driving, as he boasted,
a stake through his body, had finally reduced him to the state
of quiet becoming a tenant of the tomb.   Having chanted
the triumphant account of his contest and victory, this
mangled conqueror fell dead before them.   The body of
Assueit was taken out of the tomb, burnt, and the ashes dispersed to heaven ; whilst that of the victor, now lifeless and
without a companion, was deposited there, so that it was hoped
his slumbers might remain undisturbed.*   The precautions
taken against Assueit's reviving a second time, remind us of
those adopted in the Greek islands and in the Turkish provinces against the vampire.   It affords also a derivation of
the ancient English law in case of suicide, when a stake was
driven through the body, originally to keep it secure in the
tomb.

The Northern people also acknowledged a kind of ghosts,
who, when they had obtained possession of a building, or
the right of haunting it, did not defend themselves against
mortals on the knightly principle of duel, like Assueit, nor

* See Saxo Grammaticus, "Hist. Dan.," lib. v.

were amenable to the prayers of the priest or the spells of the sorcerer, but became tractable when properly convened in a legal process. The Eyrbiggia Saga acquaints us, that the mansion of a respectable landholder in Iceland was, soon after the settlement of that island, exposed to a persecution of this kind. The molestation was produced by the concurrence of certain mystical and spectral phenomena, calculated to introduce such persecution. About the commencement of winter, with that slight exchange of darkness and twilight which constitutes night and day in these latitudes, a contagious disease arose in a family of consequence and in the neighbourhood, which, sweeping off several members of the family at different times, seemed to threaten them all with death. But the death of these persons was attended with the singular consequence that their spectres were seen to wander in the neighbourhood of the mansion-house, terrifying, and even assaulting, those of the living family who ventured abroad. As the number of the dead members of the devoted household seemed to increase in proportion to that of the survivors, the ghosts took it upon them to enter the house, and produce their aërial forms and wasted physiognomy, even in the stove where the fire was maintained for the general use of the inhabitants, and which, in an Iceland winter, is the only comfortable place of assembling the family. But the remaining inhabitants of the place, terrified by the intrusion of these spectres, chose rather to withdraw to the other extremity of the house, and abandon their warm seats, than to endure the neighbourhood of the phantoms. Complaints were at length made to a pontiff of the god Thor, named Snorro, who exercised considerable influence in the island. By his counsel, the young proprietor of the haunted mansion assembled a jury, or inquest, of his neighbours, constituted in the usual judicial form, as if to judge an ordinary civil matter, and proceeded, in their presence, to cite individually the various phantoms and resemblances of the deceased members of the family, to show by what warrant they disputed with him and his servants the quiet possession of his property, and what defence they could plead for thus interfering with and incommoding the living. The spectres of the dead, by name, and in order as summoned, appeared on their being·called, and muttering some regrets at being obliged to abandon their dwelling, departed, or vanished, from the astonished inquest. Judgment then went against the ghosts by default; and the trial by jury, of which we here can trace the origin, obtained a triumph unknown to any of the great writers who have made it the subject of eulogy.*

It was not only with the spirits of the dead that the war-like people of the North made war without timidity, and successfully entered into suits of ejectment. These daring champions often braved the indignation even of the superior deities of their mythology, rather than allow that there existed any being before whom their boldness could quail. Such is the singular story how a young man of high courage, in crossing a desolate ridge of mountains, met with a huge waggon, in which the goddess Freya (*i.e.*, a gigantic idol formed to represent her), together with her shrine, and the wealthy offerings attached to it, was travelling from one dis-trict of the country to another. The shrine, or sanctuary of the idol, was, like a modern caravan travelling with a show, screened by boards and curtains from the public gaze, and the equipage was under the immediate guidance of the priestess of Freya, a young, good-looking, and attractive woman. The traveller naturally associated himself with the priestess, who, as she walked on foot, apparently was in no degree displeased with the company of a powerful and hand-some young man, as a guide and companion on the journey. It chanced, however, that the presence of the champion, and his discourse with the priestess, was less satisfactory to the goddess than to the parties principally concerned. By a

* Eyrbiggia Saga. See "Northern Antiquities."

certain signal the divinity summoned the priestess to the sanctuary, who presently returned, with tears in her eyes and terror in her countenance, to inform her companion that it was the will of Freya that he should depart, and no longer travel in their company. "You must have mistaken the meaning of the goddess," said the champion; "Freya cannot have formed a wish so unreasonable as to desire I should abandon the straight and good road, which leads me directly on my journey, to choose precipitous paths and by-roads, where I may break my neck." "Nevertheless," said the priestess, "the goddess will be highly offended if you disobey her commands, nor can I conceal from you that she may personally assault you." "It will be at her own peril if she should be so audacious," said the champion, "for I will try the power of this axe against the strength of beams and boards." The priestess chid him for his impiety; but being unable to compel him to obey the goddess's mandate, they again relapsed into familiarity, which advanced to such a point that a clattering noise within the tabernacle, as of machinery put in motion, intimated to the travellers that Freya, who perhaps had some qualities in common with the classical Vesta, thought a personal interruption of this tête-à-tête ought to be deferred no longer. The curtains flew open, and the massive and awkward idol, who, we may suppose, resembled in form the giant created by Frankenstein, leapt lumbering from the carriage, and, rushing on the intrusive traveller, dealt him, with its wooden hands and arms, such tremendous blows, as were equally difficult to parry or to endure. But the champion was armed with a double-edged Danish axe, with which he bestirred himself with so much strength and activity, that at length he split the head of the image, and with a severe blow hewed off its left leg. The image of Freya then fell motionless to the ground, and the demon which had animated it fled yelling from the battered tenement. The champion was now victor; and, according to the law of arms, took possession of the female and the baggage. The priestess, the divinity of whose patroness had been by the event of the combat sorely lessened in her eyes, was now easily induced to become the associate and concubine of the conqueror. She accompanied him to the district whither he was travelling, and there displayed the shrine of Freya, taking care to hide the injuries which the goddess had received in the brawl. The champion came in for a share of a gainful trade driven by the priestess, besides appropriating to himself most of the treasures which the sanctuary had formerly contained. Neither does it appear that Freya, having, perhaps, a sensible recollection of the power of the axe, ever again ventured to appear in person for the purpose of calling her false stewards to account.

The national estimation of deities, concerning whom such stories could be told and believed, was, of course, of no deep or respectful character. The Icelanders abandoned Odin, Freya, Thor, and their whole pagan mythology, in consideration of a single disputation between the heathen priests and the Christian missionaries. The priests threatened the island with a desolating eruption of the volcano called Hecla, as the necessary consequence of the vengeance of their deities. Snorro, the same who advised the inquest against the ghosts, had become a convert to the Christian religion, and was present on the occasion, and as the conference was held on the surface of what had been a stream of lava, now covered with vegetable substances, he answered the priests with much readiness, " To what was the indignation of the gods owing when the substance on which we stand was fluid and scorching ? Believe me, men of Iceland, the eruption of the volcano depends on natural circumstances now as it did then, and is not the engine of vengeance intrusted to Thor and Odin." It is evident that men who reasoned with so much accuracy concerning the imbecility of Odin and Thor were well prepared, on abandoning their worship, to consider their former deities, of whom they believed so much that was impious, in the light of evil demons.

But there were some particulars of the Northern creed in which it corresponded so exactly with that of the classics as leaves room to doubt whether the original Asæ, or Asiatics, the founders of the Scandinavian system, had, before their migration from Asia, derived them from some common source with those of the Greeks and Romans ; or whether, on the other hand, the same proneness of the human mind to superstition has caused that similar ideas are adopted in different regions, as the same plants are found in distant countries without the one, as far as can be discovered, having obtained the seed from the others.

The classical fiction, for example, of the satyrs and other subordinate deities of wood and wild, whose power is rather delusive than formidable, and whose supernatural pranks intimate rather a wish to inflict terror than to do hurt, was received among the Northern people, and perhaps transferred by them to the Celtic tribes. It is an idea which seems common to many nations. The existence of a satyr, in the silvan form, is even pretended to be proved by the evidence of Saint Anthony, to whom one is said to have appeared in the desert. The Scottish Gael have an idea of the same kind, respecting a goblin called *Ourisk*, whose form is like that of Pan, and his attendants something between a man and a goat, the nether extremities being in the latter form. A species of cavern, or rather hole, in the rock, affords to the wildest retreat in the romantic neighbourhood of Loch Katrine a name taken from classical superstition. It is not the least curious circumstance that from this silvan deity the modern nations of Europe have borrowed the degrading and unsuitable emblems of the goat's visage and form, the horns, hoofs, and tail, with which they have depicted the author of evil when it pleased him to show himself on earth. So that the alteration of a single word would render Pope's well-known line more truly adapted to the fact, should we venture to read—

" And Pan to *Satan* lends his heathen horn."

We cannot attribute the transferrence of the attributes of the Northern satyr, or Celtic ourisk, to the arch-fiend, to any particular resemblance between the character of these deities and that of Satan.   On the contrary, the ourisk of the Celts was a creature by no means peculiarly malevolent or formidably powerful, but rather a melancholy spirit, which dwelt in wildernesses far removed from men.   If we are to identify him with the Brown Dwarf of the Border moors, the ourisk has a mortal term of life and a hope of salvation, as indeed the same high claim was made by the satyr who appeared to St. Anthony.   Moreover, the Highland ourisk was a species of lubber fiend, and capable of being over-reached by those who understood philology.   It is related of one of these goblins which frequented a mill near the foot of Loch Lomond, that the miller, desiring to get rid of this meddling spirit, who injured the machinery by setting the water on the wheel when there was no grain to be grinded, contrived to have a meeting with the goblin by watching in his mill till night.   The ourisk then entered, and demanded the miller's name, and was informed that he was called *Myself ;* on which is founded a story almost exactly like that of OUTIS in the " Odyssey," a tale which, though classic, is by no means an elegant or ingenious fiction, but which we are astonished to find in an obscure district, and in the Celtic tongue, seeming to argue some connexion or communication between these remote Highlands of Scotland and the readers of Homer in former days, which we cannot account for.   After all, perhaps, some Churchman more learned than his brethren may have transferred the legend from Sicily to Duncrune, from the shores of the Mediterranean to those of Loch Lomond.   I have heard it also told that the celebrated freebooter, Rob Roy, once gained a victory by disguising a part of his men with goat-skins, so as to resemble the *ourisk* or Highland satyr.

There was an individual satyr called, I think, Meming, belonging to the Scandinavian mythology, of a character different from the ourisk, though similar in shape, whom it was the boast of the highest champions to seek out in the solitudes which he inhabited. He was an armourer of extreme. dexterity, and the weapons which he forged were of the highest value. But as club-law pervaded the ancient system of Scandinavia, Meming had the humour of refusing to work for any customer save such as compelled him to it with force of arms. He may be, perhaps, identified with the recusant smith who fled before Fingal from Ireland to the Orkneys, and being there overtaken, was compelled to forge the sword which Fingal afterwards wore in all his battles, and which was called the Son of the dark brown Luno, from the name of the armourer who forged it.*

From this it will appear that there were originals enough in the mythology of the Goths, as well as Celts, to furnish the modern attributes ascribed to Satan in later times, when the object of painter or poet was to display him in his true form and with all his terrors. Even the genius of Guido and of Tasso have been unable to surmount this prejudice, the more rooted, perhaps, that the wicked are described as goats in Scripture, and that the devil is called the old dragon. In Raffael's famous painting of the archangel Michael binding Satan, the dignity, power, and angelic character expressed by the seraph form an extraordinary contrast to the poor conception of a being who ought not, even in that lowest degradation, to have seemed so unworthy an antagonist. Neither has Tasso been more happy, where he represents the divan of darkness in the enchanted forest as presided over by a monarch having a

* The weapon is often mentioned in Mr. MacPherson's paraphrases; but the Irish ballad, which gives a spirited account of the debate between the champion and the armourer, is nowhere introduced.

huge tail, hoofs, and all the usual accompaniments of popular diablerie. The genius of Milton alone could discard all these vulgar puerilities, and assign to the author of evil the terrible dignity of one who should seem not "less than archangel ruined." This species of degradation is yet grosser when we take into consideration the changes which popular opinions have wrought respecting the taste, habits, powers, modes of tempting, and habits of tormenting, which are such as might rather be ascribed to some stupid superannuated and doting ogre of a fairy tale, than to the powerful-minded demon who fell through pride and rebellion, not through folly or incapacity.

Having, however, adopted our present ideas of the devil as they are expressed by his nearest acquaintances, the witches, from the accounts of satyrs, which seem to have been articles of faith both among the Celtic and Gothic tribes, we must next notice another fruitful fountain of demonological fancies. But as this source of the mythology of the Middle Ages must necessarily comprehend some account of the fairy folk, to whom much of it must be referred, it is necessary to make a pause before we enter upon the mystic and marvellous connexion supposed to exist between the impenitent kingdom of Satan and those merry dancers by moonlight.

LETTER IV.

The Fairy Superstition is derived from different sources—The Classical Worship of the Silvans, or Rural Deities, proved by Roman Altars discovered—The Gothic Duergar, or Dwarfs—Supposed to be derived from the Northern Laps, or Fins—" The Niebelungen-Lied" —King Laurin's Adventure—Celtic Fairies of a gayer character, yet their pleasures empty and illusory—Addicted to carry off Human Beings, both Infants and Adults—Adventures of a Butler in Ireland —The Elves supposed to pay a Tax to Hell—The Irish, Welsh, Highlanders, and Manxmen held the same belief—It was rather rendered more gloomy by the Northern Traditions—Merlin and Arthur carried off by the Fairies—Also Thomas of Erceldoune— His Amour with the Queen of Elfland—His re-appearance in latter times—Another account from Reginald Scot—Conjectures on the derivation of the word Fairy.

WE may premise by observing, that the classics had not forgotten to enrol in their mythology a certain species of subordinate deities, resembling the modern elves in their habits. Good old Mr. Gibb, of the Advocates' Library (whom all lawyers whose youth he assisted in their studies, by his knowledge of that noble collection, are bound to name with gratitude), used to point out, amongst the ancient altars under his charge, one which is consecrated, *Diis campestribus*, and usually added, with a wink, " The fairies, ye ken."* This relic of antiquity was discovered near Roxburgh Castle, and a vicinity more delightfully appropriate to the abode of the silvan deities can hardly be found.

* Another altar of elegant form and perfectly preserved, was, within these few weeks, dug up near the junction of the Leader and the Tweed, in the neighbourhood of the village of Newstead, to the east of Melrose. It was inscribed by Carrius Domitianus, the prefect of the twentieth legion, to the god Sylvanus, forming another instance how much the wild and silvan character of the country disposed the feelings of the Romans to acknowledge the presence of the rural deities. The altar is preserved ot Drygrange, the seat of Mr. Tod.

Two rivers of considerable size, made yet more remarkable by the fame which has rendered them in some sort classical, unite their streams beneath the vestiges of an extensive castle, renowned in the wars with England, and for the valiant, noble, and even royal blood, which has been shed around and before it—a landscape ornamented with the distant village and huge abbey tower of Kelso, arising out of groves of aged trees—the modern mansion of Fleurs, with its terrace, its woods, and its extensive lawn—form altogether a kingdom for Oberon and Titania to reign in, or any spirit who, before their time, might love scenery, of which the majesty, and even the beauty, impress the mind with a sense of awe mingled with pleasure. These silvans, satyrs, and fauns with whom superstition peopled the lofty banks and tangled copses of this romantic country, were obliged to give place to deities very nearly resembling themselves in character, who probably derive some of their attributes from their classic predecessors, although more immediately allied to the barbarian conquerors. We allude to the fairies, which, as received into the popular creed, and as described by the poets who have made use of them as machinery, are certainly among the most pleasing legacies of fancy.

Dr. Leyden, who exhausted on this subject, as upon most others, a profusion of learning, found the first idea of the elfin people in the Northern opinions concerning the duergar, or dwarfs.* These were, however, it must be owned, spirits of a coarser sort, more laborious vocation, and more malignant temper, and in all respects less propitious to humanity, than the fairies (properly so called), which were the invention of the Celtic people, and displayed that superiority of taste and fancy which, with the love of music and poetry, has been generally ascribed to their race, through its various classes and modifications.

* See the essay on the Fairy Superstition, in the "Minstrelsy of the Scottish Border," of which many of the materials were contributed by Dr. Leyden, and the whole brought into its present form by the author.

In fact, there seems reason to conclude that these duergar were originally nothing else than the diminutive natives of the Lappish, Lettish, and Finnish nations, who, flying before the conquering weapons of the Asæ, sought the most retired regions of the North, and there endeavoured to hide themselves from their Eastern invaders. They were a little, diminutive race, but possessed of some skill probably in mining or smelting minerals, with which the country abounds. Perhaps also they might, from their acquaintance with the changes of the clouds, or meteorological phenomena, be judges of weather, and so enjoy another title to supernatural skill. At any rate, it has been plausibly supposed that these poor people, who sought caverns and hiding-places from the persecution of the Asæ, were in some respects compensated for inferiority in strength and stature by the art and power with which the superstition of the enemy invested them. These oppressed yet dreaded fugitives obtained, naturally enough, the character of the German spirits called Kobold, from which the English goblin and the Scottish bogle, by some inversion and alteration of pronunciation, are evidently derived.

The Kobolds were a species of gnomes, who haunted the dark and solitary places, and were often seen in the mines, where they seemed to imitate the labours of the miners, and sometimes took pleasure in frustrating their objects and rendering their toil unfruitful. Sometimes they were malignant, especially if neglected or insulted; but sometimes also they were indulgent to individuals whom they took under their protection. When a miner, therefore, hit upon a rich vein of ore, the inference commonly was, not that he possessed more skill, industry, or even luck, than his fellow-workmen, but that the spirits of the mine had directed him to the treasure. The employment and apparent occupation of these subterranean gnomes or fiends, led very naturally to identify the Fin, or Laplander, with the Kobold ; but it was a bolder stretch of the imagination which confounded this reserved and sullen race with the livelier and gayer spirit which bears correspondence with the British fairy. Neither can we be surprised that the duergar, ascribed by many persons to this source, should exhibit a darker and more malignant character than the elves that revel by moonlight in more southern climates.

According to the old Norse belief, these dwarfs form the current machinery of the Northern Sagas, and their inferiority in size is represented as compensated by skill and wisdom superior to those of ordinary mortals. In the "Niebelungen-Lied," one of the oldest romances of Germany, and compiled, it would seem, not long after the time of Attila, Theodorick of Bern, or of Verona, figures among a cycle of champions over whom he presides, like the Charlemagne of France or Arthur of England. Among others vanquished by him is the Elf King, or Dwarf Laurin, whose dwelling was in an enchanted garden of roses, and who had a body-guard of giants, a sort of persons seldom supposed to be themselves conjurers. He becomes a formidable opponent to Theodorick and his chivalry ; but as he attempted by treachery to attain the victory, he is, when overcome, condemned to fill the dishonourable yet appropriate office of buffoon and juggler at the Court of Verona.*

Such possession of supernatural wisdom is still imputed by the natives of the Orkney and Zetland Islands to the people called *Drows*, being a corruption of duergar or *dwarfs*, and who may, in most other respects, be identified with the Caledonian fairies. Lucas Jacobson Debes, who dates his description of Feroe from his Pathmos, in Thorshaven, March 12, 1670, dedicates a long chapter to the spectres who disturbed his congregation, and sometimes carried off his hearers. The actors in these disturbances he states to be the *Skow*, or *Biergen-Trold—i.e.*, the spirits

---

* See an abstract, by the late learned Henry Weber, of " A Lay on this subject of King Laurin," complied by Henry of Osterdingen. "Northern Antiquities," Edinburgh, 1814.

of the woods and mountains, sometimes called subterranean people, and adds, they appeared in deep caverns and among horrid rocks ; as also, that they haunted the places where murders or other deeds of mortal sin had been acted. They appear to have been the genuine northern dwarfs, or Trows, another pronunciation of Trollds, and are considered by the reverend author as something very little better than actual fiends.

But it is not only, or even chiefly, to the Gothic race that we must trace the opinions concerning the elves of the middle ages ; these, as already hinted, were deeply blended with the attributes which the Celtic tribes had, from the remotest ages, ascribed to their deities of rocks, valleys, and forests. We have already observed, what indeed makes a great feature of their national character, that the power of the imagination is peculiarly active among the Celts, and leads to an enthusiasm concerning national music and dancing, national poetry and song, the departments in which fancy most readily indulges herself. The Irish, the Welsh, the Gael, or Scottish Highlander, all tribes of Celtic descent, assigned to the Men of Peace, Good Neighbours, or by whatever other names they called these sylvan pigmies, more social habits, and a course of existence far more gay, than the sullen and heavy toils of the more saturnine Duergar. Their elves did not avoid the society of men, though they behaved to those who associated with them with caprice, which rendered it dangerous to displease them ; and although their gifts were sometimes valuable, they were usually wantonly given and unexpectedly resumed.

The employment, the benefits, the amusements of the Fairy court, resembled the aerial people themselves. Their government was always represented as monarchical. A King, more frequently a Queen of Fairies, was acknowledged ; and sometimes both held their court together. Their pageants and court entertainments comprehended all that the imagination could conceive of what was, by that age, accounted gallant and splendid. At their processions they paraded more beautiful steeds than those of mere earthly parentage—the hawks and hounds which they employed in their chase were of the first race. At their daily banquets, the board was set forth with a splendour which the proudest kings of the earth dared not aspire to; and the hall of their dancers echoed to the most exquisite music. But when viewed by the eye of a seer the illusion vanished. The young knights and beautiful ladies showed themselves as wrinkled carles and odious hags—their wealth turned into slate-stones—their splendid plate into pieces of clay fantastically twisted—and their victuals, unsavoured by salt (prohibited to them, we are told, because an emblem of eternity), became tasteless and insipid—the stately halls were turned into miserable damp caverns—all the delights of the Elfin Elysium vanished at once. In a word, their pleasures were showy, but totally unsubstantial— their activity unceasing, but fruitless and unavailing—and their condemnation appears to have consisted in the necessity of maintaining the appearance of constant industry or enjoyment, though their toil was fruitless and their pleasures shadowy and unsubstantial. Hence poets have designed them as "*the crew that never rest.*" Besides the unceasing and useless bustle in which these spirits seemed to live, they had propensities unfavourable and distressing to mortals.

One injury of a very serious nature was supposed to be constantly practised by the fairies against "the human mortals," that of carrying off their children, and breeding them as beings of their race. Unchristened infants were chiefly exposed to this calamity; but adults were also liable to be abstracted from earthly commerce, notwithstanding it was their natural sphere. With respect to the first, it may be easily conceived that the want of the sacred ceremony of introduction into the Christian church rendered them the more obnoxious to the power of those creatures, who, if not to be in all respects considered as fiends, had nevertheless, considering their constant round of idle occupation, little right to rank themselves among good spirits, and were accounted by most divines as belonging to a very different class. An adult, on the other hand, must have been engaged in some action which exposed him to the power of the spirits, and so, as the legal phrase went, " taken in the manner." Sleeping on a fairy mount, within which the Fairy court happened to be held for the time, was a very ready mode of obtaining a pass for Elfland. It was well for the individual if the irate elves were contented, on such occasions, with transporting him through the air to a city at some forty miles' distance, and leaving, perhaps, his hat or bonnet on some steeple between, to mark the direct line of his course. Others, when engaged in some unlawful action, or in the act of giving way to some headlong and sinful passion, exposed themselves also to become inmates of Fairyland.

The same belief on these points obtained in Ireland. Glanville, in his " Eighteenth Relation," tells us of the butler of a gentleman, a neighbour of the Earl of Orrery, who was sent to purchase cards. In crossing the fields, he saw a table surrounded by people apparently feasting and making merry. They rose to salute him, and invited him to join in their revel; but a friendly voice from the party whispered in his ear, " Do nothing which this company invite you to." Accordingly, when he refused to join in feasting, the table vanished, and the company began to dance and play on musical instruments; but the butler would not take part in these recreations. They then left off dancing, and betook themselves to work; but neither in this would the mortal join them. He was then left alone for the present; but in spite of the exertions of my Lord Orrery, in spite of two bishops who were his guests at the time, in spite of the celebrated Mr. Greatrix, it was all they could do to prevent the butler from being carried off bodily from amongst them by the fairies, who considered him as their lawful prey. They raised him in the air above the heads of the mortals, who could only run beneath, to break his fall when they pleased to let him go. The spectre which formerly advised the poor man continued to haunt him, and at length discovered himself to be the ghost of an acquaintance who had been dead for seven years. "You know," added he, "I lived a loose life, and ever since have I been hurried up and down in a restless condition, with the company you saw, and shall be till the day of judgment." He added, "that if the butler had acknowledged God in all his ways, he had not suffered so much by their means; he reminded him that he had not prayed to God in the morning before he met with this company in the field, and, moreover, that he was then going on an unlawful business.

It is pretended that Lord Orrery confirmed the whole of this story, even to having seen the butler raised into the air by the invisible beings who strove to carry him off. Only he did not bear witness to the passage which seems to call the purchase of cards an unlawful errand.*

Individuals, whose lives had been engaged in intrigues of politics or stratagems of war, were sometimes surreptitiously carried off to Fairyland; as Alison Pearson, the sorceress who cured Archbishop Adamson, averred that she had recognised in the Fairy court the celebrated Secretary Lethington and the old Knight of Buccleuch, the one of whom had been the most busy politician, the other one of the most unwearied partisans of Queen Mary, during the reign of that unfortunate queen. Upon the whole, persons carried off by sudden death were usually suspected of having fallen into the hands of the fairies, and unless redeemed from their power, which it was not always safe to attempt, were doomed to conclude their lives with them. We must not omit to state that those who had an intimate

* " Sadducismus Triumphatus," by Joseph Glanville, p. 131. Edinburgh, 1790.

communication with these spirits, while they were yet inhabitants of middle earth, were most apt to be seized upon and carried off to Elfland before their death.

The reason assigned for this kidnapping of the human race, so peculiar to the elfin people, is said to be that they were under a necessity of paying to the infernal regions a yearly tribute out of their population, which they were willing to defray by delivering up to the prince of these regions the children of the human race, rather than their own. From this it must be inferred, that they have off-spring among themselves, as it is said by some authorities, and particularly by Mr. Kirke, the minister of Aberfoyle. He indeed adds that, after a certain length of life, these spirits are subject to the universal lot of mortality—a position, however, which has been controverted, and is scarcely reconcilable to that which holds them amenable to pay a tax to hell, which infers existence as eternal as the fire which is not quenched. The opinions on the subject of the fairy people here expressed, are such as are entertained in the Highlands and some remote quarters of the Lowlands of Scotland. We know, from the lively and entertaining legends published by Mr. Crofton Croker—which, though in most cases told with the wit of the editor and the humour of his country, contain points of curious antiquarian information—that the opinions of the Irish are conformable to the account we have given of the general creed of the Celtic nations respecting elves. If the Irish elves are any-wise distinguished from those of Britain, it seems to be by their disposition to divide into factions and fight among themselves—a pugnacity characteristic of the Green Isle. The Welsh fairies, according to John Lewis, barrister-at-law, agree in the same general attributes with those of Ireland and Britain. We must not omit the creed of the Manxmen, since we find, from the ingenious researches of Mr. Waldron, that the Isle of Man, beyond other places in Britain, was a peculiar depository of the fairy traditions, which, on the island being conquered by the Norse, became, in all probability, chequered with those of Scandinavia from a source peculiar and more direct than that by which they reached Scotland or Ireland.

Such as it was, the popular system of the Celts easily received the northern admixture of Drows and Duergar, which gave the belief, perhaps, a darker colouring than originally belonged to the British fairyland. It was from the same source also, in all probability, that additional legends were obtained of a gigantic and malignant female, the Hecate of this mythology, who rode on the storm and marshalled the rambling host of wanderers under her grim banner. This hag (in all respects the reverse of the Mab or Titania of the Celtic creed) was called Nicneven in that later system which blended the faith of the Celts and of the Goths on this subject. The great Scottish poet Dunbar has made a spirited description of this Hecate riding at the head of witches and good neighbours (fairies, namely), sorceresses and elves, indifferently, upon the ghostly eve of All-Hallow Mass.* In Italy we hear of the hags arraying themselves under the orders of Diana (in her triple character of Hecate, doubtless) and Herodias, who were the joint leaders of their choir. But we return to the more simple fairy belief, as entertained by the Celts before they were conquered by the Saxons.

Of these early times we can know little ; but it is singular to remark what light the traditions of Scotland throw upon the poetry of the Britons of Cumberland, then called Reged. Merlin Wyllt, or the wild, is mentioned by both ; and that renowned wizard, the son of an elf or fairy, with King Arthur, the dubious champion of Britain at that early period, were both said by tradition to have been abstracted by the fairies, and to have vanished without having suffered death, just at the time when it was supposed that the magic of the wizard and the celebrated sword of the monarch, which had

* See " Flyting of Dunbar and Kennedy."

done so much to preserve British independence, could no longer avert the impending ruin. It may be conjectured that there was a desire on the part of Arthur or his surviving champions to conceal his having received a mortal wound in the fatal battle of Camlan ; and to that we owe the wild and beautiful incident so finely versified by Bishop Percy, in which, in token of his renouncing in future the use of arms, the monarch sends his attendant, sole survivor of the field, to throw his sword Excalibar into the lake hard by. Twice eluding the request, the esquire at last complied, and threw the far-famed weapon into the lonely mere. A hand and arm arose from the water and caught Excalibar by the hilt, flourished it thrice, and then sank into the lake.* The astonished messenger returned to his master to tell him the marvels he had seen, but he only saw a boat at a distance push from the land, and heard shrieks of females in agony :—

> " And whether the king was there or not
> He never knew, he never colde
> For never since that doleful day
> Was British Arthur seen on molde."

The circumstances attending the disappearance of Merlin would probably be found as imaginative as those of Arthur's removal, but they cannot be recovered ; and what is singular enough, circumstances which originally belonged to the history of this famous bard, said to be the son of the Demon himself, have been transferred to a later poet, and surely one of scarce inferior name, Thomas of Erceldoune. The legend was supposed to be only preserved among the inhabitants of his native valleys, but a copy as old as the reign of Henry VII. has been recovered. The story is interesting and beautifully told, and, as one of the oldest fairy legends, may well be quoted in this place.

Thomas of Erceldoune, in Lauderdale, called the Rhymer, on account of his producing a poetical romance on the

* See "Percy's Reliques of Ancient English Poetry."

subject of Tristrem and Yseult, which is curious as the earliest
specimen of English verse known to exist, flourished in the
reign of Alexander III. of Scotland.   Like other men of
talent of the period, Thomas was suspected of magic.   He
was said also to have the gift of prophecy, which was
accounted for in the following peculiar manner, referring
entirely to the elfin superstition :—As True Thomas (we
give him the epithet by anticipation) lay on Huntly Bank,
a place on the descent of the Eildon Hills, which raise their
triple crest above the celebrated Monastery of Melrose, he
saw a lady so extremely beautiful that he imagined it must
be the Virgin Mary herself.   Her appointments, however,
were rather those of an Amazon or goddess of the woods.
Her steed was of the highest beauty and spirit, and at
his mane hung thirty silver bells and nine, which made
music to the wind as she paced along.   Her saddle was
of *royal bone* (ivory), laid over with *orfeverie—i.e.*, gold-
smith's work.   Her stirrups, her dress, all corresponded
with her extreme beauty and the magnificence of her array.
The fair huntress had her bow in her hand, and her arrows at
her belt.   She led three greyhounds in a leash, and three
raches, or hounds of scent, followed her closely.   She rejected and disclaimed the homage which Thomas desired
to pay to her ; so that, passing from one extremity to the
other, Thomas became as bold as he had at first been
humble.   The lady warns him that he must become her
slave if he should prosecute his suit towards her in the
manner he proposes.   Before their interview terminates,
the appearance of the beautiful lady is changed into that of
the most hideous hag in existence.   One side is blighted
and wasted, as if by palsy ; one eye drops from her head ;
her colour, as clear as the virgin silver, is now of a dun
leaden hue.   A witch from the spital or almshouse would
have been a goddess in comparison to the late beautiful
huntress.   Hideous as she was, Thomas's irregular desires
had placed him under the control of this hag, and when she

bade him take leave of sun, and of the leaf that grew on tree, he felt himself under the necessity of obeying her. A cavern received them, in which, following his frightful guide, he for three days travelled in darkness, sometimes hearing the booming of a distant ocean, sometimes walking through rivers of blood, which crossed their subterranean path. At length they emerged into daylight, in a most beautiful orchard. Thomas, almost fainting for want of food, stretches out his hand towards the goodly fruit which hangs around him, but is forbidden by his conductress, who informs him these are the fatal apples which were the cause of the fall of man. He perceives also that his guide had no sooner entered this mysterious ground, and breathed its magic air, than she was revived in beauty, equipage, and splendour, as fair, or fairer, than he had first seen her on the mountain. She then commands him to lay his head upon her knee, and proceeds to explain to him the character of the country. "Yonder right-hand path," she says, "conveys the spirits of the blessed to Paradise ; yon downward and well-worn way leads sinful souls to the place of everlasting punishment ; the third road, by yonder dark brake, conducts to the milder place of pain from which prayer and mass may release offenders. But see you yet a fourth road, sweeping along the plain to yonder splendid castle ? Yonder is the road to Elfland, to which we are now bound. The lord of the castle is king of the country, and I am his queen. But, Thomas, I would rather be drawn with wild horses, than he should know what hath passed between you and me. Therefore, when we enter yonder castle, observe strict silence, and answer no question that is asked at you, and I will account for your silence by saying I took your speech when I brought you from middle earth."

Having thus instructed her lover, they journeyed on to the castle, and entering by the kitchen, found themselves in the midst of such a festive scene as might become the mansion of a great feudal lord or prince. Thirty carcases of deer were lying on the massive kitchen board, under the hands of numerous cooks, who toiled to cut them up and dress them, while the gigantic greyhounds which had taken the spoil lay lapping the blood, and enjoying the sight of the slain game. They came next to the royal hall, where the king received his loving consort without censure or suspicion. Knights and ladies, dancing by threes (reels perhaps), occupied the floor of the hall, and Thomas, the fatigues of his journey from the Eildon hills forgotten, went forward and joined in the revelry. After a period, however, which seemed to him a very short one, the queen spoke with him apart, and bade him prepare to return to his own country. " Now," said the queen, " how long think you that you have been here ?" " Certes, fair lady," answered Thomas, " not above these seven days." " You are deceived," answered the queen, " you have been seven *years* in this castle; and it is full time you were gone. Know, Thomas, that the fiend of hell will come to this castle to-morrow to demand his tribute, and so handsome a man as you will attract his eye. For all the world would I not suffer you to be betrayed to such a fate ; therefore up, and let us be going." These terrible news reconciled Thomas to his departure from Elfin land, and the queen was not long in placing him upon Huntly bank, where the birds were singing. She took a tender leave of him, and to ensure his reputation, bestowed on him the tongue which *could not lie*. Thomas in vain objected to this inconvenient and involuntary adhesion to veracity, which would make him, as he thought, unfit for church or for market, for king's court or for lady's bower. But all his remonstrances were disregarded by the lady, and Thomas the Rhymer, whenever the discourse turned on the future, gained the credit of a prophet whether he would or not ; for he could say nothing but what was sure to come to pass. It is plain that had Thomas been a legislator instead of a poet, we have here the story of Numa and Egeria.

Thomas remained several years in his own tower near Erceldoune, and enjoyed the fame of his predictions, several of which are current among the country people to this day. At length, as the prophet was entertaining the Earl of March in his dwelling, a cry of astonishment arose in the village, on the appearance of a hart and hind,* which left the forest and, contrary to their shy nature, came quietly onward, traversing the village towards the dwelling of Thomas. The prophet instantly rose from the board ; and, acknowledging the prodigy as the summons of his fate, he accompanied the hart and hind into the forest, and though occasionally seen by individuals to whom he has chosen to show himself, has never again mixed familiarly with mankind.

Thomas of Erceldoune, during his retirement, has been supposed, from time to time, to be levying forces to take the field in some crisis of his country's fate. The story has often been told of a daring horse-jockey having sold a black horse to a man of venerable and antique appearance, who appointed the remarkable hillock upon Eildon hills, called the Lucken-hare, as the place where, at twelve o'clock at night, he should receive the price. He came, his money was paid in ancient coin, and he was invited by his customer to view his residence. The trader in horses followed his guide in the deepest astonishment through several long ranges of stalls, in each of which a horse stood motionless, while an armed warrior lay equally still at the charger's feet. "All these men," said the wizard in a whisper, " will awaken at the battle of Sheriffmoor." At the extremity of this extraordinary depôt hung a sword and a horn, which the prophet pointed out to the horse-dealer as containing the means of dissolving the spell. The man in confusion took the horn, and attempted to wind it. The horses

* This last circumstance seems imitated from a passage in the " Life of Merlin," by Jeffrey of Monmouth. See Ellis's " Ancient Romances," vol. i. p. 73.

instantly started in their stalls, stamped, and shook their bridles, the men arose and clashed their armour, and the mortal, terrified at the tumult he had excited, dropped the horn from his hand. A voice like that of a giant, louder even than the tumult around, pronounced these words :—

> " Woe to the coward that ever he was born,
> That did not draw the sword before he blew the horn !"

A whirlwind expelled the horse-dealer from the cavern, the entrance to which he could never again find. A moral might be perhaps extracted from the legend—namely, that it is best to be armed against danger before bidding it defiance. But it is a circumstance worth notice, that although this edition of the tale is limited to the year 1715, by the very mention of the Sheriffmoor, yet a similar story appears to have been current during the reign of Queen Elizabeth, which is given by Reginald Scot. The narrative is edifying as peculiarly illustrative of the mode of marring a curious tale in telling it, which was one of the virtues professed by Caius when he hired himself to King Lear. Reginald Scot, incredulous on the subject of witchcraft, seems to have given some weight to the belief of those who thought that the spirits of famous men do, after death, take up some particular habitations near cities, towns, and countries, and act as tutelary and guardian spirits to the places which they loved while in the flesh.

" But more particularly to illustrate this conjecture," says he, " I could name a person who hath lately appeared thrice since his decease, at least some ghostly being or other that calls itself by the name of such a person who was dead above a hundred years ago, and was in his lifetime accounted as a prophet or predicter by the assistance of sublunary spirits ; and now, at his appearance, did also give strange predictions respecting famine and plenty, war and bloodshed, and the end of the world. By the information of the person that had communication with him, the last of his appearances was in the following manner :—" I had been," said he, "to sell a horse at the next market town, but not attaining my price, as I returned home by the way I met this man, who began to be familiar with me, asking what news, and how affairs moved through the country. I answered as I thought fit; withal, I told him of my horse, whom he began to cheapen, and proceeded with me so far that the price was agreed upon. So he turned back with me, and told me that if I would go along with him I should receive my money. On our way we went, I upon my horse, and he on another milk-white beast. After much travel I asked him where he dwelt and what his name was. He told me that his dwelling was a mile off, at a place called *Farran,* of which place I had never heard, though I knew all the country round about.* He also told me that he himself was that person of the family of Learmonths† so much spoken of as a prophet. At which I began to be somewhat fearful, perceiving we were on a road which I never had been on before, which increased my fear and amazement more. Well, on we went till he brought me under ground, I knew not how, into the presence of a beautiful woman, who paid the money without a word speaking. He conducted me out again through a large and long entry, where I saw above six hundred men in armour laid prostrate on the ground as if asleep. At last I found myself in the open field by the help of the moonlight, in the very place where I first met him, and made a shift to get home by three in the morning. But the money I had received was just double of what I esteemed it when the woman paid me, of which at this instant I have several pieces to show, consisting of ninepennies, thirteen pence-halfpennies," &c.‡

* In this the author is in the same ignorance as his namesake Reginald, though having at least as many opportunities of information.

† In popular tradition, the name of Thomas the Rhymer was always averred to be Learmonth, though he neither uses it himself, nor is described by his son other than Le Rymour. The Learmonths of Dairsie, in Fife, claimed descent from the prophet.

‡ "Discourse of Devils and Spirits appended to the Discovery of Witchcraft," by Reginald Scot, Esq., book ii. chap. 3, sec. 19.

It is a great pity that this horse-dealer, having specimens of the fairy coin, of a quality more permanent than usual, had not favoured us with an account of an impress so valuable to medalists. It is not the less edifying, as we are deprived of the more picturesque parts of the story, to learn that Thomas's payment was as faithful as his prophecies. The beautiful lady who bore the purse must have been undoubtedly the Fairy Queen, whose affection, though, like that of his own heroine Yseult, we cannot term it altogether laudable, seems yet to have borne a faithful and firm character.

I have dwelt at some length on the story of Thomas the Rhymer, as the oldest tradition of the kind which has reached us in detail, and as pretending to show the fate of the first Scottish poet, whose existence, and its date, are established both by history and records ; and who, if we consider him as writing in the Anglo-Norman language, was certainly one among the earliest of its versifiers. But the legend is still more curious, from its being the first and most distinguished instance of a man alleged to have obtained supernatural knowledge by means of the fairies.

Whence or how this singular community derived their more common popular name, we may say has not as yet been very clearly established. It is the opinion of the learned that the Persian word Peri, expressing an unearthly being, of a species very similar, will afford the best derivation, if we suppose it to have reached Europe through the medium of the Arabians, in whose alphabet the letter P does not exist, so that they pronounce the word Feri instead of Peri. Still there is something uncertain in this etymology. We hesitate to ascribe either to the Persians or the Arabians the distinguishing name of an ideal commonwealth, the notion of which they certainly did not contribute to us. Some are, therefore, tempted to suppose that the elves may have obtained their most frequent name from their being *par excellence* a *fair* or *comely* people, a quality which they affected on all occasions ; while the superstition of the Scottish was likely enough to give them a name which might propitiate the vanity for which they deemed the race remarkable ; just as, in other instances, they called the fays "men of peace," "good neighbours," and by other titles of the like import. It must be owned, at the same time, that the words *fay* and *fairy* may have been mere adoptions of the French *fee* and *feerie*, though these terms, on the other side of the Channel, have reference to a class of spirits corresponding, not to our fairies, but with the far different Fata of the Italians. But this is a question which we willingly leave for the decision of better etymologists than ourselves.

LETTER V.

Those who dealt in fortune-telling, mystical cures by charms, and the like, often claimed an intercourse with Fairyland—Hudhart or Hudikin—Pitcairn's "Scottish Criminal Trials"—Story of Bessie Dunlop and her Adviser—Her Practice of Medicine—And of Discovery of Theft—Account of her Familiar, Thome Reid—Trial of Alison Pearson—Account of her Familiar, William Sympson—Trial of the Lady Fowlis, and of Hector Munro, her Stepson—Extraordinary species of Charm used by the latter—Confession of John Stewart, a Juggler, of his Intercourse with the Fairies—Trial and Confession of Isobel Gowdie—Use of Elf-arrow Heads—Parish of Aberfoyle—Mr. Kirke, the Minister of Aberfoyle's Work on Fairy Superstitions—He is himself taken to Fairyland—Dr. Grahame's interesting Work, and his Information on Fairy Superstitions—Story of a Female in East Lothian carried off by the Fairies—Another instance from Pennant.

To return to Thomas the Rhymer, with an account of whose legend I concluded last letter, it would seem that the example which it afforded of obtaining the gift of prescience, and other supernatural powers, by means of the fairy people, became the common apology of those who attempted to cure diseases, to tell fortunes, to revenge injuries, or to engage in traffic with the invisible world, for the purpose of satisfying their own wishes, curiosity, or revenge, or those of others. Those who practised the petty arts of deception in such mystic cases, being naturally desirous to screen their own impostures, were willing to be supposed to derive from the fairies, or from mortals transported to fairyland the power necessary to effect the displays of art which they pretended to exhibit. A confession of direct communication and league with Satan, though the accused were too frequently compelled by torture to admit and avow such horrors, might, the poor wretches hoped, be avoided by the avowal of a less disgusting intercourse with sublunary spirits, a race which might be described by negatives, being neither angels, devils, nor the souls of deceased men ; nor would it, they might flatter themselves, be considered as any criminal alliance, that they held communion with a race not properly hostile to man, and willing, on certain conditions, to be useful and friendly to him. Such an intercourse was certainly far short of the witch's renouncing her salvation, delivering herself personally to the devil, and at once ensuring condemnation in this world, together with the like doom in the next.

Accordingly, the credulous, who, in search of health, knowledge, greatness, or moved by any of the numberless causes for which men seek to look into futurity, were anxious to obtain superhuman assistance, as well as the numbers who had it in view to dupe such willing clients, became both cheated and cheaters, alike anxious to establish the possibility of a harmless process of research into futurity, for laudable, or at least innocent objects, as healing diseases and the like ; in short, of the existence of white magic, as it was called, in opposition to that black art exclusively and directly derived from intercourse with Satan. Some endeavoured to predict a man's fortune in marriage or his success in life by the aspect of the stars ; others pretended to possess spells, by which they could reduce and compel an elementary spirit to enter within a stone, a looking-glass, or some other local place of abode, and confine her there by the power of an especial charm, conjuring her to abide and answer the questions of her master. Of these we shall afterwards say something ; but the species of evasion now under our investigation is that of the fanatics or impostors who pretended to draw information from the equivocal spirits called fairies ; and the number of instances before us is so great as induces us to believe that the pretence of communicating with Elfland, and not with the actual demon, was the manner in which the persons accused of witchcraft most frequently endeavoured to excuse themselves, or at least to alleviate the charges brought against them of practising sorcery. But the Scottish law did not acquit those who accomplished even praiseworthy actions, such as remarkable cures by mysterious remedies; and the proprietor of a patent medicine who should in those days have attested his having wrought such miracles as we see sometimes advertised, might perhaps have forfeited his life before he established the reputation of his drop, elixir, or pill.

Sometimes the soothsayers, who pretended to act on this information from sublunary spirits, soared to higher matters than the practice of physic, and interfered in the fate of nations. When James I. was murdered at Perth in 1437, a Highland woman prophesied the course and purpose of the conspiracy, and had she been listened to, it might have been disconcerted. Being asked her source of knowledge, she answered Hudhart had told her; which might either be the same with Hudkin, a Dutch spirit somewhat similar to Friar Rush or Robin Goodfellow,* or with the red-capped demon so powerful in the case of Lord Soulis, and other wizards, to whom the Scots assigned rather more serious influenee.

The most special account which I have found of the intercourse between Fairyland and a female professing to have some influence in that court, combined with a strong desire to be useful to the distressed of both sexes, occurs in the early part of a work to which I have been exceedingly obliged in the present and other publications.* The

---

* Hudkin is a very familiar devil, who will do nobody hurt, except he receive injury; but he cannot abide that, nor yet be mocked. He talketh with men friendly, sometimes visibly, sometimes invisibly. There go as many tales upon this Hudkin in some parts of Germany as there did in England on Robin Goodfellow.—"Discourse concerning Devils," annexed to "The Discovery of Witchcraft," by Reginald Scot, book i. chap. 21.

† The curious collection of trials, from "The Criminal Records of Scotland," now in the course of publication, by Robert Pitcairn, Esq., affords so singular a picture of the manners and habits of our ancestors, while yet a semibarbarous people, that it is equally worth the attention of the historian, the antiquary, the philosopher, and the poet.

details of the evidence, which consists chiefly of the unfortunate woman's own confession, are more full than usual, and comprehend some curious particulars. To spare technical repetitions, I must endeavour to select the principal facts in evidence in detail, so far as they bear upon the present subject.

On the 8th November, 1576, Elizabeth or Bessie Dunlop, spouse to Andro Jak, in Lyne, in the Barony of Dalry, Ayrshire, was accused of sorcery and witchcraft and abuse of the people. Her answers to the interrogatories of the judges or prosecutors ran thus : It being required of her by what art she could tell of lost goods or prophesy the event of illness, she replied that of herself she had no knowledge or science of such matters, but that when questions were asked at her concerning such matters, she was in the habit of applying to one Thome Reid, who died at the battle of Pinkie (10th September, 1547), as he himself affirmed, and who resolved her any questions which she asked at him. This person she described as a respectable elderly-looking man, grey-bearded, and wearing a grey coat, with Lombard sleeves of the auld fashion. A pair of grey breeches and white stockings gartered above the knee, a black bonnet on his head, close behind and plain before, with silken laces drawn through the lips thereof, and a white wand in his hand, completed the description of what we may suppose a respectable-looking man of the province and period. Being demanded concerning her first interview with this mysterious Thome Reid, she gave rather an affecting account of the disasters with which she was then afflicted, and a sense of which perhaps aided to conjure up the imaginary counsellor. She was walking between her own house and the yard of Monkcastle, driving her cows to the common pasture, and making heavy moan with herself, weeping bitterly for her cow that was dead, her husband and child that were sick of the land-ill (some contagious sickness of the time), while she herself was in a very infirm state, having lately borne a

child. On this occasion she met Thome Reid for the first
time, who saluted her courteously, which she returned.
"Sancta Maria, Bessie !" said the apparition, "why must
thou make such dole and weeping for any earthly thing?"
" Have I not reason for great sorrow," said she, "since our
property is going to destruction, my husband is on the point
of death, my baby will not live, and I am myself at a weak
point?   Have I not cause to have a sore heart?"   " Bessie,"
answered the spirit, "thou hast displeased God in asking
something that thou should not, and I counsel you to amend
your fault.   I tell thee, thy child shall die ere thou get home ;
thy two sheep shall also die ; but thy husband shall recover,
and be as well and feir as ever he was."   The good woman
was something comforted to hear that her husband was to
be spared in such her general calamity, but was rather
alarmed to see her ghostly counsellor pass from her and
disappear through a hole in the garden wall, seemingly too
narrow to admit of any living person passing through it.
Another time he met her at the Thorn of Dawmstarnik, and
showed his ultimate purpose by offering her plenty of every
thing if she would but deny Christendom and the faith she
took at the font-stone.   She answered, that rather than do
that she would be torn at horses' heels, but that she would
be conformable to his advice in less matters.   He parted
with her in some displeasure.   Shortly afterwards he appeared in her own house about noon, which was at the time
occupied by her husband and three tailors.   But neither
Andrew Jak nor the three tailors were sensible of the presence of the phantom warrior who was slain at Pinkie ; so
that, without attracting their observation, he led out the
good-wife to the end of the house near the kiln.   Here he
showed her a company of eight women and four men.   The
women were busked in their plaids, and very seemly.   The
strangers saluted her, and said, " Welcome, Bessie ; wilt
thou go with us ?"   But Bessie was silent, as Thome Reid
had previously recommended.   After this she saw their lips

move, but did not understand what they said ; and in a short time they removed from thence with a hideous ugly howling sound, like that of a hurricane. Thome Reid then acquainted her that these were the good wights (fairies) dwelling in the court of Elfland, who came to invite her to go thither with them. Bessie answered that, before she went that road, it would require some consideration. Thome answered, "Seest thou not me both meat-worth, clothes-worth, and well enough in person ?" and engaged she should be easier than ever she was. But she replied, she dwelt with her husband and children, and would not leave them; to which Thome Reid replied, in very ill-humour, that if such were her sentiments, she would get little good of him.

Although they thus disagreed on the principal object of Thome Reid's visits, Bessie Dunlop affirmed he continued to come to her frequently, and assist her with his counsel ; and that if any one consulted her about the ailments of human beings or of cattle, or the recovery of things lost and stolen, she was, by the advice of Thome Reid, always able to answer the querists. She was also taught by her (literally ghostly) adviser how to watch the operation of the ointments he gave her, and to presage from them the recovery or death of the patient. She said Thome gave her herbs with his own hand, with which she cured John Jack's bairn and Wilson's of the Townhead. She also was helpful to a waiting-woman of the young Lady Stanlie, daughter of the Lady Johnstone, whose disease, according to the opinion of the infallible Thome Reid, was "a cauld blood that came about her heart," and frequently caused her to swoon away. For this Thome mixed a remedy as generous as the balm of Gilead itself. It was composed of the most potent ale, concocted with spices and a little white sugar, to be drunk every morning before taking food. For these prescriptions Bessie Dunlop's fee was a peck of meal and some cheese. The young woman recovered. But the poor old Lady Kilbowie could get no help for her leg, which had been crooked for years; for Thome Reid said the marrow of the limb was perished and the blood benumbed, so that she would never recover, and if she sought further assistance, it would be the worse for her. These opinions indicate common sense and prudence at least, whether we consider them as originating with the *umquhile* Thome Reid, or with the culprit whom he patronized. The judgments given in the case of stolen goods were also well chosen; for though they seldom led to recovering the property, they generally alleged such satisfactory reasons for its not being found as effectually to cover the credit of the prophetess. Thus Hugh Scott's cloak could not be returned, because the thieves had gained time to make it into a kirtle. James Jamieson and James Baird would, by her advice, have recovered their plough-irons, which had been stolen, had it not been the will of fate that William Dougal, sheriff's officer, one of the parties searching for them, should accept a bribe of three pounds not to find them. In short, although she lost a lace which Thome Reid gave her out of his own hand, which, tied round women in childbirth, had the power of helping their delivery, Bessy Dunlop's profession of a wise woman seems to have flourished indifferently well till it drew the evil eye of the law upon her.

More minutely pressed upon the subject of her familiar, she said she had never known him while among the living, but was aware that the person so calling himself was one who had, in his lifetime, actually been known in middle earth as Thome Reid, officer to the Laird of Blair, and who died at Pinkie. Of this she was made certain, because he sent her on errands to his son, who had succeeded in his office, and to others his relatives, whom he named, and commanded them to amend certain trespasses which he had done while alive, furnishing her with sure tokens by which they should know that it was he who had sent her. One of these errands was somewhat remarkable. She was to remind a neighbour of some particular which she was to recall to his memory by the token that Thome Reid and he had set out together to go to the battle which took place on the Black Saturday; that the person to whom the message was sent was inclined rather to move in a different direction, but that Thome Reid heartened him to pursue his journey, and brought him to the Kirk of Dalry, where he bought a parcel of figs, and made a present of them to his companion, tying them in his handkerchief; after which they kept company till they came to the field upon the fatal Black Saturday, as the battle of Pinkie was long called.

Of Thome's other habits, she said that he always behaved with the strictest propriety, only that he pressed her to go to Elfland with him, and took hold of her apron as if to pull her along. Again, she said she had seen him in public places, both in the churchyard at Dalry and on the street of Edinburgh, where he walked about among other people, and handled goods that were exposed to sale, without attracting any notice. She herself did not then speak to him, for it was his command that, upon such occasions, she should never address him unless he spoke first to her. In his theological opinions, Mr. Reid appeared to lean to the Church of Rome, which, indeed, was most indulgent to the fairy folk. He said that the *new law, i.e.,* the Reformation, was not good, and that the old faith should return again, but not exactly as it had been before. Being questioned why this visionary sage attached himself to her more than to others, the accused person replied, that when she was confined in childbirth of one of her boys, a stout woman came into her hut, and sat down on a bench by her bed, like a mere earthly gossip; that she demanded a drink, and was accommodated accordingly; and thereafter told the invalid that the child should die, but that her husband, who was then ailing, should recover. This visit seems to have been previous to her meeting Thome Reid near Monkcastle garden, for that worthy explained to her that her stout visitant was Queen of Fairies, and that he had since attended her by the express command of that lady, his queen and mistress. This reminds us of the extreme doting attachment which the Queen of the Fairies is represented to have taken for Dapper in " The Alchemist." Thome Reid attended her, it would seem, on being summoned thrice, and appeared to her very often within four years. He often requested her to go with him on his return to Fairyland, and when she refused, he shook his head, and said she would repent it.

If the delicacy of the reader's imagination be a little hurt at imagining the elegant Titania in the disguise of a *stout* woman, a heavy burden for a clumsy bench, drinking what Christopher Sly would have called very sufficient small-beer with a peasant's wife, the following description of the fairy host may come more near the idea he has formed of that invisible company :—Bessie Dunlop declared that as she went to tether her nag by the side of Restalrig Loch (Lochend, near the eastern port of Edinburgh), she heard a tremendous sound of a body of riders rushing past her with such a noise as if heaven and earth would come to gether; that the sound swept past her and seemed to rush into the lake with a hideous rumbling noise. All this while she saw nothing ; but Thome Reid showed her that the noise was occasioned by the wights, who were performing one of their cavalcades upon earth.

The intervention of Thome Reid as a partner in her trade of petty sorcery did not avail poor Bessie Dunlop, although his affection to her was apparently entirely platonic—the greatest familiarity on which he ventured was taking hold of her gown as he pressed her to go with him to Elfland. Neither did it avail her that the petty sorcery which she practised was directed to venial or even bene-ficial purposes. The sad words on the margin of the record, " Convict and burnt," sufficiently express the tragic conclusion of a curious tale.

Alison Pearson, in Byrehill, was, 28th May, 1588, tried for invocation of the spirits of the devil, specially in the vision of one Mr. William Sympson, her cousin and her mother's brother's son, who she affirmed was a great scholar and doctor of medicine, dealing with charms and abusing the ignorant people. Against this poor woman her own confession, as in the case of Bessie Dunlop, was the principal evidence.

As Bessie Dunlop had Thome Reid, Alison Pearson had also a familiar in the court of Elfland. This was her relative, William Sympson aforesaid, born in Stirling, whose father was king's smith in that town. William had been taken away, she said, by a man of Egypt (a Gipsy), who carried him to Egypt along with him; that he remained there twelve years, and that his father died in the meantime for opening a priest's book and looking upon it. She declared that she had renewed her acquaintance with her kinsman so soon as he returned. She further confessed that one day as she passed through Grange Muir she lay down in a fit of sickness, and that a green man came to her, and said if she would be faithful he might do her good. In reply she charged him, in the name of God and by the law he lived upon, if he came for her soul's good to tell his errand. On this the green man departed. But he afterwards appeared to her with many men and women with him, and against her will she was obliged to pass with them farther than she could tell, with piping, mirth, and good cheer; also that she accompanied them into Lothian, where she saw puncheons of wine with tasses or drinking-cups. She declared that when she told of these things she was sorely tormented, and received a blow that took away the power of her left side, and left on it an ugly mark which had no feeling. She also confessed that she had seen before sunrise the good neighbours make their salves with pans and fires. Sometimes, she said, they came in such fearful forms as frightened her very much. At other times they spoke her fair, and promised her that she should never want if faithful, but if she told of them and their doings, they threatened to martyr her. She also boasted of her favour with the Queen of Elfland and the good friends she hadat that court, notwithstanding that she was sometimes in disgrace there, and had not seen the queen for seven years. She said William Sympson is with the fairies, and that he lets her know when they are coming; and that he taught her what remedies to use, and how to apply them. She declared that when a whirlwind blew the fairies were commonly there, and that her cousin Sympson confessed that every year the tithe of them were taken away to hell. The celebrated Patrick Adamson, an excellent divine and accomplished scholar, created by James VI. Archbishop of St. Andrews, swallowed the prescriptions of this poor hypochondriac with good faith and will, eating a stewed fowl, and drinking out at two draughts a quart of claret, medicated with the drugs she recommended. According to the belief of the time, this Alison Pearson transferred the bishop's indisposition from himself to a white palfrey, which died in consequence. There is a very severe libel on him for this and other things unbecoming his order, with which he was charged, and from which we learn that Lethington and Buccleuch were seen by Dame Pearson in the Fairyland.* This poor woman's kinsman, Sympson, did not give better shelter to her than Thome Reid had done to her predecessor. The margin of the court-book again bears the melancholy and brief record, " *Convicta et combusta.*"

The two poor women last mentioned are the more to be pitied as, whether enthusiasts or impostors, they practised their supposed art exclusively for the advantage of mankind. The following extraordinary detail involves persons of far higher quality, and who sought to familiars for more baneful purposes.

Katherine Munro, Lady Fowlis, by birth Katherine Ross of Balnagowan, of high rank, both by her own family and that of her husband, who was the fifteenth Baron of Fowlis,

* See " Scottish Poems," edited by John G. Dalzell, p. 321.

and chief of the warlike clan of Munro, had a stepmother's quarrel with Robert Munro, eldest son of her husband, which she gratified by forming a scheme for compassing his death by unlawful arts. Her proposed advantage in this was, that the widow of Robert, when he was thus removed, should marry with her brother, George Ross of Balnagowan; and for this purpose, her sister-in-law, the present Lady Balnagowan, was also to be removed. Lady Fowlis, if the indictment had a syllable of truth, carried on her practices with the least possible disguise. She assembled persons of the lowest order, stamped with an infamous celebrity as witches; and, besides making pictures or models in clay, by which they hoped to bewitch Robert Munro and Lady Balnagowan, they brewed, upon one occasion, poison so strong that a page tasting of it immediately took sickness. Another earthen jar (Scotticè *pig*) of the same deleterious liquor was prepared by the Lady Fowlis, and sent with her own nurse for the purpose of administering it to Robert Munro. The messenger having stumbled in the dark, broke the jar, and a rank grass grew on the spot where it fell, which sheep and cattle abhorred to touch; but the nurse, having less sense than the brute beasts, and tasting of the liquor which had been spilled, presently died. What is more to our present purpose, Lady Fowlis made use of the artillery of Elfland in order to destroy her stepson and sister-in-law. Laskie Loncart, one of the assistant hags, produced two of what the common people call elf-arrow heads, being, in fact, the points of flint used for arming the ends of arrow-shafts in the most ancient times, but accounted by the superstitious the weapons by which the fairies were wont to destroy both man and beast. The pictures of the intended victims were then set up at the north end of the apartment, and Christian Ross Malcolmson, an assistant hag, shot two shafts at the image of Lady Balnagowan, and three against the picture of Robert Munro, by which shots they were broken, and Lady Fowlis commanded new figures to be modelled. Many similar acts

of witchcraft and of preparing poisons were alleged against
Lady Fowlis.

Her son-in-law, Hector Munro, one of his stepmother's
prosecutors, was, for reasons of his own, active in a similar
conspiracy against the life of his own brother. The rites
that he practised were of an uncouth, barbarous, and unusual nature. Hector, being taken ill, consulted on his
case some of the witches or soothsayers, to whom this
family appears to have been partial. The answer was
unanimous that he must die unless the principal man of his
blood should suffer death in his stead. It was agreed that
the vicarious substitute for Hector must mean George
Munro, brother to him by the half-blood (the son of the
Katherine Lady Fowlis before commemorated). Hector
sent at least seven messengers for this young man, refusing
to receive any of his other friends till he saw the substitute
whom he destined to take his place in the grave. When
George at length arrived, Hector, by advice of a notorious
witch, called Marion MacIngarach, and of his own foster-
mother, Christian Neil Dalyell, received him with peculiar
coldness and restraint. He did not speak for the space of
an hour, till his brother broke silence and asked, "How he
did?" Hector replied, "That he was the better George
had come to visit him," and relapsed into silence, which
seemed singular when compared with the anxiety he had
displayed to see his brother ; but it was, it seems, a necessary part of the spell. After midnight the sorceress Marion
MacIngarach, the chief priestess or Nicneven of the company, went forth with her accomplices, carrying spades with
them. They then proceeded to dig a grave not far from
the seaside, upon a piece of land which formed the boun-
dary betwixt two proprietors. The grave was made as
nearly as possible to the size of their patient Hector Munro,
the earth dug out of the grave being laid aside for the time.
After ascertaining that the operation of the charm on George
Munro, the destined victim, should be suspended for a

time, to avoid suspicion, the conspirators proceeded to work their spell in a singular, impressive, and, I believe, unique manner. The time being January, 1588, the patient, Hector Munro, was borne forth in a pair of blankets, accompanied with all who were entrusted with the secret, who were warned to be strictly silent till the chief sorceress should have received her information from the angel whom they served. Hector Munro was carried to his grave and laid therein, the earth being filled in on him, and the grave secured with stakes as at a real funeral. Marion Mac-Ingarach, the Hecate of the night, then sat down by the grave, while Christian Neil Dalyell, the foster-mother, ran the breadth of about nine ridges distant, leading a boy in her hand, and, coming again to the grave where Hector Munro was interred alive, demanded of the witch which victim she would choose, who replied that she chose Hector to live and George to die in his stead. This form of incantation was thrice repeated ere Mr. Hector was removed from his chilling bed in a January grave and carried home, all remaining mute as before. The consequence of a process which seems ill-adapted to produce the former effect was that Hector Munro recovered, and after the intervention of twelve months George Munro, his brother, died. Hector took the principal witch into high favour, made her keeper of his sheep, and evaded, it is said, to present her to trial when charged at Aberdeen to produce her. Though one or two inferior persons suffered death on account of the sorceries practised in the house of Fowlis, the Lady Katharine and her stepson Hector had both the unusual good fortune to be found not guilty. Mr. Pitcairn remarks that the juries, being composed of subordinate persons not suitable to the rank or family of the person tried, has all the appearance of having been packed on purpose for acquittal. It might also, in some interval of good sense, creep into the heads of Hector Munro's assize that the enchantment being performed in January, 1588, and the deceased being only taken ill of his fatal disease in April, 1590, the distance between the events might seem too great to admit the former being regarded as the cause of the latter.*

Another instance of the skill of a sorcerer being traced to the instructions of the elves is found in the confession of John Stewart, called a vagabond, but professing skill in palmistry and jugglery, and accused of having assisted Margaret Barclay, or Dein, to sink or cast away a vessel belonging to her own good brother. It being demanded of him by what means he professed himself to have knowledge of things to come, the said John confessed that the space of twenty-six years ago, he being travelling on All-Hallow Even night, between the towns of Monygoif (so spelled) and Clary, in Galway, he met with the King of the Fairies and his company, and that the King of the Fairies gave him a stroke with a white rod over the forehead, which took from him the power of speech and the use of one eye, which he wanted for the space of three years. He declared that the use of speech and eyesight was restored to him by the King of Fairies and his company, on an Hallowe'en night, at the town of Dublin, in Ireland, and that since that time he had joined these people every Saturday at seven o'clock, and remained with them all the night; also, that they met every Hallow-tide, sometimes on Lanark Hill (Tintock, perhaps), sometimes on Kilmaurs Hill, and that he was then taught by them. He pointed out the spot of his forehead on which, he said, the King of the Fairies struck him with a white rod, whereupon the prisoner, being blindfolded, they pricked the spot with a large pin, whereof he expressed no sense or feeling. He made the usual declaration, that he had seen many persons at the Court of Fairy, whose names he rehearsed particularly, and declared that all such persons as are taken away by sudden death go with the King of Elfland. With this man's evidence we have at

* Pitcairn's "Trials," vol. i. pp. 191–201.

present no more to do, though we may revert to the
execrable proceedings which then took place against this
miserable juggler and the poor women who were accused of
the same crime. At present it is quoted as another instance
of a fortune-teller referring to Elfland as the source of his
knowledge.

At Auldearne, a parish and burgh of barony in the
county of Nairne, the epidemic terror of witches seems to
have gone very far. The confession of a woman called
Isobel Gowdie, of date April, 1662, implicates, as usual, the
Court of Fairy, and blends the operations of witchcraft with
the facilities afforded by the fairies. These need be the less
insisted upon in this place, as the arch-fiend, and not the
elves, had the immediate agency in the abominations which
she narrates. Yet she had been, she said, in the Dounie
Hills, and got meat there from the Queen of Fairies more
than she could eat. She added, that the queen is bravely
clothed in white linen and in white and brown cloth, that
the King of Fairy is a brave man ; and there were elf-bulls
roaring and *skoilling* at the entrance of their palace, which
frightened her much. On another occasion this frank
penitent confesses her presence at a rendezvous of witches,
Lammas, 1659, where, after they had rambled through the
country in different shapes—of cats, hares, and the like—
eating, drinking, and wasting the goods of their neighbours
into whose houses they could penetrate, they at length
came to the dounie Hills, where the mountain opened to
receive them, and they entered a fair big room, as bright as
day. At the entrance ramped and roared the large fairy
bulls, which always alarmed Isobel Gowdie. These animals
are probably the water-bulls, famous both in Scottish and
Irish tradition, which are not supposed to be themselves
altogether *canny* or safe to have concern with. In their
caverns the fairies manufactured those elf-arrow heads
with which the witches and they wrought so much evil.
The elves and the arch-fiend laboured jointly at this task,

the former forming and sharpening the dart from the rough flint, and the latter perfecting and finishing (or, as it is called, *dighting*) it. Then came the sport of the meeting. The witches bestrode either corn-straws, bean-stalks, or rushes, and calling, " Horse and Hattock, in the Devil's name !" which is the elfin signal for mounting, they flew wherever they listed. If the little whirlwind which accompanies their transportation passed any mortal who neglected to bless himself, all such fell under the witches' power, and they acquired the right of shooting at him. The penitent prisoner gives the names of many whom she and her sisters had so slain, the death for which she was most sorry being that of William Brown, in the Milntown of Mains. A shaft was also aimed at the Reverend Harrie Forbes, a minister who was present at the examination of Isobel, the confessing party. The arrow fell short, and the witch would have taken aim again, but her master forbade her, saying the reverend gentleman's life was not subject to their power. To this strange and very particular confession we shall have occasion to recur when witchcraft is the more immediate subject. What is above narrated marks the manner in which the belief in that crime was blended with the fairy superstition.

To proceed to more modern instances of persons supposed to have fallen under the power of the fairy race, we must not forget the Reverend Robert Kirke, minister of the Gospel, the first translator of the Psalms into Gaelic verse. He was, in the end of the seventeenth century, successively minister of the Highland parishes of Balquidder and Aberfoyle, lying in the most romantic district of Perthshire, and within the Highland line. These beautiful and wild regions, comprehending so many lakes, rocks, sequestered valleys, and dim copsewoods, are not even yet quite abandoned by the fairies, who have resolutely maintained secure footing in a region so well suited for their residence. Indeed, so much was this the case formerly, that Mr. Kirke, while in his latter charge of Aberfoyle, found materials for collecting and compiling his Essay on the "Subterranean and for the most part Invisible People heretofore going under the name of Elves, Fawnes, and Fairies, or the like."* In this discourse, the author, " with undoubting mind," describes the fairy race as a sort of astral spirits, of a kind betwixt humanity and angels—says, that they have children, nurses, marriages, deaths, and burials, like mortals in appearance; that, in some respect, they represent mortal men, and that individual apparitions, or double-men, are found among them, corresponding with mortals existing on earth. Mr. Kirke accuses them of stealing the milk from the cows, and of carrying away, what is more material, the women in pregnancy, and new-born children from their nurses. The remedy is easy in both cases. The milk cannot be stolen if the mouth of the calf, before he is permitted to suck, be rubbed with a certain balsam, very easily come by; and the woman in travail is safe if a piece of cold iron is put into the bed. Mr. Kirke accounts for this by informing us that the great northern mines of iron, lying adjacent to the place of eternal punishment, have a savour odious to these "fascinating creatures." They have, says the reverend author, what one would not expect, many light toyish books (novels and plays, doubtless), others on Rosycrucian subjects, and of an abstruse mystical character; but they have no Bibles or works of devotion. The essayist fails not to mention the elf-arrow heads, which have something of the subtlety of thunderbolts, and can mortally wound the vital parts without breaking the skin. These wounds, he says, he has himself observed in beasts, and felt the fatal lacerations which he could not see.

* The title continues :—" Among the Low Country Scots, as they are described by those who have the second sight, and now, to occasion farther enquiry, collected and compared by a circumspect enquirer residing among the Scottish-Irish (*i.e.*, the Gael, or Highlanders) in Scotland." It was printed with the author's name in 1691, and reprinted, Edinburgh, 1815, for Longman & Co.

It was by no means to be supposed that the elves, so jealous and irritable a race as to be incensed against those who spoke of them under their proper names, should be less than mortally offended at the temerity of the reverend author, who had pryed so deeply into their mysteries, for the purpose of giving them to the public. Although, therefore, the learned divine's monument, with his name duly inscribed, is to be seen at the east end of the churchyard at Aberfoyle, yet those acquainted with his real history do not believe that he enjoys the natural repose of the tomb. His successor, the Rev. Dr. Grahame, has informed us of the general belief that, as Mr. Kirke was walking one evening in his night-gown upon a *Dun-shi*, or fairy mount, in the vicinity of the manse or parsonage, behold! he sunk down in what seemed to be a fit of apoplexy, which the unenlightened took for death, while the more understanding knew it to be a swoon produced by the supernatural influence of the people whose precincts he had violated. After the ceremony of a seeming funeral, the form of the Rev. Robert Kirke appeared to a relation, and commanded him to go to Grahame of Duchray, ancestor of the present General Graham Stirling. "Say to Duchray, who is my cousin as well as your own, that I am not dead, but a captive in Fairyland, and only one chance remains for my liberation. When the posthumous child, of which my wife has been delivered since my disappearance, shall be brought to baptism, I will appear in the room, when, if Duchray shall throw over my head the knife or dirk which he holds in his hand, I may be restored to society; but if this opportunity is neglected, I am lost for ever." Duchray was apprised of what was to be done. The ceremony took place, and the apparition of Mr. Kirke was visibly seen while they were seated at table; but Grahame of Duchray, in his astonishment, failed to perform the ceremony enjoined, and it is to be feared that Mr. Kirke still "drees his weird in Fairyland," the Elfin state declaring to him, as the Ocean to poor Falconer, who perished at sea after having written his popular poem of "The Shipwreck"—

"Thou hast proclaimed our power—be thou our prey!"

Upon this subject the reader may consult a very entertaining little volume, called "Sketches of Perthshire,"* by the Rev. Dr. Grahame of Aberfoyle. The terrible visitation of fairy vengeance which has lighted upon Mr. Kirke has not intimidated his successor, an excellent man and good antiquary, from affording us some curious information on fairy superstition. He tells us that these capricious elves are chiefly dangerous on a Friday, when, as the day of the Crucifixion, evil spirits have most power, and mentions their displeasure at any one who assumes their accustomed livery of green, a colour fatal to several families in Scotland, to the whole race of the gallant Grahames in particular; insomuch that we have heard that in battle a Grahame is generally shot through the green check of his plaid; moreover, that a veteran sportsman of the name, having come by a bad fall, he thought it sufficient to account for it, that he had a piece of green whip-cord to complete the lash of his hunting-whip. I remember, also, that my late amiable friend, James Grahame, author of "The Sabbath," would not break through this ancient prejudice of his clan, but had his library table covered with blue or black cloth, rather than use the fated colour commonly employed on such occasions.

To return from the Perthshire fairies, I may quote a story of a nature somewhat similar to that of Mas Robert Kirke. The life of the excellent person who told it was, for the benefit of her friends and the poor, protracted to an unusual duration; so I conceive that this adventure, which took place in her childhood, might happen before the middle of last century. She was residing with some relations near the small seaport town of North Berwick, when the place and its vicinity were alarmed by the following story:—

* Edinburgh, 1812.

An industrious man, a weaver in the little town, was married to a beautiful woman, who, after bearing two or three children, was so unfortunate as to die during the birth of a fourth child. The infant was saved, but the mother had expired in convulsions; and as she was much disfigured after death, it became an opinion among her gossips that, from some neglect of those who ought to have watched the sick woman, she must have been carried off by the elves, and this ghastly corpse substituted in the place of the body. The widower paid little attention to these rumours, and, after bitterly lamenting his wife for a year of mourning, began to think on the prudence of forming a new marriage, which, to a poor artisan with so young a family, and without the assistance of a housewife, was almost a matter of necessity. He readily found a neighbour with whose good looks he was satisfied, whilst her character for temper seemed to warrant her good usage of his children. He proposed himself and was accepted, and carried the names of the parties to the clergyman (called, I believe, Mr. Matthew Reid) for the due proclamation of banns. As the man had really loved his late partner, it is likely that this proposed decisive alteration of his condition brought back many reflections concerning the period of their union, and with these recalled the extraordinary rumours which were afloat at the time of her decease, so that the whole forced upon him the following lively dream :—As he lay in his bed, awake as he thought, he beheld, at the ghostly hour of midnight, the figure of a female dressed in white, who entered his hut, stood by the side of his bed, and appeared to him the very likeness of his late wife. He conjured her to speak, and with astonishment heard her say, like the minister of Aberfoyle, that she was not dead, but the unwilling captive of the Good Neighbours. Like Mr. Kirke, too, she told him that if all the love which he once had for her was not entirely gone, an opportunity still remained of recovering her, or *winning her back*, as it was usually termed, from the comfortless realms of Elfland.

She charged him on a certain day of the ensuing week that he should convene the most respectable housekeepers in the town, with the clergyman at their head, and should disinter the coffin in which she was supposed to have been buried. "The clergyman is to recite certain prayers, upon which," said the apparition, "I will start from the coffin and fly with great speed round the church, and you must have the fleetest runner of the parish (naming a man famed for swiftness) to pursue me, and such a one, the smith, renowned for his strength, to hold me fast after I am over-taken; and in that case I shall, by the prayers of the church, and the efforts of my loving husband and neighbours, again recover my station in human society." In the morning the poor widower was distressed with the recollection of his dream, but, ashamed and puzzled, took no measures in consequence. A second night, as is not very surprising, the visitation was again repeated. On the third night she appeared with a sorrowful and displeased countenance, upbraided him with want of love and affection, and conjured him, for the last time, to attend to her instructions, which, if he now neglected, she would never have power to visit earth or communicate with him again. In order to convince him there was no delusion, he "saw in his dream" that she took up the nursling at whose birth she had died, and gave it suck; she spilled also a drop or two of her milk on the poor man's bed-clothes, as if to assure him of the reality of the vision.

The next morning the terrified widower carried a statement of his perplexity to Mr. Matthew Reid, the clergyman. This reverend person, besides being an excellent divine in other respects, was at the same time a man of sagacity, who under-stood the human passions. He did not attempt to combat the reality of the vision which had thrown his parishioner into this tribulation, but he contended it could be only an illusion of the devil. He explained to the widower that no created being could have the right or power to imprison or detain the soul of a Christian—conjured him not to believe that his wife was otherwise disposed of than according to God's pleasure—assured him that Protestant doctrine utterly denies the existence of any middle state in the world to come—and explained to him that he, as a clergyman of the Church of Scotland, neither could nor dared authorize opening graves or using the intervention of prayer to sanction rites of a suspicious character. The poor man, confounded and perplexed by various feelings, asked his pastor what he should do. " I will give you my best advice," said the clergyman. " Get your new bride's consent to be married to-morrow, or to-day, if you can ; I will take it on me to dispense with the rest of the banns, or proclaim them three times in one day. You will have a new wife, and, if you think of the former, it will be only as of one from whom death has separated you, and for whom you may have thoughts of affection and sorrow, but as a saint in Heaven, and not as a prisoner in Elfland." The advice was taken, and the perplexed widower had no more visitations from his former spouse.

An instance, perhaps the latest which has been made public, of communication with the Restless People—(a more proper epithet than that of *Daoine Shi*, or Men of Peace, as they are called in Gaelic)—came under Pennant's notice so late as during that observant traveller's tour in 1769. Being perhaps the latest news from the invisible commonwealth, we give the tourist's own words.

" A poor visionary who had been working in his cabbage-garden (in Breadalbane) imagined that he was raised suddenly up into the air, and conveyed over a wall into an adjacent corn-field ; that he found himself surrounded by a crowd of men and women, many of whom he knew to have been dead for some years, and who appeared to him skimming over the tops of the unbending corn, and mingling together like bees going to hive ; that they spoke an unknown language, and with a hollow sound ; that they very roughly pushed him to and fro, but on his uttering the name of God all vanished, but a female sprite, who, seizing him by the shoulder, obliged him to promise an assignation at that very hour that day seven-night; that he then found his hair was all tied in double knots (well known by the name of elf-locks), and that he had almost lost his speech; that he kept his word with the spectre, whom he soon saw floating through the air towards him; that he spoke to her, but she told him she was at that time in too much haste to attend to him, but bid him go away and no harm should befall him, and so the affair rested when I left the country. But it is incredible the mischief these *ægri somnia* did in the neighbourhood. The friends and neighbours of the deceased, whom the old dreamer had named, were in the utmost anxiety at finding them in such bad company in the other world; the almost extinct belief of the old idle tales began to gain ground, and the good minister will have many a weary discourse and exhortation before he can eradicate the absurd ideas this idle story has revived."*

It is scarcely necessary to add that this comparatively recent tale is just the counterpart of the story of Bessie Dunlop, Alison Pearson, and of the Irish butler who was so nearly carried off, all of whom found in Elfland some friend, formerly of middle earth, who attached themselves to the child of humanity, and who endeavoured to protect a fellow-mortal against their less philanthropic companions.

These instances may tend to show how the fairy superstition, which, in its general sense of worshipping the *Dii Campestres*, was much the older of the two, came to bear upon and have connexion with that horrid belief in witchcraft which cost so many innocent persons and crazy impostors their lives for the supposed commission of impossible crimes. In the next chapter I propose to trace how the general disbelief in the fairy creed began to take place, and gradually brought into discredit the supposed feats of witchcraft, which afforded pretext for such cruel practical consequences.

* Pennant's "Tour in Scotland," vol. i. p. 110.

LETTER VI.

Immediate Effect of Christianity on Articles of Popular Superstition—
Chaucer's Account of the Roman Catholic Priests banishing the
Fairies—Bishop Corbett imputes the same Effect to the Reformation
—His Verses on that Subject—His Iter Septentrionale—Robin
Goodfellow and other Superstitions mentioned by Reginald Scot—
Character of the English Fairies—The Tradition had become obsolete
in that Author's Time—That of Witches remained in vigour—But
impugned by various Authors after the Reformation, as Wierus,
Naudæus, Scot, and others—Demonology defended by Bodinus,
Remigius, &c.—Their mutual Abuse of each other—Imperfection
of Physical Science at this Period, and the Predominance of Mys-
ticism in that Department.

ALTHOUGH the influence of the Christian religion was not
introduced to the nations of Europe with such radiance as
to dispel at once those clouds of superstition which continued to obscure the understanding of hasty and ill-
instructed converts, there can be no doubt that its immediate operation went to modify the erroneous and
extravagant articles of credulity which lingered behind the
old pagan faith, and which gave way before it, in proportion as its light became more pure and refined from the
devices of men.

The poet Chaucer, indeed, pays the Church of Rome,
with its monks and preaching friars, the compliment of
having, at an early period, expelled from the land all spirits
of an inferior and less holy character. The verses are
curious as well as picturesque, and may go some length to
establish the existence of doubts concerning the general
belief in fairies among the well-instructed in the time of
Edward III.

The fairies of whom the bard of Woodstock talks are, it
will be observed, the ancient Celtic breed, and he seems to

refer for the authorities of his tale to Bretagne, or Armorica,
a genuine Celtic colony :—

> " In old time of the King Artour,
> Of which that Bretons speken great honour,
> All was this land fulfilled of faerie ;
> The Elf queen, with her joly company,
> Danced full oft in many a grene mead.
> This was the old opinion, as I rede—
> I speake of many hundred years ago,
> But now can no man see no elves mo.
> For now the great charity and prayers
> Of limitours,* and other holy freres,
> That searchen every land and every stream,
> As thick as motes in the sunne-beam,
> Blessing halls, chambers, kitchenes, and boures,
> Cities and burghes, castles high and towers,
> Thropes and barnes, sheep-pens and dairies,
> This maketh that there ben no fairies.
> For there as wont to walken was an elf,
> There walketh now the limitour himself,
> In under nichtes and in morwenings,
> And saith his mattins and his holy things,
> As he goeth in his limitation.
> Women may now go safely up and doun ;
> In every bush, and under every tree,
> There is no other incubus than he,
> And he ne will don them no dishonour."†

When we see the opinion which Chaucer has expressed
of the regular clergy of his time, in some of his other tales,
we are tempted to suspect some mixture of irony in the
compliment which ascribes the exile of the fairies, with
which the land was "fulfilled" in King Arthur's time,
to the warmth and zeal of the devotion of the limitary
friars. Individual instances of scepticism there might exist
among scholars, but a more modern poet, with a vein
of humour not unworthy of Geoffrey himself, has with
greater probability delayed the final banishment of the
fairies from England, that is, from popular faith, till the

---

* Friars limited to beg within a certain district.
† " Wife of Bath's Tale."

reign of Queen Elizabeth, and has represented their expulsion as a consequence of the change of religion. Two or three verses of this lively satire may be very well worth the reader's notice, who must, at the same time, be informed that the author, Dr. Corbett, was nothing less than the Bishop of Oxford and Norwich in the beginning of the seventeenth century. The poem is named "A proper new Ballad, entitled the Fairies' Farewell, to be sung or whistled to the tune of the Meadow Brow by the learned; by the unlearned to the tune of Fortune:"—

"Farewell, rewards and fairies,
　　Good housewives now may say,
For now foul sluts in dairies
　　Do fare as well as they;
And though they sweep their hearths no less
　　Than maids were wont to do,
Yet who of late for cleanliness
　　Finds sixpence in her shoe?

"Lament, lament, old abbies,
　　The fairies' lost command;
They did but change priests' babies,
　　But some have changed your land;
And all your children sprung from hence
　　Are now grown Puritans,
Who live as changelings ever since
　　For love of your domains.

"At morning and at evening both,
　　You merry were and glad,
So little care of sleep and sloth
　　Those pretty ladies had.
When Tom came home from labour,
　　Or Cis to milking rose,
Then merrily, merrily went their tabor,
　　And merrily went their toes.

"Witness those rings and roundelays
　　Of theirs, which yet remain,
Were footed, in Queen Mary's days,
　　On many a grassy plain;

> But since of late Elizabeth,
>   And later James came in,
> They never danced on any heath
>   As when the time hath bin.

> " By which we note, the fairies
>   Were of the old profession,
> Their songs were Ave Maries,
>   Their dances were procession.
> But now, alas ! they all are dead,
>   Or gone beyond the seas ;
> Or farther for religion fled,
>   Or else they take their ease."

The remaining part of the poem is dedicated to the praise and glory of old William Chourne of Staffordshire, who remained a true and stanch evidence in behalf of the departed elves, and kept, much it would seem to the amusement of the witty bishop, an inexhaustible record of their pranks and feats, whence the concluding verse—

> " To William all give audience,
>   And pray ye for his noddle,
> For all the fairies' evidence
>   Were lost if that were addle."*

This William Chourne appears to have attended Dr. Corbett's party on the *iter septentrionale*, " two of which were, and two desired to be, doctors ;" but whether William was guide, friend, or domestic seems uncertain. The travellers lose themselves in the mazes of Chorley Forest on their way to Bosworth, and their route becomes so confused that they return on their steps and labour—

> " As in a conjuror's circle—William found
> A mean for our deliverance,—' Turn your cloaks,'
> Quoth he, ' for Puck is busy in these oaks ;
> If ever you at Bosworth would be found,
> Then turn your cloaks, for this is fairy ground.'
> But ere this witchcraft was performed, we meet
> A very man who had no cloven feet.
> Though William, still of little faith, has doubt,

---

* Corbett's Poems, edited by Octavius Gilchrist, p. 213.

'Tis Robin, or some sprite that walks about.
'Strike him,' quoth he, 'and it will turn to air—
Cross yourselves thrice and strike it.'—'Strike that dare,'
Thought I, 'for sure this massy forester,
In strokes will prove the better conjuror.'
But 'twas a gentle keeper, one that knew
Humanity and manners, where they grew,
And rode along so far, till he could say,
'See, yonder Bosworth stands, and this your way.'"*

In this passage the bishop plainly shows the fairies maintained their influence in William's imagination, since the courteous keeper was mistaken by their associate champion for Puck or Robin Goodfellow. The spells resorted to to get rid of his supposed delusions are alternatively that of turning the cloak—(recommended in visions of the second-sight or similar illusions as a means of obtaining a certainty concerning the being which is before imperfectly seen†)—and that of exorcising the spirit with a cudgel; which last, Corbett prudently thinks, ought not to be resorted to unless under an absolute conviction that the exorcist is the stronger party. Chaucer, therefore, could not be serious in averring that the fairy superstitions were obsolete in his day, since they were found current three centuries afterwards.

It is not the less certain that, as knowledge and religion became more widely and brightly displayed over any country, the superstitious fancies of the people sunk gradually in esteem and influence ; and in the time of Queen Elizabeth the unceasing labour of many and popular preachers, who declaimed against the "splendid miracles" of the Church of Rome, produced also its natural effect upon the other stock of superstitions. "Certainly," said Reginald Scot, talking of times before his own, "some one

---

* Corbett's Poems, p. 191.
† A common instance is that of a person haunted with a resemblance whose face he cannot see. If he turn his cloak or plaid, he will obtain the full sight which he desires, and may probably find it to be his own fetch, or wraith, or double-ganger.

knave in a white sheet hath cozened and abused many thousands, specially when Robin Goodfellow kept such a coil in the country. In our childhood our mothers' maids have so terrified us with an ugly devil having horns on his head, fire in his mouth, and a tail at his breech ; eyes like a basin, fangs like a dog, claws like a bear, a skin like a negro, and a voice roaring like a lion, whereby we start and are afraid when we hear one cry, Boh ! and they have so frayd us with bull-beggars, spirits, witches, urchins, elves, hags, fairies, satyrs, Pans, faunes, sylvans, Kitt-with-the-candlestick, tritons, centaurs, dwarfs, giants, imps, calcars, conjurers, nymphs, changelings, incubus, Robin Goodfellow, the spoorn, the man-in-the-oak, the hellwain, the fire-drake, the puckle, Tom Thumb, Hob-goblin, Tom Tumbler, Boneless, and such other bugbears, that we are afraid of our own shadows, insomuch that some never fear the devil but on a dark night ; and then a polled sheep is a perilous beast, and many times is taken for our father's soul, specially in a churchyard, where a right hardy man heretofore durst not to have passed by night but his hair would stand upright. Well, thanks be to God, this wretched and cowardly infidelity, since the preaching of the Gospel, is in part forgotten, and doubtless the rest of these illusions will in a short time, by God's grace, be detected and vanish away."*

It would require a better demonologist than I am to explain the various obsolete superstitions which Reginald Scot has introduced as articles of the old English faith, into the preceding passage. I might indeed say the Phuca is a Celtic superstition, from which the word Pook or Puckle was doubtless derived ; and I might conjecture that the man-in-the-oak was the same with the Erl-König of the Germans ; and that the hellwain were a kind of wandering spirits, the descendants of a champion named Hellequin, who are introduced into the romance of Richard sans Peur. But

---

* Reginald Scot's " Discovery of Witchcraft," book vii. chap. 15.

most antiquaries will be at fault concerning the spoorn, Kitt-with-the-candlestick, Boneless, and some others. The catalogue, however, serves to show what progress the English have made in two centuries, in forgetting the very names of objects which had been the sources of terror to their ancestors of the Elizabethan age.

Before leaving the subject of fairy superstition in England we may remark that it was of a more playful and gentle, less wild and necromantic character, than that received among the sister people. The amusements of the southern fairies were light and sportive ; their resentments were satisfied with pinching or scratching the objects of their displeasure ; their peculiar sense of cleanliness rewarded the housewives with the silver token in the shoe ; their nicety was extreme concerning any coarseness or negligence which could offend their delicacy ; and I cannot discern, except, perhaps, from the insinuations of some scrupulous divines, that they were vassals to or in close alliance with the infernals, as there is too much reason to believe was the case with their North British sisterhood.* The common nursery story cannot be forgotten, how, shortly after the death of what is called a nice tidy housewife, the Elfin band was shocked to see that a person of different character, with whom the widower had filled his deserted arms, instead of the nicely arranged little loaf of the whitest bread, and a basin of sweet cream, duly placed for their refreshment by the deceased, had substituted a brown loaf and a cobb of herrings. Incensed at such a coarse regale, the elves dragged the peccant housewife out of bed, and pulled her down the wooden stairs by the heels, repeating, at the same time, in scorn of her churlish hospitality—

---

* Dr. Jackson, in his "Treatise on Unbelief," opines for the severe opinion. "Thus are the Fayries, from difference of events ascribed to them, divided into good and bad, when as it is but one and the same malignant fiend that meddles in both ; seeking sometimes to be feared, otherwhiles to be loued as God, for the bodily harmes or good turnes supposed to be in his power."—Jackson on Unbelief, p. 178, edit. 1625.

" Brown bread and herring cobb !
    Thy fat sides shall have many a bob !"

But beyond such playful malice they had no desire to extend their resentment.

The constant attendant upon the English Fairy court was the celebrated Puck, or Robin Goodfellow, who to the elves acted in some measure as the jester or clown of the company—(a character then to be found in the establishment of every person of quality)—or to use a more modern comparison, resembled the Pierrot of the pantomime. His jests were of the most simple and at the same time the broadest comic character—to mislead a clown on his path homeward, to disguise himself like a stool, in order to induce an old gossip to commit the egregious mistake of sitting down on the floor when she expected to repose on a chair, were his special enjoyments. If he condescended to do some work for the sleeping family, in which he had some resemblance to the Scottish household spirit called a Brownie, the selfish Puck was far from practising this labour on the disinterested principle of the northern goblin, who, if raiment or food was left in his way and for his use, departed from the family in displeasure. Robin Goodfellow, on the contrary, must have both his food and his rest, as Milton informs us, amid his other notices of country superstitions, in the poem of L'Allegro. And it is to be noticed that he represents these tales of the fairies, told round the cottage hearth, as of a cheerful rather than a serious cast ; which illustrates what I have said concerning the milder character of the southern superstitions, as compared with those of the same class in Scotland—the stories of which are for the most part of a frightful and not seldom of a disgusting quality.

Poor Robin, however, between whom and King Oberon Shakespeare contrives to keep a degree of distinct subordination, which for a moment deceives us by its appearance of reality, notwithstanding his turn for wit and humour, had been obscured by oblivion even in the days of Queen Bess.

We have already seen, in a passage quoted from Reginald Scot, that the belief was fallen into abeyance; that which follows from the same author affirms more positively that Robin's date was over:—

"Know ye this, by the way, that heretofore Robin Goodfellow and Hobgoblin were as terrible, and also as credible, to the people as hags and witches be now; and in time to come a witch will be as much derided and condemned, and as clearly perceived, as the illusion and knavery of Robin Goodfellow, upon whom there have gone as many and as credible tales as witchcraft, saving that it hath not pleased the translators of the Bible to call spirits by the name of Robin Goodfellow, as they have diviners, soothsayers, poisoners, and cozeners by the name of witches."* In the same tone Reginald Scot addresses the reader in the preface:—"To make a solemn suit to you that are partial readers to set aside partiality, to take in good part my writings, and with indifferent eyes to look upon my book, were labour lost and time ill-employed; for I should no more prevail herein than if, a hundred years since, I should have entreated your predecessors to believe that Robin Goodfellow, that great and ancient bull-beggar, had been but a cozening merchant, and no devil indeed. But Robin Goodfellow ceaseth now to be much feared, and Popery is sufficiently discovered; nevertheless, witches' charms and conjurers' cozenage are yet effectual." This passage seems clearly to prove that the belief in Robin Goodfellow and his fairy companions was now out of date; while that as to witchcraft, as was afterwards but too well shown, kept its ground against argument and controversy, and survived "to shed more blood."

We are then to take leave of this fascinating article of the popular creed, having in it so much of interest to the imagination that we almost envy the credulity of those who, in the gentle moonlight of a summer night in England, amid

* Reginald Scot's "Discovery of Witchcraft," book vii. chap. ii.

the tangled glades of a deep forest, or the turfy swell of her romantic commons, could fancy they saw the fairies tracing their sportive ring. But it is in vain to regret illusions which, however engaging, must of necessity yield their place before the increase of knowledge, like shadows at the advance of morn. These superstitions have already survived their best and most useful purpose, having been embalmed in the poetry of Milton and of Shakespeare, as well as writers only inferior to these great names. Of Spenser we must say nothing, because in his "Faery Queen" the title is the only circumstance which connects his splendid allegory with the popular superstition, and, as he uses it, means nothing more than an Utopia or nameless country.

With the fairy popular creed fell, doubtless, many subordinate articles of credulity in England, but the belief in witches kept its ground. It was rooted in the minds of the common people, as well by the easy solution it afforded of much which they found otherwise hard to explain, as in reverence to the Holy Scriptures, in which the word *witch*, being used in several places, conveyed to those who did not trouble themselves about the nicety of the translation from the Eastern tongues, the inference that the same species of witches were meant as those against whom modern legislation had, in most European nations, directed the punishment of death. These two circumstances furnished the numerous believers in witchcraft with arguments in divinity and law which they conceived irrefragable. They might say to the theologist, Will you not believe in witches? the Scriptures aver their existence ;—to the jurisconsult, Will you dispute the existence of a crime against which our own statute-book, and the code of almost all civilized countries, have attested, by laws upon which hundreds and thousands have been convicted, many or even most of whom have, by their judicial confessions, acknowledged their guilt and the justice of their punishment?

It is a strange scepticism, they might add, which rejects the evidence of Scripture, of human legislature, and of the accused persons themselves.

Notwithstanding these specious reasons, the sixteenth and seventeenth centuries were periods when the revival of learning, the invention of printing, the fearless investigations of the Reformers into subjects thought formerly too sacred for consideration of any save the clergy, had introduced a system of doubt, enquiry, disregard of authority, when unsupported by argument, and unhesitating exercise of the private judgment, on subjects which had occupied the bulls of popes and decrees of councils. In short, the spirit of the age was little disposed to spare error, however venerable, or countenance imposture, however sanctioned by length of time and universal acquiescence. Learned writers arose in different countries to challenge the very existence of this imaginary crime, to rescue the reputation of the great men whose knowledge, superior to that of their age, had caused them to be suspected of magic, and to put a stop to the horrid superstition whose victims were the aged, ignorant, and defenceless, and which could only be compared to that which sent victims of old through the fire to Moloch.

The courageous interposition of those philosophers who opposed science and experience to the prejudices of superstition and ignorance, and in doing so incurred much misrepresentation, and perhaps no little ill-will, in the cause of truth and humanity, claim for them some distinction in a work on Demonology. The pursuers of exact science to its coy retreats, were sure to be the first to discover that the most remarkable phenomena in Nature are regulated by certain fixed laws, and cannot rationally be referred to supernatural agency, the sufficing cause to which superstition attributes all that is beyond her own narrow power of explanation. Each advance in natural knowledge teaches us that it is the pleasure of the Creator to govern the world by the laws which he has imposed, and which are not in our times interrupted or suspended.

The learned Wier, or Wierus, was a man of great research in physical science, and studied under the celebrated Cornelius Agrippa, against whom the charge of sorcery was repeatedly alleged by Paulus Jovius and other authors, while he suffered, on the other hand, from the persecution of the inquisitors of the Church, whose accusation against this celebrated man was, that he denied the existence of spirits, a charge very inconsistent with that of sorcery, which consists in corresponding with them. Wierus, after taking his degree as a doctor of medicine, became physician to the Duke of Cleves, at whose court he practised for thirty years with the highest reputation. This learned man, disregarding the scandal which, by so doing, he was likely to bring upon himself, was one of the first who attacked the vulgar belief, and boldly assailed, both by serious arguments and by ridicule, the vulgar credulity on the subject of wizards and witches.

Gabriel Naudé, or Naudæus, as he termed himself, was a perfect scholar and man of letters, busied during his whole life with assembling books together, and enjoying the office of librarian to several persons of high rank, amongst others, to Queen Christina of Sweden. He was, besides, a beneficed clergyman, leading a most unblemished life, and so temperate as never to taste any liquor stronger than water; yet did he not escape the scandal which is usually flung by their prejudiced contemporaries upon those disputants whom it is found more easy to defame than to answer. He wrote an interesting work, entitled " Apologie pour les Grands Hommes Accusés de Magie ;" and as he exhibited a good deal of vivacity of talent, and an earnestness in pleading his cause, which did not always spare some of the superstitions of Rome herself, he was charged by his contemporaries as guilty of heresy and scepticism, when justice could only accuse him of an incautious eagerness to make good his argument.

Among persons who, upon this subject, purged their eyes with rue and euphrasie, besides the Rev. Dr. Harsnet and many others (who wrote rather on special cases of Demonology than on the general question), Reginald Scot ought to be distinguished. Webster assures us that he was a "person of competent learning, pious, and of a good family." He seems to have been a zealous Protestant, and much of his book, as well as that of Harsnet, is designed to throw upon the Papists in particular those tricks in which, by confederacy and imposture, the popular ideas concerning witchcraft, possession, and other supernatural fancies, were maintained and kept in exercise ; but he also writes on the general question with some force and talent, considering that his subject is incapable of being reduced into a regular form, and is of a nature particularly seductive to an excursive talent. He appears to have studied legerdemain for the purpose of showing how much that is apparently unaccountable can nevertheless be performed without the intervention of supernatural assistance, even when it is impossible to persuade the vulgar that the devil has not been consulted on the occasion. Scot also had intercourse with some of the celebrated fortune-tellers, or Philomaths, of the time ; one of whom he brings forward to declare the vanity of the science which he himself had once professed.

To defend the popular belief of witchcraft there arose a number of advocates, of whom Bodin and some others neither wanted knowledge nor powers of reasoning. They pressed the incredulous party with the charge that they denied the existence of a crime against which the law had denounced a capital punishment. As that law was understood to emanate from James himself, who was reigning monarch during the hottest part of the controversy, the English authors who defended the opposite side were obliged to entrench themselves under an evasion, to avoid maintaining an argument unpalatable to a degree to those in power, and which might perchance have proved unsafe to those who used it. With a certain degree of sophistry they answered that they did not doubt the possibility of witches, but only demurred to what is their nature, and how they came to be such—according to the scholastic jargon, that the question in respect to witches was not *de existentia,* but only *de modo existendi.*

By resorting to so subtle an argument those who impugned the popular belief were obliged, with some inconsistency, to grant that witchcraft had existed, and might exist, only insisting that it was a species of witchcraft consisting of they knew not what, but certainly of something different from that which legislators, judges, and juries had hitherto considered the statute as designed to repress.

In the meantime (the rather that the debate was on a subject particularly difficult of comprehension) the debating parties grew warm, and began to call names. Bodin, a lively Frenchman of an irritable habit, explained the zeal of Wierus to protect the tribe of sorcerers from punishment, by stating that he himself was a conjurer and the scholar of Cornelius Agrippa, and might therefore well desire to save the lives of those accused of the same league with Satan. Hence they threw on their antagonists the offensive names of witch-patrons and witch-advocates, as if it were impossible for any to hold the opinion of Naudæus, Wierus, Scot, &c., without patronizing the devil and the witches against their brethren of mortality. Assailed by such heavy charges, the philosophers themselves lost patience, and retorted abuse in their turn, calling Bodin, Delrio, and others who used their arguments, witch-advocates, and the like, as the affirming and defending the existence of the crime seemed to increase the number of witches, and assuredly augmented the list of executions. But for a certain time the preponderance of the argument lay on the side of the Demonologists, and we may briefly observe the causes which gave their opinions, for a period, greater influence than their opponents on the public mind.

It is first to be observed that Wierus, for what reason cannot well be conjectured, except to show the extent of his cabalistical knowledge, had introduced into his work against witchcraft the whole Stenographia of Trithemius, which he had copied from the original in the library of Cornelius Agrippa; and which, suspicious from the place where he found it, and from the long catalogue of fiends which it contained, with the charms for raising and for binding them to the service of mortals, was considered by Bodin as containing proof that Wierus himself was a sorcerer; not one of the wisest, certainly, since he thus unnecessarily placed at the disposal of any who might buy the book the whole secrets which formed his stock-in-trade.

Secondly, we may notice that, from the state of physical science at the period when Van Helmont, Paracelsus, and others began to penetrate into its recesses, it was an unknown, obscure, and ill-defined region, and did not permit those who laboured in it to give that precise and accurate account of their discoveries which the progress of reasoning experimentally and from analysis has enabled the late discoverers to do with success. Natural magic—a phrase used to express those phenomena which could be produced by a knowledge of the properties of matter—had so much in it that was apparently uncombined and uncertain, that the art of chemistry was accounted mystical, and an opinion prevailed that the results now known to be the consequence of laws of matter, could not be traced through their various combinations even by those who knew the effects themselves. Physical science, in a word, was cumbered by a number of fanciful and incorrect opinions, chiefly of a mystical character. If, for instance, it was observed that a flag and a fern never grew near each other, the circumstance was imputed to some antipathy between these vegetables; nor was it for some time resolved by the natural rule, that the flag has its nourishment in marshy ground, whereas the fern loves a deep dryish soil. The attributes of the divining-rod were fully credited; the discovery of the philosopher's stone was daily hoped for; and electricity, magnetism, and other remarkable and misconceived phenomena were appealed to as proof of the reasonableness of their expectations. Until such phenomena were traced to their sources, imaginary and often mystical causes were assigned to them, for the same reason that, in the wilds of a partially discovered country, according to the satirist,

> " Geographers on pathless downs
> Place elephants for want of towns."

This substitution of mystical fancies for experimental reasoning gave, in the sixteenth and seventeenth centuries, a doubtful and twilight appearance to the various branches of physical philosophy. The learned and sensible Dr. Webster, for instance, writing in detection of supposed witchcraft, assumes, as a string of undeniable facts, opinions which our more experienced age would reject as frivolous fancies; " for example, the effects of healing by the weapon-salve, the sympathetic powder, the curing of various diseases by apprehensions, amulets, or by transplantation." All of which undoubted wonders he accuses the age of desiring to throw on the devil's back—an unnecessary load certainly, since such things do not exist, and it is therefore in vain to seek to account for them. It followed that, while the opposers of the ordinary theory might have struck the deepest blows at the witch hypothesis by an appeal to common sense, they were themselves hampered by articles of philosophical belief which they must have been sensible contained nearly as deep draughts upon human credulity as were made by the Demonologists, against whose doctrine they protested. This error had a doubly bad effect, both as degrading the immediate department in which it occurred, and as affording a protection for falsehood in other branches of science. The champions who, in their own province, were obliged by the imperfect knowledge of the times to admit much that was mystical and inexplicable—those who

opined, with Bacon, that warts could be cured by sympathy
—who thought, with Napier, that hidden treasures could be
discovered by the mathematics—who salved the weapon
instead of the wound, and detected murders as well as
springs of water by the divining-rod, could not consistently
use, to confute the believers in witches, an argument turning
on the impossible or the incredible.

Such were the obstacles arising from the vanity of philosophers and the imperfection of their science, which suspended the strength of their appeal to reason and common
sense against the condemning of wretches to a cruel death
on account of crimes which the nature of things rendered
in modern times totally impossible. We cannot doubt
that they suffered considerably in the contest, which was
carried on with much anger and malevolence; but the good
seed which they had sown remained uncorrupted in the soil,
to bear fruit so soon as the circumstances should be altered
which at first impeded its growth. In the next letter I
shall take a view of the causes which helped to remove these
impediments, in addition, it must always be remembered,
to the general increase of knowledge and improvement of
experimental philosophy.

LETTER VII.

Penal Laws unpopular when rigidly exercised—Prosecution of Witches placed in the hand of Special Commissioners, *ad inquirendum*—Prosecution for Witchcraft not frequent in the Elder Period of the Roman Empire—Nor in the Middle Ages—Some Cases took place, however—The Maid of Orleans—The Duchess of Gloucester—Richard the Third's Charge against the Relations of the Queen Dowager—But Prosecutions against Sorcerers became more common in the end of the Fourteenth Century—Usually united with the Charge of Heresy—Monstrelet's Account of the Persecution against the Waldenses, under pretext of Witchcraft—Florimond's Testimony concerning the Increase of Witches in his own Time—Bull of Pope Innocent VIII.—Various Prosecutions in Foreign Countries under this severe Law—Prosecutions in Labourt by the Inquisitor De Lancre and his Colleague—Lycanthropy—Witches in Spain—In Sweden—and particularly those Apprehended at Mohra.

PENAL laws, like those of the Middle Ages, denounced against witchcraft, may be at first hailed with unanimous acquiescence and approbation, but are uniformly found to disgust and offend at least the more sensible part of the public when the punishments become frequent and are relentlessly inflicted. Those against treason are no exception. Each reflecting government will do well to shorten that melancholy reign of terror which perhaps must necessarily follow on the discovery of a plot or the defeat of an insurrection. They ought not, either in humanity or policy, to wait till the voice of the nation calls to them, as Mecænas to Augustus, " *Surge tandem carnifex !*"

It is accordingly remarkable, in different countries, how often at some particular period of their history there occurred an epidemic of terror of witches, which, as fear is always cruel and credulous, glutted the public with seas of innocent blood ; and how uniformly men loathed the gore after having swallowed it, and by a reaction natural to the human mind desired, in prudence, to take away or restrict those laws which had been the source of carnage, in order that their posterity might neither have the will nor the means to enter into similar excesses.

A short review of foreign countries, before we come to notice the British Islands and their Colonies, will prove the truth of this statement.   In Catholic countries on the Continent, the various kingdoms adopted readily that part of the civil law, already mentioned, which denounces sorcerers and witches as rebels to God, and authors of sedition in the empire.   But being considered as obnoxious equally to the canon and civil law, Commissions of Inquisition were especially empowered to weed out of the land the witches and those who had intercourse with familiar spirits, or in any other respect fell under the ban of the Church, as well as the heretics who promulgated or adhered to false doctrine. Special warrants were thus granted from time to time in behalf of such inquisitors, authorizing them to visit those provinces of Germany, France, or Italy where any report concerning witches or sorcery had alarmed the public mind ; and those Commissioners, proud of the trust reposed in them, thought it becoming to use the utmost exertions on their part, that the subtlety of the examinations, and the severity of the tortures they inflicted, might wring the truth out of all suspected persons, until they rendered the province in which they exercised their jurisdiction a desert from which the inhabitants fled.   It would be impossible to give credit to the extent of this delusion, had not some of the inquisitors themselves been reporters of their own judicial exploits : the same hand which subscribed the sentence has recorded the execution.

In the earlier period of the Church of Rome witchcraft is frequently alluded to, and a capital punishment assigned to those who were supposed to have accomplished by sorcery the death of others, or to have attempted, by false prophecies or otherwise, under pretext of consulting with the spiritual world, to make innovation in the state. But no general denunciation against witchcraft itself, as a league with the Enemy of Man, or desertion of the Deity, and a crime *sui generis*, appears to have been so acted upon, until the later period of the sixteenth century, when the Papal system had attained its highest pitch of power and of corruption. The influence of the Churchmen was in early times secure, and they rather endeavoured, by the fabrication of false miracles, to prolong the blind veneration of the people, than to vex others and weary themselves by secret investigations into dubious and mystical trespasses, in which probably the higher and better instructed members of the clerical order put as little faith at that time as they do now. Did there remain a mineral fountain, respected for the cures which it had wrought, a huge oak-tree, or venerated mount, which beauty of situation had recommended to traditional respect, the fathers of the Roman Church were in policy reluctant to abandon such impressive spots, or to represent them as exclusively the rendezvous of witches or of evil spirits. On the contrary, by assigning the virtues of the spring or the beauty of the tree to the guardianship of some saint, they acquired, as it were, for the defence of their own doctrine, a frontier fortress which they wrested from the enemy, and which it was at least needless to dismantle, if it could be conveniently garrisoned and defended. Thus the Church secured possession of many beautiful pieces of scenery, as Mr. Whitfield is said to have grudged to the devil the monopoly of all the fine tunes.

It is true that this policy was not uniformly observed. The story of the celebrated Jeanne d'Arc, called the Maid of Orleans, preserves the memory of such a custom, which was in that case turned to the prejudice of the poor woman who observed it.

It is well known that this unfortunate female fell into the hands of the English, after having, by her courage and

enthusiasm manifested on many important occasions, revived the drooping courage of the French, and inspired
them with the hope of once more freeing their country.
The English vulgar regarded her as a sorceress—the French
as an inspired heroine; while the wise on both sides
considered her as neither the one nor the other, but a tool
used by the celebrated Dunois to play the part which
he assigned her. The Duke of Bedford, when the ill-
starred Jeanne fell into his hands, took away her life in
order to stigmatize her memory with sorcery and to destroy
the reputation she had acquired among the French. The
mean recurrence to such a charge against such a person
had no more success than it deserved, although Jeanne was
condemned both by the Parliament of Bordeux and the
University of Paris. Her indictment accused her of having
frequented an ancient oak-tree, and a fountain arising under
it, called the Fated or Fairy Oak of Bourlemont. Here she
was stated to have repaired during the hours of divine
service, dancing, skipping, and making gestures, around the
tree and fountain, and hanging on the branches chaplets
and garlands of flowers, gathered for the purpose, reviving,
doubtless, the obsolete idolatry which in ancient times had
been rendered on the same spot to the *Genius Loci*. The
charmed sword and blessed banner, which she had represented as signs of her celestial mission, were in this hostile
charge against her described as enchanted implements,
designed by the fiends and fairies whom she worshipped to
accomplish her temporary success. The death of the
innocent, high-minded, and perhaps amiable enthusiast, was
not, we are sorry to say, a sacrifice to a superstitious fear of
witchcraft, but a cruel instance of wicked policy mingled
with national jealousy and hatred.

To the same cause, about the same period, we may impute the trial of the Duchess of Gloucester, wife of the
good Duke Humphrey, accused of consulting witches concerning the mode of compassing the death of her husband's

nephew, Henry VI. The Duchess was condemned to do penance, and thereafter banished to the Isle of Man, while several of her accomplices died in prison or were executed. But in this instance also the alleged witchcraft was only the ostensible cause of a procedure which had its real source in the deep hatred between the Duke of Gloucester and Cardinal Beaufort, his half-brother. The same pretext was used by Richard III. when he brought the charge of sorcery against the Queen Dowager, Jane Shore, and the queen's kinsmen ; and yet again was by that unscrupulous prince directed against Morton, afterwards Archbishop of Canterbury, and other adherents of the Earl of Richmond. The accusation in both cases was only chosen as a charge easily made and difficult to be eluded or repelled.

But in the meanwhile, as the accusation of witchcraft thus afforded to tyranny or policy the ready means of assailing persons whom it might not have been possible to convict of any other crime, the aspersion itself was gradually considered with increase of terror as spreading wider and becoming more contagious. So early as the year 1398 the University of Paris, in laying down rules for the judicial prosecuting of witches, express their regret that the crime was growing more frequent than in any former age. The more severe enquiries and frequent punishments by which the judges endeavoured to check the progress of this impious practice seem to have increased the disease, as indeed it has been always remarked that those morbid affections of mind which depend on the imagination are sure to become more common in proportion as public attention is fastened on stories connected with their display.

In the same century schisms arising from different causes greatly alarmed the Church of Rome. The universal spirit of enquiry which was now afloat, taking a different direction in different countries, had in almost all of them stirred up a sceptical dissatisfaction with the dogmas of the Church— such views being rendered more credible to the poorer classes through the corruption of manners among the clergy, too many of whom wealth and ease had caused to neglect that course of morality which best recommends religious doctrine. In almost every nation in Europe there lurked in the crowded cities, or the wild solitude of the country, sects who agreed chiefly in their animosity to the supremacy of Rome and their desire to cast off her domination. The Waldenses and Albigenses were parties existing in great numbers through the south of France. The Romanists became extremely desirous to combine the doctrine of the heretics with witchcraft, which, according to their account, abounded especially where the Protestants were most numerous; and, the bitterness increasing, they scrupled not to throw the charge of sorcery, as a matter of course, upon those who dissented from the Catholic standard of faith. The Jesuit Delrio alleges several reasons for the affinity which he considers as existing between the Protestant and the sorcerer; he accuses the former of embracing the opinion of Wierus and other defenders of the devil (as he calls all who oppose his own opinions concerning witchcraft), thus fortifying the kingdom of Satan against that of the Church.*

A remarkable passage in Monstrelet puts in a clear view the point aimed at by the Catholics in thus confusing and blending the doctrines of heresy and the practice of witchcraft, and how a meeting of inoffensive Protestants could be cunningly identified with a Sabbath of hags and fiends.

"In this year (1459), in the town of Arras and county of Artois, arose, through a terrible and melancholy chance, an opinion called, I know not why, the Religion of Vaudoisie. This sect consisted, it is said, of certain persons, both men and women, who, under cloud of night, by the power of the devil, repaired to some solitary spot, amid woods and deserts, where the devil appeared before them in a human

---

* Delrio, " De Magia." See the Preface.

form—save that his visage is never perfectly visible to them —read to the assembly a book of his ordinances, informing them how he would be obeyed ; distributed a very little money and a plentiful meal, which was concluded by a scene of general profligacy ; after which each one of the party was conveyed home to her or his own habitation.

" On accusations of access to such acts of madness," continues Monstrelet, " several creditable persons of the town of Arras were seized and imprisoned along with some foolish women and persons of little consequence. These were so horribly tortured that some of them admitted the truth of the whole accusations, and said, besides, that they had seen and recognised in their nocturnal assembly many persons of rank, prelates, seigneurs, and governors of bailliages and cities, being such names as the examinators had suggested to the persons examined, while they constrained them by torture to impeach the persons to whom they belonged. Several of those who had been thus informed against were arrested, thrown into prison, and tortured for so long a time that they also were obliged to confess what was charged against them. After this those of mean condition were executed and inhumanly burnt, while the richer and more powerful of the accused ransomed themselves by sums of money, to avoid the punishment and the shame attending it. Many even of those also confessed being persuaded to take that course by the interrogators, who promised them indemnity for life and fortune. Some there were, of a truth, who suffered with marvellous patience and constancy the torments inflicted on them, and would confess nothing imputed to their charge ; but they, too, had to give large sums to the judges, who exacted that such of them as, notwithstanding their mishandling, were still able to move, should banish themselves from that part of the country." Monstrelet winds up this shocking narrative by informing us " that it ought not to be concealed that the whole accusation was a stratagem of wicked men for their own covetous purposes, and in order, by these false accusations and forced confessions, to destroy the life, fame, and fortune of wealthy persons."

Delrio himself confesses that Franciscus Balduinus gives an account of the pretended punishment, but real persecution, of these Waldenses, in similar terms with Monstrelet, whose suspicions are distinctly spoken out, and adds that the Parliament of Paris, having heard the affair by appeal, had declared the sentence illegal and the judges iniquitous, by an arrét dated 20th May, 1491. The Jesuit Delrio quotes the passage, but adheres with lingering reluctance to the truth of the accusation. "The Waldenses (of whom the Albigenses are a species) were," he says, "never free from the most wretched excess of fascination ;" and finally, though he allows the conduct of the judges to have been most odious, he cannot prevail on himself to acquit the parties charged by such interested accusers with horrors which should hardly have been found proved even upon the most distinct evidence. He appeals on this occasion to Florimond's work on Antichrist. The introduction of that work deserves to be quoted, as strongly illustrative of the condition to which the country was reduced, and calculated to make an impression the very reverse probably of that which the writer would have desired :—

"All those who have afforded us some signs of the approach of Antichrist agree that the increase of sorcery and witchcraft is to distinguish the melancholy period of his advent; and was ever age so afflicted with them as ours ? The seats destined for criminals before our judicatories are blackened with persons accused of this guilt. There are not judges enough to try them. Our dungeons are gorged with them. No day passes that we do not render our tribunals bloody by the dooms which we pronounce, or in which we do not return to our homes discountenanced and terrified at the horrible contents of the confessions which it has been our duty to hear. And the devil is accounted so good a master that we cannot commit so great a number of his slaves to the flames but what there shall arise from their ashes a number sufficient to supply their place."*

This last statement, by which it appears that the most active and unsparing inquisition was taking place, corresponds with the historical notices of repeated persecutions upon this dreadful charge of sorcery. A bull of Pope Innocent VIII. rang the tocsin against this formidable crime, and set forth in the most dismal colours the guilt, while it stimulated the inquisitors to the unsparing discharge of their duty in searching out and punishing the guilty. " It is come to our ears," says the bull, " that numbers of both sexes do not avoid to have intercourse with the infernal fiends, and that by their sorceries they afflict both man and beast; that they blight the marriage-bed, destroy the births of women, and the increase of cattle ; they blast the corn on the ground, the grapes of the vineyard, the fruits of the trees, the grass and herbs of the field." For which reasons the inquisitors were armed with the apostolic power, and called upon to "convict, imprison, and punish," and so forth.

Dreadful were the consequences of this bull all over the Continent, especially in Italy, Germany, and France.† About 1485 Cumanus burnt as witches forty-one poor women in one year in the county of Burlia. In the ensuing years he continued the prosecution with such unremitting zeal that many fled from the country.

Alciatus states that an inquisitor, about the same period, burnt an hundred sorcerers in Piedmont, and persevered in his inquiries till human patience was exhausted, and the people arose and drove him out of the country, after which the jurisdiction was deferred to the archbishop. That prelate consulted Alciatus himself, who had just then obtained his doctor's degree in civil law, to which he was afterwards an

* Florimond, "Concerning the Antichrist," cap. 7, n. 5, quoted by Delrio, " De Magia," p. 820.
† Dr. Hutchinson quotes " H. Institor," 105, 161.

honour. A number of unfortunate wretches were brought for judgment, fitter, according to the civilian's opinion, for a course of hellebore than for the stake. Some were accused of having dishonoured the crucifix and denied their salvation ; others of having absconded to keep the Devil's Sabbath, in spite of bolts and bars; others of having merely joined in the choral dances around the witches' tree of rendezvous. Several of their husbands and relatives swore that they were in bed and asleep during these pretended excursions. Alciatus recommended gentle and temperate measures ; and the minds of the country became at length composed.*

In 1488, the country four leagues around Constance was laid waste by lightning and tempest, and two women being, by fair means or foul, made to confess themselves guilty as the cause of the devastation, suffered death.

About 1515, 500 persons were executed at Geneva, under the character of "Protestant witches," from which we may suppose many suffered for heresy. Forty-eight witches were burnt at Ravensburgh within four years, as Hutchison reports, on the authority of Mengho, the author of the "Malleus Malleficarum." In Lorraine the learned inquisitor, Remigius, boasts that he put to death 900 people in fifteen years. As many were banished from that country, so that whole towns were on the point of becoming desolate. In 1524, 1,000 persons were put to death in one year at Como, in Italy, and about 100 every year after for several years.†

In the beginning of the next century the persecution of witches broke out in France with a fury which was hardly conceivable, and multitudes were burnt amid that gay and lively people. Some notion of the extreme prejudice of their judges may be drawn from the words of one of the inquisitors themselves. Pierre de Lancre, royal councillor in the Parliament of Bourdeaux, with whom the President

* Alciat. "Parerg. Juris," lib. viii. chap. 22.
† Bart. de Spina, de Strigilibus.

Espaignel was joined in a commission to enquire into certain acts of sorcery, reported to have been committed in Labourt and its neighbourhood, at the foot of the Pyrenees, about the month of May, 1619. A few extracts from the preface will best evince the state of mind in which he proceeded to the discharge of his commission.

His story assumes the form of a narrative of a direct war between Satan on the one side and the Royal Commissioners on the other, "because," says Councillor de Lancre, with self-complaisance, "nothing is so calculated to strike terror into the fiend and his dominions as a commission with such plenary powers."

At first, Satan endeavoured to supply his vassals who were brought before the judges with strength to support the examinations, so that if, by intermission of the torture, the wretches should fall into a doze, they declared, when they were recalled from it to the question, that the profound stupor "had something of Paradise in it, being gilded," said the judge, "with the immediate presence of the devil;" though, in all probability, it rather derived its charms from the natural comparison between the insensibility of exhaustion and the previous agony of acute torture. The judges took care that the fiend seldom obtained any advantage in the matter by refusing their victims, in most cases, any interval of rest or sleep. Satan then proceeded, in the way of direct defiance, to stop the mouth of the accused openly, and by mere force, with something like a visible obstruction in their throat. Notwithstanding this, to put the devil to shame, some of the accused found means, in spite of him, to confess and be hanged, or rather burnt. The fiend lost much credit by his failure on this occasion. Before the formidable Commissioners arrived, he had held his *cour plénière* before the gates of Bourdeaux, and in the square of the palace of Galienne, whereas he was now insulted publicly by his own vassals, and in the midst of his festival of the Sabbath the children and relations of the witches who had suffered not sticking to say to him, "Out upon you ! Your promise was that our mothers who were prisoners should not die ; and look how you have kept your word with us ! They have been burnt, and are a heap of ashes." To appease this mutiny Satan had two evasions. He produced illusory fires, and encouraged the mutinous to walk through them, assuring them that the judicial pile was as frigid and inoffensive as those which he exhibited to them. Again, taking his refuge in lies, of which he is well known to be the father, he stoutly affirmed that their parents, who seemed to have suffered, were safe in a foreign country, and that if their children would call on them they would receive an answer. They made the invocation accordingly, and Satan answered each of them in a tone which resembled the voice of the lamented parent almost as successfully as Monsieur Alexandre could have done.

Proceeding to a yet more close attack, the Commissioners, on the eve of one of the Fiend's Sabbaths, placed the gibbet on which they executed their victims just on the spot where Satan's gilded chair was usually stationed. The devil was much offended at such an affront, and yet had so little power in the matter that he could only express his resentment by threats that he would hang Messieurs D'Amon and D'Urtubbe, gentlemen who had solicited and promoted the issuing of the Commission, and would also burn the Commissioners themselves in their own fire. We regret to say that Satan was unable to execute either of these laudable resolutions. Ashamed of his excuses, he abandoned for three or four sittings his attendance on the Sabbaths, sending as his representative an imp of subordinate account, and in whom no one reposed confidence. When he took courage again to face his parliament, the Arch-fiend covered his defection by assuring them that he had been engaged in a lawsuit with the Deity, which he had gained with costs, and that six score of infant children were to be delivered up to him in name of damages, and the witches were directed to procure such victims accordingly. After this grand fiction he confined himself to the petty vengeance of impeding the access of confessors to the condemned, which was the more easy as few of them could speak the Basque language. I have no time to detail the ingenious method by which the learned Councillor de Lancre explains why the district of Labourt should be particularly exposed to the pest of sorcery. The chief reason seems to be that it is a mountainous, a sterile, and a border country, where the men are all fishers and the women smoke tobacco and wear short petticoats.

To a person who, in this presumptuous, trifling, and conceited spirit, has composed a quarto volume full of the greatest absurdities and grossest obscenities ever impressed on paper, it was the pleasure of the most Christian Monarch to consign the most absolute power which could be exercised on these poor people ; and he might with as much prudence have turned a ravenous wolf upon an undefended flock, of whom the animal was the natural enemy, as they were his natural prey. The priest, as well as the ignorant peasant, fell under the suspicion of this fell Commission ; and De Lancre writes, with much complacency, that the accused were brought to trial to the number of forty in one day— with what chance of escape, when the judges were blinded with prejudice, and could only hear the evidence and the defence through the medium of an interpreter, the understanding of the reader may easily anticipate.

Among other gross transgressions of the most ordinary rules, it may be remarked that the accused, in what their judges called confessions, contradicted each other at every turn respecting the description of the Domdaniel in which they pretended to have been assembled, and the fiend who presided there. All spoke to a sort of gilded throne ; but some saw a hideous wild he-goat seated there ; some a man disfigured and twisted, as suffering torture ; some, with better taste, beheld a huge indistinct form, resembling one of those mutilated trunks of trees found in ancient forests.

But De Lancre was no "Daniel come to judgment," and the discrepancy of evidence, which saved the life and fame of Susannah, made no impression in favour of the sorcerers of Labourt.

Instances occur in De Lancre's book of the trial and condemnation of persons accused of the crime of *lycanthropy*, a superstition which was chiefly current in France, but was known in other countries, and is the subject of great debate between Wier, Naudé, Scot, on the one hand, and their demonological adversaries on the other.   The idea, said the one party, was that a human being had the power, by sorcery, of transforming himself into the shape of a wolf, and in that capacity, being seized with a species of fury, he rushed out and made havoc among the flocks, slaying and wasting, like the animal whom he represented, far more than he could devour.   The more incredulous reasoners would not allow of a real transformation, whether with or without the enchanted hide of a wolf, which in some cases was supposed to aid the metamorphosis, and contended that lycanthropy only subsisted as a woful species of disease, a melancholy state of mind, broken with occasional fits of insanity, in which the patient imagined that he committed the ravages of which he was accused.   Such a person, a mere youth, was tried at Besançon, who gave himself out for a servant, or yeoman pricker, of the Lord of the Forest—so he called his superior—who was judged to be the devil.   He was, by his master's power, transformed into the likeness and performed the usual functions of a wolf, and was attended in his course by one larger, which he supposed the Lord of the Forest himself.   These wolves, he said, ravaged the flocks, and throttled the dogs which stood in their defence.   If either had not seen the other, he howled, after the manner of the animal, to call his comrade to his share of the prey ; if he did not come upon this signal, he proceeded to bury it the best way he could.

Such was the general persecution under Messieurs Espiagnel and De Lancre.   Many similar scenes occurred in France, till the edict of Louis XIV. discharging all future prosecutions for witchcraft, after which the crime itself was heard of no more.*

While the spirit of superstition was working such horrors in France, it was not, we may believe, more idle in other countries of Europe. In Spain, particularly, long the residence of the Moors, a people putting deep faith in all the day-dreams of witchcraft, good and evil genii, spells and talismans, the ardent and devotional temper of the old Christians dictated a severe research after sorcerers as well as heretics, and relapsed Jews or Mahommedans. In former times, during the subsistence of the Moorish kingdoms in Spain, a school was supposed to be kept open in Toboso for the study, it is said, of magic, but more likely of chemistry, algebra, and other sciences, which, altogether mistaken by the ignorant and vulgar, and imperfectly understood even by those who studied them, were supposed to be allied to necromancy, or at least to natural magic. It was, of course, the business of the Inquisition to purify whatever such pursuits had left of suspicious Catholicism, and their labours cost as much blood on accusations of witchcraft and magic as for heresy and relapse.

Even the colder nations of Europe were subject to the same epidemic terror for witchcraft, and a specimen of it was exhibited in the sober and rational country of Sweden about the middle of last century, an account of which, being translated into English by a respectable clergyman, Doctor Horneck, excited general surprise how a whole people could be imposed upon to the degree of shedding much blood, and committing great cruelty and injustice, on account of the idle falsehoods propagated by a crew of lying children, who in this case were both actors and witnesses.

The melancholy truth that "the human heart is deceitful above all things, and desperately wicked," is by nothing proved so strongly as by the imperfect sense displayed by children of the sanctity of moral truth. Both the gentlemen

* The reader may sup full on such wild horrors in the *causes célèbres.*

and the mass of the people, as they advance in years, learn
to despise and avoid falsehood ; the former out of pride,
and from a remaining feeling, derived from the days of
chivalry, that the character of a liar is a deadly stain on
their honour ; the other, from some general reflection upon
the necessity of preserving a character for integrity in the
course of life, and a sense of the truth of the common
adage, that " honesty is the best policy." But these are
acquired habits of thinking. The child has no natural love
of truth, as is experienced by all who have the least
acquaintance with early youth. If they are charged with a
fault while they can hardly speak, the first words they
stammer forth are a falsehood to excuse it. Nor is this all :
the temptation of attracting attention, the pleasure of
enjoying importance, the desire to escape from an unpleasing task, or accomplish a holiday, will at any time
overcome the sentiment of truth, so weak is it within them.
Hence thieves and housebreakers, from a surprisingly early
period, find means of rendering children useful in their
mystery ; nor are such acolytes found to evade justice with
less dexterity than the more advanced rogues. Where
a number of them are concerned in the same mischief,
there is something resembling virtue in the fidelity with
which the common secret is preserved. Children, under the
usual age of their being admitted to give evidence, were
necessarily often examined in witch trials ; and it is terrible
to see how often the little impostors, from spite or in mere
gaiety of spirit, have by their art and perseverance made
shipwreck of men's lives. But it would be hard to discover
a case which, supported exclusively by the evidence of
children (the confessions under torture excepted), and
obviously existing only in the young witnesses' own
imagina tion,has been attended with such serious consequences, or given cause to so extensive and fatal a
delusion, as that which occurred in Sweden.

The scene was the Swedish village of Mohra, in the province of Elfland, which district had probably its name from

some remnant of ancient superstition. The delusion had come to a great height ere it reached the ears of government, when, as was the general procedure, Royal Commissioners were sent down, men well fitted for the duty entrusted to them ; that is, with ears open to receive the incredibilities with which they were to be crammed, and hearts hardened against every degree of compassion to the accused. The complaints of the common people, backed by some persons of better condition, were that a number of persons, renowned as witches, had drawn several hundred children of all classes under the devil's authority. They demanded, therefore, the punishment of these agents of hell, reminding the judges that the province had been clear of witches since the burning of some on a former occasion. The accused were numerous, so many as threescore and ten witches and sorcerers being seized in the village of Mohra ; three-and-twenty confessed their crimes, and were sent to Faluna, where most of them were executed. Fifteen of the children were also led to death. Six-and-thirty of those who were young were forced to run the gauntlet, as it is called, and were, besides, lashed weekly at the church doors for a whole year. Twenty of the youngest were condemned to the same discipline for three days only.

The process seems to have consisted in confronting the children with the witches, and hearing the extraordinary story which the former insisted upon maintaining. The children, to the number of three hundred, were found more or less perfect in a tale as full of impossible absurdities as ever was told around a nursery fire. Their confession ran thus :—

They were taught by the witches to go to a cross way, and with certain ceremonies to invoke the devil by the name of Antecessor, begging him to carry them off to Blockula, meaning, perhaps, the Brockenberg, in the Hartz forest, a mountain infamous for being the common scene of witches' meetings, and to which Goethe represents the spirit Mephistopheles as conducting his pupil Faustus. The devil courteously appeared at the call of the children in various forms, but chiefly as a mad Merry-Andrew, with a grey coat, red and blue stockings, a red beard, a high-crowned hat, with linen of various colours wrapt round it, and garters of peculiar length. He set each child on some beast of his providing, and anointed them with a certain unguent composed of the scrapings of altars and the filings of church clocks. There is here a discrepancy of evidence which in another court would have cast the whole. Most of the children considered their journey to be corporeal and actual. Some supposed, however, that their strength or spirit only travelled with the fiend, and that their body remained behind. Very few adopted this last hypothesis, though the parents unanimously bore witness that the bodies of the children remained in bed, and could not be awakened out of a deep sleep, though they shook them for the purpose of awakening them. So strong was, nevertheless, the belief of nurses and mothers in their actual transportation, that a sensible clergyman, mentioned in the preface, who had resolved he would watch his son the whole night and see what hag or fiend would take him from his arms, had the utmost difficulty, notwithstanding, in convincing his mother that the child had not been transported to Blockula during the very night he held him in his embrace.

The learned translator candidly allows, " out of so great a multitude as were accused, condemned, and executed, there might be some who suffered unjustly, and owed their death more to the malice of their enemies than to their skill in the black art, I will readily admit. Nor will I deny," he continues, " but that when the news of these transactions and accounts, how the children bewitched fel into fits and strange unusual postures, spread abroad in the kingdom, some fearful and credulous people, if they saw their children any way disordered, might think they were bewitched or ready to be carried away by imps."* The learned gentleman here stops short in a train of reasoning,

---

* Translator's preface to Horneck's " Account of what happened in the Kingdom of Sweden." See appendix to Glanville's work.

which, followed out, would have deprived the world of the benefit of his translation. For if it was possible that some of these unfortunate persons fell a sacrifice to the malice of their neighbours or the prejudices of witnesses, as he seems ready to grant, is it not more reasonable to believe that the whole of the accused were convicted on similar grounds, than to allow, as truth, the slightest part of the gross and vulgar impossibilities upon which alone their execution can be justified?

The Blockula, which was the object of their journey, was a house having a fine gate painted with divers colours, with a paddock, in which they turned the beasts to graze which had brought them to such scenes of revelry. If human beings had been employed they were left slumbering against the wall of the house. The plan of the devil's palace consisted of one large banqueting apartment and several withdrawing-rooms. Their food was homely enough, being broth made of coleworts and bacon, with bread and butter, and milk and cheese. The same acts of wickedness and profligacy were committed at Blockula which are usually supposed to take place upon the devil's Sabbath elsewhere; but there was this particular, that the witches had sons and daughters by the fiends, who were married together, and produced an offspring of toads and serpents.

These confessions being delivered before the accused witches, they at first stoutly denied them. At last some of them burst into tears, and acquiesced in the horrors imputed to them. They said the practice of carrying off children had been enlarged very lately (which shows the whole rumours to have arisen recently); and the despairing wretches confirmed what the children said, with many other extravagant circumstances, as the mode of elongating a goat's back by means of a spit, on which we care not to be particular. It is worth mentioning that the devil, desirous of enjoying his own reputation among his subjects, pretended at one time to be dead, and was much lamented at Blockula—but he soon revived again.

Some attempts these witches had made to harm individuals on middle earth, but with little success. One old sorceress, indeed, attempted to strike a nail, given her by the devil for that purpose, into the head of the minister of Elfland; but as the skull was of unusual solidity, the reverend gentleman only felt a headache from her efforts. They could not be persuaded to exhibit any of their tricks before the Commissioners, excusing themselves by alleging that their witchcraft had left them, and that the devil had amused them with the vision of a burning pit, having a hand thrust out of it.

The total number who lost their lives on this singular occasion was fourscore and four persons, including fifteen children; and at this expense of blood was extinguished a flame that arose as suddenly, burned as fiercely, and decayed as rapidly, as any portent of the kind within the annals of superstition. The Commissioners returned to Court with the high approbation of all concerned; prayers were ordered through the churches weekly, that Heaven would be pleased to restrain the powers of the devil, and deliver the poor creatures who hitherto had groaned under it, as well as the innocent children, who were carried off by hundreds at once.

If we could ever learn the true explanation of this story, we should probably find that the cry was led by some clever mischievous boy, who wished to apologise to his parents for lying an hour longer in the morning by alleging he had been at Blockula on the preceding night; and that the desire to be as much distinguished as their comrade had stimulated the bolder and more acute of his companions to the like falsehoods; whilst those of weaker minds assented, either from fear of punishment or the force of dreaming over at night the horrors which were dinned into their ears all day. Those who were ingenuous, as it was termed, in their confessions, received praise and encouragement; and those who denied or were silent, and, as it was considered, impenitent, were sure to bear the harder share of the punishment which was addressed to all. It is worth while also to observe, that the smarter children began to improve their evidence and add touches to the general picture of Blockula. " Some of the children talked much of a white angel, which used to forbid them what the devil bid them do, and told them that these doings should not last long. And (they added) this better being would place himself sometimes at the door betwixt the witches and the children, and when they came to Blockula he pulled the children back, but the witches went in."

This additional evidence speaks for itself, and shows the whole tale to be the fiction of the children's imagination, which some of them wished to improve upon. The reader may consult " An Account of what happened in the Kingdom of Sweden in the years 1669 and 1670, and afterwards translated out of High Dutch into English by Dr. Antony Horneck," attached to Glanville's "Sadducismus Triumphatus." The translator refers to the evidence of Baron Sparr, Ambassador from the Court of Sweden to the Court of England in 1672 ; and that of Baron Lyonberg, Envoy Extraordinary of the same power, both of whom attest the confession and execution of the witches. The King of Sweden himself answered the express inquiries of the Duke of Holstein with marked reserve. " His judges and commissioners," he said, " had caused divers men, women, and children, to be burnt and executed on such pregnant evidence as was brought before them. But whether the actions confessed and proved against them were real, or only the effects of strong imagination, he was not as yet able to determine"— a sufficient reason, perhaps, why punishment should have been at least deferred by the interposition of the royal authority.

We must now turn our eyes to Britain, in which our knowledge as to such events is necessarily more extensive, and where it is in a high degree more interesting to our present purpose.

LETTER VIII.

The Effects of the Witch Superstition are to be traced in the Laws of a
Kingdom—Usually punished in England as a Crime connected with
Politics—Attempt at Murder for Witchcraft not in itself Capital—-
Trials of Persons of Rank for Witchcraft, connected with State
Crimes—Statutes of Henry VIII.—How Witchcraft was regarded
by the three Leading Sects of Religion in the Sixteenth Century;
first, by the Catholics; second, by the Calvinists; third, by the
Church of England and Lutherans—Impostures unwarily coun-
tenanced by individual Catholic Priests, and also by some Puritanic
Clergymen—Statute of 1562, and some cases upon it—Case of
Dugdale—Case of the Witches of Warbois, and the execution of the
Family of Samuel—That of Jane Wenham, in which some Church
of England Clergymen insisted on the Prosecution—Hutchison's
Rebuke to them—James the First's Opinion of Witchcraft—His
celebrated Statute, 1 Jac. I.—Canon passed by the Convocation
against Possession—Case of Mr. Fairfax's Children—Lancashire
Witches in 1613—Another Discovery in 1634—Webster's Account
of the manner in which the Imposture was managed—Superiority of
the Calvinists is followed by a severe Prosecution of Witches—
Executions in Suffolk, &c. to a dreadful extent—Hopkins, the
pretended Witchfinder, the cause of these Cruelties—His Brutal
Practices—His Letter—Execution of Mr. Lowis—Hopkins Punished
—Restoration of Charles—Trial of Coxe—Of Dunny and Callendar
before Lord Hales—Royal Society and Progress of Knowledge—
Somersetshire Witches—Opinions of the Populace—A Woman
Swum for Witchcraft at Oakly—Murder at Tring—Act against
Witchcraft abolished, and the belief in the Crime becomes forgotten
—Witch Trials in New England—Dame Glover's Trial—Affliction
of the Parvises, and frightful Increase of the Prosecutions—Suddenly
put a stop to—The Penitence of those concerned in them.

Our account of Demonology in England must naturally, as
in every other country, depend chiefly on the instances which
history contains of the laws and prosecutions against witchcraft. Other superstitions arose and decayed, were dreaded
or despised, without greater embarrassment, in the provinces

in which they have a temporary currency, than that cowards and children go out more seldom at night, while the reports of ghosts and fairies are peculiarly current. But when the alarm of witchcraft arises, Superstition dips her hand in the blood of the persons accused, and records in the annals of jurisprudence their trials and the causes alleged in vindication of their execution. Respecting other fantastic allegations, the proof is necessarily transient and doubtful, depending upon the inaccurate testimony of vague report and of doting tradition. But in cases of witchcraft we have before us the recorded evidence upon which judge and jury acted, and can form an opinion with some degree of certainty of the grounds, real or fanciful, on which they acquitted or condemned. It is, therefore, in tracing this part of Demonology, with its accompanying circumstances, that we have the best chance of obtaining an accurate view of our subject.

The existence of witchcraft was, no doubt, received and credited in England, as in the countries on the Continent, and originally punished accordingly. But after the fourteenth century the practices which fell under such a description were thought unworthy of any peculiar animadversion, unless they were connected with something which would have been of itself a capital crime, by whatever means it had been either essayed or accomplished. Thus the supposed paction between a witch and the demon was perhaps deemed in itself to have terrors enough to prevent its becoming an ordinary crime, and was not, therefore, visited with any statutory penalty. But to attempt or execute bodily harm to others through means of evil spirits, or, in a word, by the black art, was actionable at common law as much as if the party accused had done the same harm with an arrow or pistol-shot. The destruction or abstraction of goods by the like instruments, supposing the charge proved, would, in like manner, be punishable. *A fortiori*, the consulting soothsayers, familiar spirits, or the like, and the obtaining and circulating pretended prophecies to the unsettlement of the State and the endangering of the King's title, is yet a higher degree of guilt. And it may be remarked that the inquiry into the date of the King's life bears a close affinity with the desiring or compassing the death of the Sovereign, which is the essence of high treason. Upon such charges repeated trials took place in the courts of the English, and condemnations were pronounced, with sufficient justice, no doubt, where the connexion between the resort to sorcerers and the design to perpetrate a felony could be clearly proved. We would not, indeed, be disposed to go the length of so high an authority as Selden, who pronounces (in his "Table-Talk") that if a man heartily believed that he could take the life of another by waving his hat three times and crying Buzz! and should, under this fixed opinion, wave his hat and cry Buzz! accordingly, he ought to be executed as a murderer. But a false prophecy of the King's death is not to be dealt with exactly on the usual principle; because, however idle in itself, the promulgation of such a prediction has, in times such as we are speaking of, a strong tendency to work its completion.

Many persons, and some of great celebrity, suffered for the charge of trafficking with witches, to the prejudice of those in authority. We have already mentioned the instance of the Duchess of Gloucester, in Henry the Sixth's reign, and that of the Queen Dowager's kinsmen, in the Protectorate of Richard, afterwards the Third. In 1521, the Duke of Buckingham was beheaded, owing much to his having listened to the predictions of one Friar Hopkins. In the same reign, the Maid of Kent, who had been esteemed a prophetess, was put to death as a cheat. She suffered with seven persons who had managed her fits for the support of the Catholic religion, and confessed her fraud upon the scaffold. About seven years after this, Lord Hungerford was beheaded for consulting certain soothsayers concerning the length of Henry the Eighth's life. But these cases rather relate to the purpose for which the sorcery was employed, than to the fact of using it.

Two remarkable statutes were passed in the year 1541 ; one against false prophecies, the other against the act of conjuration, witchcraft, and sorcery, and at the same time against breaking and destroying crosses. The former enactment was certainly made to ease the suspicious and wayward fears of the tetchy King Henry. The prohibition against witchcraft might be also dictated by the king's jealous doubts of hazard to the succession. The enactment against breaking crosses was obviously designed to check the ravages of the Reformers, who in England as well as else-where desired to sweep away Popery with the besom of destruction. This latter statute was abrogated in the first year of Edward VI., perhaps as placing an undue restraint on the zeal of good Protestants against idolatry.

At length, in 1562, a formal statute against sorcery, as penal in itself, was actually passed ; but as the penalty was limited to the pillory for the first transgression, the legislature probably regarded those who might be brought to trial as impostors rather than wizards. There are instances of individuals tried and convicted as impostors and cheats, and who acknowledged themselves such before the court and people ; but in their articles of visitation the prelates directed enquiry to be made after those who should use enchantments, witchcraft, sorcery, or any like craft, *invented by the devil.*

But it is here proper to make a pause for the purpose of enquiring in what manner the religious disputes which occupied all Europe about this time influenced the proceedings of the rival sects in relation to Demonology.

The Papal Church had long reigned by the proud and absolute humour which she had assumed, of maintaining every doctrine which her rulers had adopted in dark ages ; but this pertinacity at length made her citadel too large to be defended at every point by a garrison whom prudence would have required to abandon positions which had been taken in times of darkness, and were unsuited to the warfare of a more enlightened age. The sacred motto of the Vatican was, " *Vestigia nulla retrorsum;*" and this rendered it impossible to comply with the more wise and moderate of her own party, who would otherwise have desired to make liberal concessions to the Protestants, and thus prevent, in its commencement, a formidable schism in the Christian world.

To the system of Rome the Calvinists offered the most determined opposition, affecting upon every occasion and on all points to observe an order of church-government, as well as of worship, expressly in the teeth of its enactments; —in a word, to be a good Protestant, they held it almost essential to be in all things diametrically opposite to the Catholic form and faith. As the foundation of this sect was laid in republican states, as its clerical discipline was settled on a democratic basis, and as the countries which adopted that form of government were chiefly poor, the preachers having lost the rank and opulence enjoyed by the Roman Church, were gradually thrown on the support of the people. Insensibly they became occupied with the ideas and tenets natural to the common people, which, if they have usually the merit of being honestly conceived and boldly expressed, are not the less often adopted with credulity and precipitation, and carried into effect with unhesitating harshness and severity.

Betwixt these extremes the Churchmen of England endeavoured to steer a middle course, retaining a portion of the ritual and forms of Rome, as in themselves admirable, and at any rate too greatly venerated by the people to be changed merely for opposition's sake. Their comparatively undilapidated revenue, the connexion of their system with the state, with views of ambition as ample as the station of a churchman ought to command, rendered them independent of the necessity of courting their flocks by any means

save regular discharge of their duty ; and the excellent provisions made for their education afforded them learning to
confute ignorance and enlighten prejudice.

Such being the general character of the three Churches,
their belief in and persecution of such crimes as witchcraft
and sorcery were necessarily modelled upon the peculiar
tenets which each system professed, and gave rise to
various results in the countries where they were severally
received.

The Church of Rome, as we have seen, was unwilling, in
her period of undisputed power, to call in the secular arm
to punish men for witchcraft—a crime which fell especially
under ecclesiastical cognizance, and could, according to her
belief, be subdued by the spiritual arm alone. The learned
men at the head of the establishment might safely despise
the attempt at those hidden arts as impossible ; or, even if
they were of a more credulous disposition, they might be
unwilling to make laws by which their own enquiries in the
mathematics, algebra, chemistry, and other pursuits vulgarly
supposed to approach the confines of magic art, might be
inconveniently restricted. The more selfish part of the
priesthood might think that a general belief in the existence
of witches should be permitted to remain, as a source both
of power and of revenue—that if there were no possessions,
there could be no exorcism-fees—and, in short, that a whole-
some faith in all the absurdities of the vulgar creed as to
supernatural influences was necessary to maintain the influence of Diana of Ephesus. They suffered spells to be
manufactured, since every friar had the power of reversing
them ; they permitted poison to be distilled, because every
convent had the antidote, which was disposed of to all who
chose to demand it. It was not till the universal progress
of heresy, in the end of the fifteenth century, that the bull
of Pope Innocent VIII., already quoted, called to convict,
imprison, and condemn the sorcerers, chiefly because it was
the object to transfer the odium of these crimes to the Wal-

denses, and excite and direct the public hatred against the new sect by confounding their doctrines with the influences of the devil and his fiends. The bull of Pope Innocent was afterwards, in the year 1523, enforced by Adrian VI. with a new one, in which excommunication was directed against *sorcerers and heretics.*

While Rome thus positively declared herself against witches and sorcerers, the Calvinists, in whose numbers must be included the greater part of the English Puritans, who, though they had not finally severed from the communion of the Anglican Church, yet disapproved of her ritual and ceremonies as retaining too much of the Papal stamp, ranked themselves, in accordance with their usual policy, in diametrical opposition to the doctrine of the Mother Church. They assumed in the opposite sense whatever Rome pretended to as a proof of her omnipotent authority. The exorcisms, forms, and rites, by which good Catholics believed that incarnate fiends could be expelled and evil spirits of every kind rebuked—these, like the holy water, the robes of the priest, and the sign of the cross, the Calvinists considered either with scorn and contempt as the tools of deliberate quackery and imposture, or with horror and loathing, as the fit emblems and instruments of an idolatrous system.

Such of them as did not absolutely deny the supernatural powers of which the Romanists made boast, regarded the success of the exorcising priest, to whatever extent they admitted it, as at best a casting out of devils by the power of Beelzebub, the King of the Devils. They saw also, and resented bitterly, the attempt to confound any dissent from the doctrines of Rome with the proneness to an encouragement of rites of sorcery. On the whole, the Calvinists, generally speaking, were of all the contending sects the most suspicious of sorcery, the most undoubting believers in its existence, and the most eager to follow it up with what they conceived to be the due punishment of the most fearful of crimes.

The leading divines of the Church of England were, without doubt, fundamentally as much opposed to the doctrines of Rome as those who altogether disclaimed opinions and ceremonies merely because she had entertained them. But their position in society tended strongly to keep them from adopting, on such subjects as we are now discussing, either the eager credulity of the vulgar mind or the fanatic ferocity of their Calvinistic rivals. We have no purpose to discuss the matter in detail— enough has probably been said to show generally why the Romanist should have cried out a miracle respecting an incident which the Anglican would have contemptuously termed an imposture ; while the Calvinist, inspired with a darker zeal, and, above all, with the unceasing desire of open controversy with the Catholics, would have styled the same event an operation of the devil.

It followed that, while the divines of the Church of England possessed the upper hand in the kingdom, witchcraft, though trials and even condemnations for that offence occasionally occurred, did not create that epidemic terror which the very suspicion of the offence carried with it elsewhere; so that Reginald Scot and others alleged it was the vain pretences and empty forms of the Church of Rome, by the faith reposed in them, which had led to the belief of witchcraft or sorcery in general. Nor did prosecutions on account of such charges frequently involve a capital punishment, while learned judges were jealous of the imperfection of the evidence to support the charge, and entertained a strong and growing suspicion that legitimate grounds for such trials seldom actually existed. On the other hand, it usually happened that wherever the Calvinist interest became predominant in Britain, a general persecution of sorcerers and witches seemed to take place of consequence. Fearing and hating sorcery more than other Protestants, connecting its ceremonies and usages with those of the detested Catholic Church, the Calvinists were more eager than other sects in searching after the traces of this crime, and, of course, unusually successful, as they might suppose, in making discoveries of guilt, and pursuing it to the expiation of the fagot. In a word, a principle already referred to by Dr. Francis Hutchison will be found to rule the tide and the reflux of such cases in the different churches. The numbers of witches, and their supposed dealings with Satan, will increase or decrease according as such doings are accounted probable or impossible. Under the former supposition, charges and convictions will be found augmented in a terrific degree. When the accusations are disbelieved and dismissed as not worthy of attention, the crime becomes unfrequent, ceases to occupy the public mind, and affords little trouble to the judges.

The passing of Elizabeth's statute against witchcraft in 1562 does not seem to have been intended to increa se the number of trials, or cases of conviction at least ; and the fact is, it did neither the one nor the other. Two children were tried in 1574 for counterfeiting possession, and stood in the pillory for impostors. Mildred Norrington, called the Maid of Westwell, furnished another instance of possession ; but she also confessed her imposture, and publicly showed her fits and tricks of mimicry. The strong influence already possessed by the Puritans may probably be sufficient to account for the darker issue of certain cases, in which both juries and judges in Elizabeth's time must be admitted to have shown fearful severity.

These cases of possession were in some respects sore snares to the priests of the Church of Rome, who, while they were too sagacious not to be aware that the pretended fits, contortions, strange sounds, and other extravagances, produced as evidence of the demon's influence on the possessed person, were nothing else than marks of imposture by some idle vagabond, were nevertheless often tempted to admit them as real, and take the credit of curing them. The period was one when the Catholic Church had much occasion to rally around her all the respect that remained to her in a schismatic and heretical kingdom ; and when her fathers and doctors announced the existence of such a dreadful disease, and of the power of the church's prayers, relics, and ceremonies, to cure it, it was difficult for a priest, supposing him more tender of the interest of his order than that of truth, to avoid such a tempting opportunity as a supposed case of possession offered for displaying the high privilege in which his profession made him a partaker, or to abstain from conniving at the imposture, in order to obtain for his church the credit of expelling the demon. It was hardly to be wondered at, if the ecclesiastic was sometimes induced to aid the fraud of which such motives forbade him to be the detector. At this he might hesitate the less, as he was not obliged to adopt the suspected and degrading course of holding an immediate communication *in limine* with the impostor, since a hint or two, dropped in the supposed sufferer's presence, might give him the necessary information what was the most exact mode of performing his part, and if the patient was possessed by a devil of any acuteness or dexterity, he wanted no further instruction how to play it. Such combinations were sometimes detected, and brought more discredit on the Church of Rome than was counterbalanced by any which might be more cunningly managed. On this subject the reader may turn to Dr. Harsnett's celebrated book on Popish Impostures, wherein he gives the history of several notorious cases of detected fraud, in which Roman ecclesiastics had not hesitated to mingle themselves. That of Grace Sowerbutts, instructed by a Catholic priest to impeach her grandmother of witchcraft, was a very gross fraud.

Such cases were not, however, limited to the ecclesiastics of Rome. We have already stated that, as extremes usually approach each other, the Dissenters, in their violent opposition to the Papists, adopted some of their ideas respecting demoniacs ; and we have now to add that they also claimed, by the vehemence of prayer and the authority of their own sacred commission, that power of expelling devils which the Church of Rome pretended to exercise by rites, ceremonies, and relics.   The memorable case of Richard Dugdale, called the Surrey Impostor, was one of the most remarkable which the Dissenters brought forward.   This youth was supposed to have sold his soul to the devil, on condition of being made the best dancer in Lancashire, and during his possession played a number of fantastic tricks, not much different from those exhibited by expert posture-masters of the present day.   This person threw himself into the hands of the Dissenters, who, in their eagerness, caught at an opportunity to relieve an afflicted person, whose case the regular clergy appeared to have neglected.   They fixed a committee of their number, who weekly attended the supposed sufferer, and exercised themselves in appointed days of humiliation and fasting during the course of a whole year.   All respect for the demon seems to have abandoned the reverend gentlemen, after they had relieved guard in this manner for some little time, and they got so regardless of Satan as to taunt him with the mode in which he executed his promise to teach his vassal dancing.   The following specimen of raillery is worth commemoration :—" What, Satan ! is this the dancing that Richard gave himself to thee for? &c.   Canst thou dance no better? &c.   Ransack the old records of all past times and places in thy memory ; canst thou not there find out some better way of trampling? Pump thine invention dry ; cannot the universal seed-plot of subtile wiles and stratagems spring up one new method of cutting capers?   Is this the top of skill and pride, to shuffle feet and brandish knees thus, and to trip like a doe and skip like a squirrel ?   And wherein differ thy leapings from the hoppings of a frog, or the bouncings of a goat, or friskings of a dog, or gesticulations of a monkey?   And cannot a palsy shake such a loose leg as that ?   Dost thou not twirl like a calf that hath the turn, and twitch up thy houghs just like a springhault tit ?"* One might almost conceive the demon replying to this raillery in the words of Dr. Johnson, "This merriment of parsons is extremely offensive."

The dissenters were probably too honest, however simple, to achieve a complete cure on Dugdale by an amicable understanding ; so, after their year of vigil, they relinquished their task by degrees. Dugdale, weary of his illness, which now attracted little notice, attended a regular physician, and was cured of that part of his disease which was not affected in a regular way *par ordonnance du médecin*. But the reverend gentlemen who had taken his case in hand still assumed the credit of curing him, and if anything could have induced them to sing *Te Deum*, it would have been this occasion. They said that the effect of their public prayers had been for a time suspended, until seconded by the continued earnestness of their private devotions!

The ministers of the Church of England, though, from education, intercourse with the world, and other advantages, they were less prone to prejudice than those of other sects, are yet far from being entirely free of the charge of encouraging in particular instances the witch superstition. Even while Dr. Hutchison pleads that the Church of England has the least to answer for in that matter, he is under the necessity of acknowledging that some regular country clergymen so far shared the rooted prejudices of congregations, and of the government which established laws against it, as to be active in the persecution of the suspected, and even in countenancing the superstitious signs by which in that period the vulgar thought it possible to ascertain the existence of the afflictions by witchcraft, and obtain the knowledge of the perpetrator. A singular case is mentioned of three women, called the Witches of Warbois. Indeed, their story is a matter of solemn enough record ; for Sir Samuel Cromwell, having received the sum of forty pounds as lord of the manor, out of the estate of the poor persons

* Hutchison on Witchcraft, p. 162.

who suffered, turned it into a rent-charge of forty shillings
yearly, for the endowment of an annual lecture on the
subject of witchcraft, to be preached by a doctor or
bachelor of divinity of Queen's College, Cambridge. The
accused, one Samuel and his wife, were old and very poor
persons, and their daughter a young woman. The daughter
of a Mr. Throgmorton, seeing the poor old woman in
a black knitted cap, at a time when she was not very well,
took a whim that she had bewitched her, and was ever after
exclaiming against her. The other children of this fanciful
family caught up the same cry, and the eldest of them
at last got up a vastly pretty drama, in which she herself
furnished all the scenes and played all the parts.

Such imaginary scenes, or *make-believe* stories, are the
common amusement of lively children ; and most readers
may remember having had some Utopia of their own. But
the nursery drama of Miss Throgmorton had a horrible
conclusion. This young lady and her sisters were supposed
to be haunted by nine spirits, dispatched by the wicked
Mother Samuel for that purpose. The sapient parents
heard one part of the dialogue, when the children in their
fits returned answers, as was supposed, to the spirits who
afflicted them ; and when the patients from time to time recovered, they furnished the counterpart by telling what the
spirits had said to them. The names of the spirits were
Pluck, Hardname, Catch, Blue, and three Smacks, who were
cousins. Mrs. Joan Throgmorton, the eldest (who, like
other young women of her age, about fifteen, had some
disease on her nerves, and whose fancy ran apparently
on love and gallantry), supposed that one of the Smacks
was her lover, did battle for her with the less friendly
spirits, and promised to protect her against Mother Samuel
herself; and the following curious extract will show on what
a footing of familiarity the damsel stood with her spiritual
gallant : " From whence come you, Mr. Smack ?" says the
afflicted young lady ; " and what news do you bring ?"

Smack, nothing abashed, informed her he came from
fighting with Pluck : the weapons, great cowl-staves ; the
scene, a ruinous bakehouse in Dame Samuel's yard. "And
who got the mastery, I pray you ?" said the damsel. Smack
answered, he had broken Pluck's head. " I would," said the
damsel, " he had broken your neck also." " Is that the
thanks I am to have for my labour ?" said the disappointed
Smack. " Look you for thanks at my hand ?" said the distressed maiden. "I would you were all hanged up against
each other, with your dame for company, for you are
all naught." On this repulse, exit Smack, and enter Pluck,
Blue, and Catch, the first with his head broken, the other
limping, and the third with his arm in a sling, all trophies of
Smack's victory. They disappeared after having threatened
vengeance upon the conquering Smack. However, he soon
afterwards appeared with his laurels. He told her of his
various conflicts. " I wonder," said Mrs. Joan, or Jane,
"that you are able to beat them ; you are little, and
they very big." " He cared not for that," he replied ;
"he would beat the best two of them, and his cousins
Smacks would beat the other two." This most pitiful mirth,
for such it certainly is, was mixed with tragedy enough.
Miss Throgmorton and her sisters railed against Dame
Samuel ; and when Mr. Throgmorton brought her to his
house by force, the little fiends longed to draw blood of
her, scratch her, and torture her, as the witch-creed of that
period recommended ; yet the poor woman incurred deeper
suspicion when she expressed a wish to leave a house where
she was so coarsely treated and lay under such odious
suspicions.

It was in vain that this unhappy creature endeavoured to
avert their resentment by submitting to all the ill-usage
they chose to put upon her ; in vain that she underwent
unresistingly the worst usage at the hand of Lady Cromwell,
her landlady, who, abusing her with the worst epithets, tore
her cap from her head, clipped out some of her hair, and

gave it to Mrs. Throgmorton to burn it for a counter-charm. Nay, Mother Samuel's complaisance in the latter case only led to a new charge. It happened that the Lady Cromwell, on her return home, dreamed of her day's work, and especially of the old dame and her cat; and, as her ladyship died in a *year and quarter* from that very day, it was sagaciously concluded that she must have fallen a victim to the witcheries of the terrible Dame Samuel. Mr. Throgmorton also compelled the old woman and her daughter to use expressions which put their lives in the power of these malignant children, who had carried on the farce so long that they could not well escape from their own web of deceit but by the death of these helpless creatures. For example, the prisoner, Dame Samuel, was induced to say to the supposed spirit, "As I am a witch, and a causer of Lady Cromwell's death, I charge thee to come out of the maiden." The girl lay still; and this was accounted a proof that the poor woman, who, only subdued and crushed by terror and tyranny, did as she was bidden, was a witch. One is ashamed of an English judge and jury when it must be repeated that the evidence of these enthusiastic and giddy-pated girls was deemed sufficient to the condemnation of three innocent persons. Goody Samuel, indeed, was at length worried into a confession of her guilt by the various vexations which were practised on her. But her husband and daughter continued to maintain their innocence. The last showed a high spirit and proud value for her character. She was advised by some, who pitied her youth, to gain at least a respite by pleading pregnancy; to which she answered disdainfully, "No, I will not be both held witch and strumpet!" The mother, to show her sanity of mind and the real value of her confession, caught at the advice recommended to her daughter. As her years put such a plea out of the question, there was a laugh among the unfeeling audience, in which the poor old victim joined loudly and heartily. Some there were who thought it no joking matter, and were inclined to think they had a Joanna Southcote before them, and that the devil must be the father. These unfortunate Samuels were condemned at Huntingdon, before Mr. Justice Fenner, 4th April, 1593. It was a singular case to be commemorated by an annual lecture, as provided by Sir Samuel Cromwell, for the purposes of justice were never so perverted, nor her sword turned to a more flagrant murder.

We may here mention, though mainly for the sake of contrast, the much-disputed case of Jane Wenham, the Witch of Walkerne, as she was termed, which was of a much later date. Some of the country clergy were carried away by the land-flood of superstition in this instance also, and not only encouraged the charge, but gave their countenance to some of the ridiculous and indecent tricks resorted to as proofs of witchcraft by the lowest vulgar. But the good sense of the judge, seconded by that of other reflecting and sensible persons, saved the country from the ultimate disgrace attendant on too many of these unhallowed trials. The usual sort of evidence was brought against this poor woman, by pretences of bewitched persons vomiting fire— a trick very easy to those who chose to exhibit such a piece of jugglery amongst such as rather desire to be taken in by it than to detect the imposture. The witchfinder practised upon her the most vulgar and ridiculous tricks or charms ; and out of a perverted examination they drew what they called a confession, though of a forced and mutilated character. Under such proof the jury brought her in guilty, and she was necessarily condemned to die. More fortunate, however, than many persons placed in the like circumstances, Jane Wenham was tried before a sensible and philosophic judge, who could not understand that the life of an Englishwoman, however mean, should be taken away by a set of barbarous tricks and experiments, the efficacy of which depended on popular credulity. He reprieved the witch before he left the assize-town. The rest of the history is equally a contrast to some we have told and others we shall have to recount.   A humane and high-spirited gentleman, Colonel Plummer of Gilston, putting at defiance popular calumny, placed the poor old woman in a small house near his own and under his immediate protection.   Here she lived and died, in honest and fair reputation, edifying her visitors by her accuracy and attention in repeating her devotions ; and, removed from her brutal and malignant neighbours, never afterwards gave the slightest cause of suspicion or offence till her dying day.   As this was one of the last cases of conviction in England, Dr Hutchison has been led to dilate upon it with some strength of eloquence as well as argument.

He thus expostulates with some of the better class who were eager for the prosecution :—" (1) What single fact of sorcery did this Jane Wenham do ?   What charm did she use, or what act of witchcraft could you prove upon her ?   Laws are against evil actions that can be proved to be of the person's doing.   What single fact that was against the statute could you fix upon her ?   I ask (2) Did she so much as speak an imprudent word, or do an immoral action, that you could put into the narrative of her case ?   When she was denied a few turnips, she laid them down very submissively ; when she was called witch and bitch, she only took the proper means for the vindication of her good name ; when she saw this storm coming upon her she locked herself in her own house and tried to keep herself out of your cruel hands ; when her door was broken open, and you gave way to that barbarous usage that she met with, she protested her innocence, fell upon her knees, and begged she might not go to gaol, and, in her innocent simplicity, would have let you swim her ; and at her trial she declared herself a clear woman.   This was her behaviour.   And what could any of us have done better, excepting in that case where she complied with you too much, and offered to let you swim her ?

" (3) When you used the meanest of paganish and popish

superstitions—when you scratched and mangled and ran pins into her flesh, and used that ridiculous trial of the bottle, &c.—whom did you consult, and from whom did you expect your answers? Who was your father? and into whose hands did you put yourselves? and (if the true sense of the statute had been turned upon you) which way would you have defended yourselves? (4) Durst you have used her in this manner if she had been rich? and doth not her poverty increase rather than lessen your guilt in what you did?

"And therefore, instead of closing your book with a *liberavimus animas nostras*, and reflecting upon the court, I ask you (5) Whether you have not more reason to give God thanks that you met with a wise judge, and a sensible gentleman, who kept you from shedding innocent blood, and reviving the meanest and cruelest of all superstitions amongst us?"*

But although individuals of the English Church might on some occasions be justly accused of falling into lamentable errors on a subject where error was so general, it was not an usual point of their professional character; and it must be admitted that the most severe of the laws against witchcraft originated with a Scottish King of England, and that the only extensive persecution following that statute occurred during the time of the Civil Wars, when the Calvinists obtained for a short period a predominating influence in the councils of Parliament.

James succeeded to Elizabeth amidst the highest expectations on the part of his new people, who, besides their general satisfaction at coming once more under the rule of a king, were also proud of his supposed abilities and real knowledge of books and languages, and were naturally, though imprudently, disposed to gratify him by deferring to his judgment in matters wherein his studies were supposed to have rendered him a special proficient. Unfortunately,

* Hutchison's "Essay on Witchcraft," p. 166.

besides the more harmless freak of becoming a prentice in the art of poetry, by which words and numbers were the only sufferers, the monarch had composed a deep work upon Demonology, embracing in their fullest extent the most absurd and gross of the popular errors on this subject. He considered his crown and life as habitually aimed at by the sworn slaves of Satan. Several had been executed for an attempt to poison him by magical arts; and the turbulent Francis Stewart, Earl of Bothwell, whese repeated attempts on his person had long been James's terror, had begun his course of rebellion by a consultation with the weird sisters and soothsayers. Thus the king, who had proved with his pen the supposed sorcerers to be the direct enemies of the Deity, and who conceived he knew them from experience to be his own—who, moreover, had upon much lighter occasions (as in the case of Vorstius) showed no hesitation at throwing his royal authority into the scale to aid his arguments—very naturally used his influence, when it was at the highest, to extend and enforce the laws against a crime which he both hated and feared.

The English statute against witchcraft, passed in the very first year of that reign, is therefore of a most special nature, describing witchcraft by all the various modes and ceremonies in which, according to King James's fancy, that crime could be perpetrated; each of which was declared felony, without benefit of clergy.

This gave much wider scope to prosecution on the statute than had existed under the milder acts of Elizabeth. Men might now be punished for the practice of witchcraft, as itself a crime, without necessary reference to the ulterior objects of the perpetrator. It is remarkable that in the same year, when the legislature rather adopted the passions and fears of the king than expressed their own by this fatal enactment, the Convocation of the Church evinced a very different spirit; for, seeing the ridicule brought on their sacred profession by forward and presumptuous men, in the attempt to relieve demoniacs from a disease which was commonly occasioned by natural causes, if not the mere creature of imposture, they passed a canon, establishing that no minister or ministers should in future attempt to expel any devil or devils, without the license of his bishop; thereby virtually putting a stop to a fertile source of knavery among the people, and disgraceful folly among the inferior churchmen.

The new statute of James does not, however, appear to have led at first to many prosecutions. One of the most remarkable was (*proh pudor!*) instigated by a gentleman, a scholar of classical taste, and a beautiful poet, being no other than Edward Fairfax of Fayston, in Knaresborough Forest, the translator of Tasso's "Jerusalem Delivered." In allusion to his credulity on such subjects, Collins has introduced the following elegant lines :—

> " How have I sate while piped the pensive wind,
>   To hear thy harp, by British Fairfax strung ;
> Prevailing poet, whose undoubting mind
>   Believed the magic wonders which he sung !"

Like Mr. Throgmorton in the Warbois case, Mr. Fairfax accused six of his neighbours of tormenting his children by fits of an extraordinary kind, by imps, and by appearing before the afflicted in their own shape during the crisis of these operations. The admitting this last circumstance to be a legitimate mode of proof, gave a most cruel advantage against the accused, for it could not, according to the ideas of the demonologists, be confuted even by the most distinct *alibi*. To a defence of that sort it was replied that the afflicted person did not see the actual witch, whose corporeal presence must indeed have been obvious to every one in the room as well as to the afflicted, but that the evidence of the sufferers related to the appearance of their *spectre*, or apparition ; and this was accounted a sure sign of guilt in those whose forms were so manifested during the fits of the afflicted, and who were complained of and cried out upon by the victim. The obvious tendency of this doctrine, as to visionary or spectral evidence, as it was called, was to place the life and fame of the accused in the power of any hypochondriac patient or malignant impostor, who might either seem to see, or aver she saw, the *spectrum* of the accused old man or old woman, as if enjoying and urging on the afflictions which she complained of; and, strange to tell, the fatal sentence was to rest, not upon the truth of the witnesses' eyes, but that of their imagination. It happened fortunately for Fairfax's memory, that the objects of his prosecution were persons of good character, and that the judge was a man of sense, and made so wise and skilful a charge to the jury, that they brought in a verdict of not guilty.

The celebrated case of "the Lancashire witches" (whose name was and will be long remembered, partly from Shadwell's play, but more from the ingenious and well-merited compliment to the beauty of the females of that province which it was held to contain), followed soon after. Whether the first notice of this sorcery sprung from the idle head of a mischievous boy, is uncertain; but there is no doubt that it was speedily caught up and fostered for the purpose of gain. The original story ran thus :—

These Lancaster trials were at two periods, the one in 1613, before Sir James Altham and Sir Edward Bromley, Barons of Exchequer, when nineteen witches were tried at once at Lancaster, and another of the name of Preston at York. The report against these people is drawn up by Thomas Potts An obliging correspondent sent me a sight of a copy of this curious and rare book. The chief personage in the drama is Elizabeth Southam, a witch redoubted under the name of Dembdike, an account of whom may be seen in Mr. Roby's "Antiquities of Lancaster," as well as a description of Maulkins' Tower, the witches' place of meeting. It appears that this remote county was full of Popish recusants, travelling priests, and so forth; and some of their spells are given in which the holy names and things alluded to form a strange contrast with the purpose to which they were applied, as to secure a good brewing of ale or the like. The public imputed to the accused parties a long train of murders, conspiracies, charms, mischances, hellish and damnable practices, "apparent," says the editor, " on their own examinations and confessions," and, to speak the truth, visible nowhere else. Mother Dembdike had the good luck to die before conviction. Among other tales, we have one of two *female* devils, called Fancy and Tib. It is remarkable that some of the unfortunate women endeavoured to transfer the guilt from themselves to others with whom they had old quarrels, which confessions were held good evidence against those who made them, and against the alleged accomplice also. Several of the unhappy women were found not guilty, to the great displeasure of the ignorant people of the county. Such was the first edition of the Lancashire witches. In that which follows the accusation can be more clearly traced to the most villanous conspiracy.

About 1634 a boy called Edmund Robinson, whose father, a very poor man, dwelt in Pendle Forest, the scene of the alleged witching, declared that while gathering *bullees* (wild plums, perhaps) in one of the glades of the forest, he saw two greyhounds, which he imagined to belong to gentlemen in that neighbourhood. The boy reported that, seeing nobody following them, he proposed to have a course ; but though a hare was started, the dogs refused to run. On this, young Robinson was about to punish them with a switch, when one Dame Dickenson, a neighbour's wife, started up instead of the one greyhound ; a little boy instead of the other. The witness averred that Mother Dickenson offered him money to conceal what he had seen, which he refused, saying " Nay, thou art a witch." Apparently she was determined he should have full evidence of the truth of what he said, for, like the Magician Queen in the Arabian Tales, she pulled out of her pocket a bridle and shook it over the head of the boy who had so lately represented the other greyhound. He was directly changed into a horse ; Mother Dickenson mounted, and took Robinson before her. They then rode to a large house or barn called Hourstoun, into which Edmund Robinson entered with others. He there saw six or seven persons pulling at halters, from which, as they pulled them, meat ready dressed came flying in quantities, together with lumps of butter, porringers of milk, and whatever else might, in the boy's fancy, complete a rustic feast. He declared that while engaged in the charm they made such ugly faces and looked so fiendish that he was frightened. There was more to the same purpose—as the boy's having seen one of these hags sitting half-way up his father's chimney, and some such goodly matter. But it ended in near a score of persons being committed to prison ; and the consequence was that young Robinson was carried from church to church in the neighbourhood, that he might recognise the faces of any persons he had seen at the rendezvous of witches. Old Robinson, who had been an evidence against the former witches in 1613, went along with his son, and knew, doubtless, how to make his journey profitable ; and his son probably took care to recognise none who might make a handsome consideration. "This boy," says Webster, "was brought into the church at Kildwick, a parish church, where I, being then curate there, was preaching at the time, to look about him, which made some little disturbance for the time." After prayers Mr. Webster sought and found the boy, and two very unlikely persons, who, says he, "did conduct him and manage the business : I did desire some discourse with the boy in private, but that they utterly denied. In the presence of a great many many people I took the boy near me and said, 'Good boy, tell me truly and in earnest, didst thou hear and see such strange things of the motions of the witches as many do report that thou didst relate, or did not some person teach thee to say such things of thyself?' But the two men did pluck the boy from me, and said he had been examined by two able justices of peace, and they never asked him such a question. To whom I replied, ' The persons accused had the more wrong.' " The boy afterwards acknowledged, in his more advanced years, that he was instructed and suborned to swear these things against the accused persons by his father and others, and was heard often to confess that on the day which he pretended to see the said witches at the house or barn, he was gathering plums in a neighbour's orchard.*

There was now approaching a time when the law against witchcraft, sufficiently bloody in itself, was to be pushed to more violent extremities than the quiet scepticism of the Church of England clergy gave way to. The great Civil War had been preceded and anticipated by the fierce disputes of the ecclesiastical parties. The rash and ill-judged attempt to enforce upon the Scottish a compliance with the government and ceremonies of the High Church divines, and the severe prosecutions in the Star Chamber and Prerogative Courts, had given the Presbyterian system for a season a great degree of popularity in England ; and as the King's party declined during the Civil War, and the state of church-government was altered, the influence of the Calvinistic divines increased. With much strict morality and pure practice of religion, it is to be regretted these were still marked by unhesitating belief in the existence of sorcery, and a keen desire to extend and enforce the legal penalties against it. Wier has considered the clergy of every sect as being too eager in this species of persecution : *Ad gravem hanc impietatem, connivent theologi plerique omnes.* But it is not to be denied that the Presbyterian ecclesiastics who, in Scotland, were often appointed by the Privy Council Commissioners for the trial of witchcraft, evinced a very extraordinary degree of credulity in such cases, and that the temporary superiority of the same sect in England was

* Webster on Witchcraft, edition 1677, p. 278.

marked by enormous cruelties of this kind. To this general error we must impute the misfortune that good men, such as Calamy and Baxter, should have countenanced or defended such proceedings as those of the impudent and cruel wretch called Matthew Hopkins, who, in those unsettled times, when men did what seemed good in their own eyes, assumed the title of Witchfinder General, and, travelling through the counties of Essex, Sussex, Norfolk, and Huntingdon, pretended to discover witches, superintending their examination by the most unheard-of tortures, and compelling forlorn and miserable wretches to admit and confess matters equally absurd and impossible; the issue of which was the forfeiture of their lives. Before examining these cases more minutely, I will quote Baxter's own words; for no one can have less desire to wrong a devout and conscientious man, such as that divine most unquestionably was, though borne aside on this occasion by prejudice and credulity.

" The hanging of a great number of witches in 1645 and 1646 is famously known. Mr. Calamy went along with the judges on the circuit to hear their confessions, and see there was no fraud or wrong done them. I spoke with many understanding, pious, learned, and credible persons that lived in the counties, and some that went to them in the prisons, and heard their sad confessions. Among the rest an old *reading parson,* named Lowis, not far from Framlingham, was one that was hanged, who confessed that he had two imps, and that one of them was always putting him upon doing mischief; and he, being near the sea, as he saw a ship under sail, it moved him to send it to sink the ship; and he consented, and saw the ship sink before them." Mr. Baxter passes on to another story of a mother who gave her child an imp like a mole, and told her to keep it in a can near the fire, and she would never want; and more such stuff as nursery-maids tell froward children to keep them quiet.

It is remarkable that in this passage Baxter names the

Witchfinder General rather slightly as "one Hopkins," and without doing him the justice due to one who had discovered more than one hundred witches, and brought them to confessions, which that good man received as indubitable. Perhaps the learned divine was one of those who believed that the Witchfinder General had cheated the devil out of a certain memorandum-book, in which Satan, for the benefit of his memory certainly, had entered all the witches' names in England, and that Hopkins availed himself of this record.*

It may be noticed that times of misrule and violence seem to create individuals fitted to take advantage from them, and having a character suited to the seasons which raise them into notice and action ; just as a blight on any tree or vegetable calls to life a peculiar insect to feed upon and enjoy the decay which it has produced. A monster like Hopkins could only have existed during the confusion of civil dissension. He was perhaps a native of Manningtree, in Essex ; at any rate, he resided there in the year 1644, when an epidemic outcry of witchcraft arose in that town. Upon this occasion he had made himself busy, and, affecting more zeal and knowledge than other men, learned his trade of a witchfinder, as he pretends, from experiment. He was afterwards permitted to perform it as a legal profession, and moved from one place to another, with an assistant named Sterne, and a female. In his defence against an accusation of fleecing the country, he declares his regular charge was twenty shillings a town, including charges of living and journeying thither and back again with his assistants. He also affirms that he went nowhere unless called and invited. His principal mode of discovery was

---

* This reproach is noticed in a very rare tract, which was bought at Mr. Lort's sale, by the celebrated collector Mr. Bindley, and is now in the author's possession. Its full title is, "The Discovery of Witches, in Answer to several Queries lately delivered to the Judge of Assize for the County of Norfolk ; and now published by Matthew Hopkins, Witchfinder, for the Benefit of the whole Kingdom. Printed for R. Royston, at the Angel, in Inn Lane. 1647."

to strip the accused persons naked, and thrust pins into various parts of their body, to discover the witch's mark, which was supposed to be inflicted by the devil as a sign of his sovereignty, and at which she was also said to suckle her imps. He also practised and stoutly defended the trial by swimming, when the suspected person was wrapped in a sheet, having the great toes and thumbs tied together, and so dragged through a pond or river. If she sank, it was received in favour of the accused ; but if the body floated (which must have occurred ten times for once, if it was placed with care on the surface of the water), the accused was condemned, on the principle of King James, who, in treating of this mode of trial, lays down that, as witches have renounced their baptism, so it is just that the element through which the holy rite is enforced should reject them, which is a figure of speech, and no argument. It was Hopkins's custom to keep the poor wretches waking, in order to prevent them from having encouragement from the devil, and, doubtless, to put infirm, terrified, overwatched persons in the next state to absolute madness ; and for the same purpose they were dragged about by their keepers till extreme weariness and the pain of blistered feet might form additional inducements to confession. Hopkins confesses these last practices of keeping the accused persons waking, and forcing them to walk for the same purpose, had been originally used by him. But as his tract is a professed answer to charges of cruelty and oppression, he affirms that both practices were then disused, and that they had not of late been resorted to.

The boast of the English nation is a manly independence and common-sense, which will not long permit the license of tyranny or oppression on the meanest and most obscure sufferers. Many clergymen and gentlemen made head against the practices of this cruel oppressor of the defenceless, and it required courage to do so when such an unscrupulous villain had so much interest.

Mr. Gaul, a clergyman, of Houghton, in Huntingdonshire, had the courage to appear in print on the weaker side ; and Hopkins, in consequence, assumed the assurance to write to some functionaries of the place the following letter, which is an admirable medley of impudence, bullying, and cowardice :—

"My service to your worship presented.—I have this day received a letter to come to a town called Great Houghton to search for evil-disposed persons called witches (though I hear your minister is far against us, through ignorance). I intend to come, God willing, the sooner to hear his singular judgment in the behalf of such parties. I have known a minister in Suffolk as much against this discovery in a pulpit, and forced to recant it by the Committee* in the same place. I much marvel such evil men should have any (much more any of the clergy, who should daily speak terror to convince such offenders) stand up to take their parts against such as are complainants for the king, and sufferers themselves, with their families and estates. I intend to give your town a visit suddenly. I will come to Kimbolton this week, and it will be ten to one but I will come to your town first ; but I would certainly know before whether your town affords many sticklers for such cattle, or is willing to give and allow us good welcome and entertainment, as others where I have been, else I shall waive your shire (not as yet beginning in any part of it myself), and betake me to such places where I do and may punish (not only) without control, but with thanks and recompense. So I humbly take my leave, and rest your servant to be commanded,

"MATTHEW HOPKINS."

The sensible and courageous Mr. Gaul describes the tortures employed by this fellow as equal to any practised in the Inquisition. "Having taken the suspected witch, she is placed in the middle of a room, upon a stool or table,

---

* Of Parliament.

cross-legged, or in some other uneasy posture, to which, if she submits not, she is then bound with cords; there she is watched and kept without meat or sleep for four-and-twenty hours, for, they say, they shall within that time see her imp come and suck. A little hole is likewise made in the door for the imps to come in at; and lest they should come in some less discernible shape, they that watch are taught to be ever and anon sweeping the room, and if they see any spiders or flies, to kill them; and if they cannot kill them, they may be sure they are their imps."

If torture of this kind was applied to the Reverend Mr. Lewis, whose death is too slightly announced by Mr. Baxter, we can conceive him, or any man, to have indeed become so weary of his life as to acknowledge that, by means of his imps, he sunk a vessel, without any purpose of gratification to be procured to himself by such iniquity. But in another cause a judge would have demanded some proof of the *corpus delecti*, some evidence of a vessel being lost at the period, whence coming and whither bound; in short, something to establish that the whole story was not the idle imagination of a man who might have been entirely deranged, and certainly was so at the time he made the admission. John Lewis was presented to the vicarage of Brandiston, near Framlington, in Suffolk, 6th May, 1596, where he lived about fifty years, till executed as a wizard on such evidence as we have seen. Notwithstanding the story of his alleged confession, he defended himself courageously at his trial, and was probably condemned rather as a royalist and malignant than for any other cause. He showed at the execution considerable energy, and to secure that the funeral service of the church should be said over his body, he read it aloud for himself while on the road to the gibbet.

We have seen that in 1647 Hopkins's tone became lowered, and he began to disavow some of the cruelties he had formerly practised. About the same time a miserable old woman had fallen into the cruel hands of this miscreant near Hoxne, a village in Suffolk, and had confessed all the usual enormities, after being without food or rest a sufficient time. "Her imp," she said, "was called Nan." A gentleman in the neighbourhood, whose widow survived to authenticate the story, was so indignant that he went to the house, took the woman out of such inhuman hands, dismissed the witchfinders, and after due food and rest the poor old woman could recollect nothing of the confession, but that she gave a favourite pullet the name of Nan. For this Dr. Hutchison may be referred to, who quotes a letter from the relict of the humane gentleman.

In the year 1645 a Commission of Parliament was sent down, comprehending two clergymen in esteem with the leading party, one of whom, Mr. Fairclough of Kellar, preached before the rest on the subject of witchcraft; and after this appearance of enquiry the inquisitions and executions went on as before. But the popular indignation was so strongly excited against Hopkins, that some gentlemen seized on him, and put him to his own favourite experiment of swimming, on which, as he happened to float, he stood convicted of witchcraft, and so the country was rid of him. Whether he was drowned outright or not does not exactly appear, but he has had the honour to be commemorated by the author of Hudibras :—

> " Hath not this present Parliament
> A leiger to the devil sent,
> Fully empower'd to treat about
> Finding revolted witches out?
> And has he not within a year
> Hang'd threescore of them in one shire?
> Some only for not being drown'd,
> And some for sitting above ground
> Whole days and nights upon their breeches,
> And feeling pain, were hang'd for witches.
> And some for putting knavish tricks
> Upon green geese or turkey chicks;
> Or pigs that suddenly deceased
> Of griefs unnatural, as he guess'd,

> Who proved himself at length a witch,
> And made a rod for his own breech." *

The understanding reader will easily conceive that this alteration of the current in favour of those who disapproved of witch-prosecutions, must have received encouragement from some quarter of weight and influence; yet it may sound strangely enough that this spirit of lenity should have been the result of the peculiar principles of those sectarians of all denominations, classed in general as Independents, who, though they had originally courted the Presbyterians as the more numerous and prevailing party, had at length shaken themselves loose of that connexion, and finally combated with and overcome them. The Independents were distinguished by the wildest license in their religious tenets, mixed with much that was nonsensical and mystical. They disowned even the title of a regular clergy, and allowed the preaching of any one who could draw together a congregation that would support him, or who was willing, without recompense, to minister to the spiritual necessities of his hearers. Although such laxity of discipline afforded scope to the wildest enthusiasm, and room for all possible varieties of doctrine, it had, on the other hand, this inestimable recommendation, that it contributed to a degree of general toleration which was at that time unknown to any other Christian establishment. The very genius of a religion which admitted of the subdivision of sects *ad infinitum*, excluded a legal prosecution of any one of these for heresy or apostasy. If there had even existed a sect of Manichæans, who made it their practice to adore the Evil Principle, it may be doubted whether the other sectaries would have accounted them absolute outcasts from the pale of the church; and, fortunately, the same sentiment induced them to regard with horror the prosecutions against witchcraft. Thus the Independents, when, under Cromwell, they attained a supremacy over the Presbyterians, who to a certain point

* "Hudibras," part ii. canto 3.

had been their allies, were disposed to counteract the violence of such proceedings under pretence of witchcraft, as had been driven forward by the wretched Hopkins, in Essex, Norfolk, and Suffolk, for three or four years previous to 1647.

The return of Charles II. to his crown and kingdom, served in some measure to restrain the general and wholesale manner in which the laws against witchcraft had been administered during the warmth of the Civil War. The statute of the 1st of King James, nevertheless, yet subsisted ; nor is it in the least likely, considering the character of the prince, that he, to save the lives of a few old men or women, would have run the risk of incurring the odium of encouraging or sparing a crime still held in horror by a great part of his subjects. The statute, however, was generally administered by wise and skilful judges, and the accused had such a chance of escape as the rigour of the absurd law permitted.

Nonsense, it is too obvious, remained in some cases predominant. In the year 1663 an old dame, named Julian Coxe, was convicted chiefly on the evidence of a huntsman, who declared on his oath, that he laid his greyhounds on a hare, and coming up to the spot where he saw them mouth her, there he found, on the other side of a bush, Julian Coxe lying panting and breathless, in such a manner as to convince him that she had been the creature which afforded him the course. The unhappy woman was executed on this evidence.

Two years afterwards (1664), it is with regret we must quote the venerable and devout Sir Matthew Hales, as presiding at a trial, in consequence of which Amy Dunny and Rose Callender were hanged at Saint Edmondsbury. But no man, unless very peculiarly circumstanced, can extricate himself from the prejudices of his nation and age. The evidence against the accused was laid, 1st, on the effect of spells used by ignorant persons to counteract the supposed witchcraft; the use of which was, under the statute of James I., as criminal as the act of sorcery which such counter-charms were meant to neutralize. 2ndly, The two old women, refused even the privilege of purchasing some herrings, having expressed themselves with angry impatience, a child of the herring-merchant fell ill in conseqence. 3rdly, A cart was driven against the miserable cottage of Amy Dunny. She scolded, of course; and shortly after the cart—(what a good driver will scarce comprehend)—stuck fast in a gate, where its wheels touched neither of the posts, and yet was moved easily forward on one of the posts (by which it was *not* impeded) being cut down. 4thly, One of the afflicted girls being closely muffled, went suddenly into a fit upon being touched by one of the supposed witches. But upon another trial it was found that the person so blindfolded fell into the same rage at the touch of an unsuspected person. What perhaps sealed the fate of the accused was the evidence of the celebrated Sir Thomas Browne, "that the fits were natural, but heightened by the power of the devil co-operating with the malice of witches;"—a strange opinion, certainly, from the author of a treatise on "Vulgar Errors!"*

But the torch of science was now fairly lighted, and gleamed in more than one kingdom of the world, shooting its rays on every side, and catching at all means which were calculated to increase the illumination. The Royal Society, which had taken its rise at Oxford from a private association who met in Dr. Wilkin's chambers about the year 1652, was, the year after the Restoration, incorporated by royal charter, and began to publish their Transactions, and give a new and more rational character to the pursuits of philosophy.

In France, where the mere will of the government could accomplish greater changes, the consequence of an enlarged

* See the account of Sir T. Browne in No. XIV. of the "Family Library" ("Lives of British Physicians"), p. 60.

spirit of scientific discovery was, that a decisive stop was put to the witch-prosecutions which had heretofore been as common in that kingdom as in England. About the year 1672 there was a general arrest of very many shepherds and others in Normandy, and the Parliament of Rouen prepared to proceed in the investigation with the usual severity. But an order, or *arret*, from the king (Louis XIV.), with advice of his council, commanding all these unfortunate persons to be set at liberty and protected, had the most salutary effects all over the kingdom. The French Academy of Sciences was also founded ; and, in imitation, a society of learned Germans established a similar institution at Leipsic. Prejudices, however old, were overawed and controlled—much was accounted for on natural principles that had hitherto been imputed to spiritual agency— everything seemed to promise that farther access to the secrets of nature might be opened to those who should prosecute their studies experimentally and by analysis—and the mass of ancient opinions which overwhelmed the dark subject of which we treat began to be derided and rejected by men of sense and education.

In many cases the prey was now snatched from the spoiler. A pragmatical justice of peace in Somersetshire commenced a course of enquiry after offenders against the statute of James I., and had he been allowed to proceed, Mr. Hunt might have gained a name as renowned for witch-finding as that of Mr. Hopkins ; but his researches were stopped from higher authority—the lives of the poor people arrested (twelve in number) were saved, and the country remained at quiet, though the supposed witches were suffered to live. The examinations attest some curious particulars, which may be found in *Sadducismus Triumphatus:* for among the usual string of froward, fanciful, or, as they were called, afflicted children, brought forward to club their startings, starings, and screamings, there appeared also certain remarkable confessions of the accused, from which we learn that the Somerset Satan enlisted his witches, like a wily recruiting sergeant, with one shilling in hand and twelve in promises ; that when the party of weird-sisters passed to the witch-meeting they used the magic words, *Thout, tout, throughout, and about* ; and that when they departed they exclaimed, *Rentum, Tormentum !* We are further informed that his Infernal Highness, on his departure, leaves a smell, and that (in nursery-maid's phrase) not a pretty one, behind him. Concerning this fact we have a curious exposition by Mr. Glanville. " This,"—according to that respectable authority, " seems to imply the reality of the business, those ascititious particles which he held together in his sensible shape being loosened at the vanishing, and so offending the nostrils by their floating and diffusing themselves in the open air."* How much are we bound to regret that Mr. Justice Hunt's discovery " of this hellish kind of witches," in itself so clear and plain, and containing such valuable information, should have been smothered by meeting with opposition and discouragement from some then in authority !

Lord Keeper Guildford was also a stifler of the proceedings against witches. Indeed, we may generally remark, during the latter part of the seventeenth century, that where the judges were men of education and courage, sharing in the information of the times, they were careful to check the precipitate ignorance and prejudice of the juries, by giving them a more precise idea of the indifferent value of confessions by the accused themselves, and of testimony derived from the pretended visions of those supposed to be bewitched. Where, on the contrary, judges shared with the vulgar in their ideas of such fascination, or were contented to leave the evidence with the jury, fearful to withstand the general cry too common on such occasions, a verdict of guilty often followed.

We are informed by Roger North that a case of this kind happened at the assizes in Exeter, where his brother,

* Glanville's " Collection of Relations."

the Lord Chief Justice, did not interfere with the crown trials, and the other judge left for execution a poor old woman, condemned, as usual, on her own confession, and on the testimony of a neighbour, who deponed that he saw a cat jump into the accused person's cottage window at twilight, one evening, and that he verily believed the said cat to be the devil; on which precious testimony the poor wretch was accordingly hanged. On another occasion, about the same time, the passions of the great and little vulgar were so much excited by the aquittal of an aged village dame, whom the judge had taken some pains to rescue, that Sir John Long, a man of rank and fortune, came to the judge in the greatest perplexity, requesting that the hag might not be permitted to return to her miserable cottage on his estates, since all his tenants had in that case threatened to leave him. In compassion to a gentleman who apprehended ruin from a cause so whimsical, the dangerous old woman was appointed to be kept by the town where she was acquitted, at the rate of half-a-crown a week, paid by the parish to which she belonged. But behold! in the period betwixt the two assizes Sir John Long and his farmers had mustered courage enough to petition that this witch should be sent back to them in all her terrors, because they could support her among them at a shilling a week cheaper than they were obliged to pay to the town for her maintenance. In a subsequent trial before Lord Chief Justice North himself, that judge detected one of those practices which, it is to be feared, were too common at the time, when witnesses found their advantage in feigning themselves bewitched. A woman, supposed to be the victim of the male sorcerer at the bar, vomited pins in quantities, and those straight, differing from the crooked pins usually produced at such times, and less easily concealed in the mouth. The judge, however, discovered, by cross-examining a candid witness, that in counterfeiting her fits of convulsion the woman sunk her head on her breast, so as to take up with her lips the pins which she had placed ready in her stomacher. The man was acquitted, of course. A frightful old hag, who was present, distinguished herself so much by her benedictions on the judge, that he asked the cause of the peculiar interest which she took in the acquittal. " Twenty years ago," said the poor woman, " they would have hanged me for a witch, but could not ; and now, but for your lordship, they would have murdered my innocent son."*

Such scenes happened frequently on the assizes, while country gentlemen, like the excellent Sir Roger de Coverley, retained a private share in the terror with which their tenants, servants, and retainers regarded some old Moll White, who put the hounds at fault and ravaged the fields with hail and hurricanes. Sir John Reresby, after an account of a poor woman tried for a witch at York in 1686 and acquitted, as he thought, very properly, proceeds to tell us that, notwithstanding, the sentinel upon the jail where she was confined avowed " that he saw a scroll of paper creep from under the prison-door, and then change itself first into a monkey and then into a turkey, which the under-keeper confirmed. This," says Sir John, " I have heard from the mouth of both, and now leave it to be believed or disbelieved as the reader may be inclined."† We may see that Reresby, a statesman and a soldier, had not as yet " plucked the old woman out of his heart." Even Addison himself ventured no farther in his incredulity respecting this crime than to contend that although witchcraft might and did exist, there was no such thing as a modern instance competently proved.

As late as 1682 three unhappy women named Susan Edwards, Mary Trembles, and Temperance Lloyd were hanged at Exeter for witchcraft, and, as usual, on their own confession. This is believed to be the last execution of

* Roger North's "Life of Lord-Keeper Guilford."
† "Memoirs of Sir John Reresby," p. 237.

the kind in England under form of judicial sentence. But the ancient superstition, so interesting to vulgar credulity, like sediment clearing itself from water, sunk down in a deeper shade upon the ignorant and lowest classes of society in proportion as the higher regions were purified from its influence. The populace, including the ignorant of every class, were more enraged against witches when their passions were once excited in proportion to the lenity exercised towards the objects of their indignation by those who administered the laws. Several cases occurred in which the mob, impressed with a conviction of the guilt of some destitute old creatures, took the law into their own hands, and proceeding upon such evidence as Hopkins would have had recourse to, at once, in their own apprehension, ascertained their criminality and administered the deserved punishment.

The following instance of such illegal and inhuman proceedings occurred at Oakly, near Bedford, on 12th July, 1707. There was one woman, upwards of sixty years of age, who, being under an imputation of witchcraft, was desirous to escape from so foul a suspicion, and to conciliate the good-will of her neighbours, by allowing them to duck her. The parish officers so far consented to their humane experiment as to promise the poor woman a guinea if she should clear herself by sinking. The unfortunate object was tied up in a wet sheet, her thumbs and great toes were bound together, her cap torn off, and all her apparel searched for pins; for there is an idea that a single pin spoils the operation of the charm. She was then dragged through the river Ouse by a rope tied round her middle. Unhappily for the poor woman, her body floated, though her head remained under water. The experiment was made three times with the same effect. The cry to hang or drown the witch then became general, and as she lay half-dead on the bank they loaded the wretch with reproaches, and hardly forbore blows. A single humane bystander took her part, and exposed himself to rough usage for doing so. Luckily one of the mob themselves at length suggested the additional experiment of weighing the witch against the church Bible. The friend of humanity caught at this means of escape, supporting the proposal by the staggering argument that the Scripture, being the work of God himself, must outweigh necessarily all the operations or vassals of the devil. The reasoning was received as conclusive, the more readily as it promised a new species of amusement. The woman was then weighed against a church Bible of twelve pounds jockey weight, and as she was considerably preponderant, was dismissed with honour. But many of the mob counted her acquittal irregular, and would have had the poor dame drowned or hanged on the result of her ducking, as the more authentic species of trial.

At length a similar piece of inhumanity, which had a very different conclusion, led to the final abolition of the statute of James I. as affording countenance for such brutal proceedings. An aged pauper, named Osborne, and his wife, who resided near Tring, in Staffordshire, fell under the suspicion of the mob on account of supposed witchcraft. The overseers of the poor, understanding that the rabble entertained a purpose of swimming these infirm creatures, which indeed they had expressed in a sort of proclamation, endeavoured to oppose their purpose by securing the unhappy couple in the vestry-room, which they barricaded. They were unable, however, to protect them in the manner they intended. The mob forced the door, seized the accused, and, with ineffable brutality, continued dragging the wretches through a pool of water till the woman lost her life. A brute in human form, who had superintended the murder, went among the spectators, and requested money for the sport he had shown them! The life of the other victim was with great difficulty saved. Three men were tried for their share in this inhuman action. Only one of them, named Colley, was condemned and hanged. When he came to execution, the rabble, instead of crowding round the gallows as usual, stood at a distance, and abused those who were putting to death, they said, an honest fellow for ridding the parish of an accursed witch. This abominable murder was committed July 30, 1751.

The repetitition of such horrors, the proneness of the people to so cruel and heart-searing a superstition, was traced by the legislature to its source, namely, the yet un-abolished statute of James I. Accordingly, by the 9th George II. cap. 5, that odious law, so long the object of horror to all ancient and poverty-stricken females in the kingdom, was abrogated, and all criminal procedure on the subject of sorcery or witchcraft discharged in future through-out Great Britain ; reserving for such as should pretend to the skill of fortune-tellers, discoverers of stolen goods, or the like, the punishment of the correction-house, as due to rogues and vagabonds. Since that period witchcraft has been little heard of in England, and although the belief in its existence has in remote places survived the law that recognised the evidence of the crime, and assigned its punishment—yet such faith is gradually becoming forgotten since the rabble have been deprived of all pretext to awaken it by their own riotous proceedings. Some rare instances have occurred of attempts similar to that for which Colley suffered ; and I observe one is preserved in that curious register of knowledge, Mr. Hone's " Popular Amusements," from which it appears that as late as the end of last century this brutality was practised, though happily without loss of life.

The Irish statute against witchcraft still exists, as it would seem. Nothing occurred in that kingdom which recom-mended its being formally annulled ; but it is considered as obsolete, and should so wild a thing be attempted in the present day, no procedure, it is certain, would now be per-mitted to lie upon it.

If anything were wanted to confirm the general proposition that the epidemic terror of witchcraft increases and becomes general in proportion to the increase of prosecutions against witches, it would be sufficient to quote certain extraordinary occurrences in New England. Only a brief account can be here given of the dreadful hallucination under which the colonists of that province were for a time deluded and oppressed by a strange contagious terror, and how suddenly and singularly it was cured, even by its own excess ; but it is too strong evidence of the imaginary character of this hideous disorder to be altogether suppressed.

New England, as is well known, was peopled mainly by emigrants who had been disgusted with the government of Charles I. in church and state, previous to the great Civil War. Many of the more wealthy settlers were Presbyterians and Calvinists ; others, fewer in number and less influential from their fortune, were Quakers, Anabaptists, or members of the other sects who were included under the general name of Independents. The Calvinists brought with them the same zeal for religion and strict morality which everywhere distinguished them. Unfortunately, they were not wise according to their zeal, but entertained a proneness to believe in supernatural and direct personal intercourse between the devil and his vassals, an error to which, as we have endeavoured to show, their brethren in Europe had from the beginning been peculiarly subject. In a country imperfectly cultivated, and where the partially improved spots were embosomed in inaccessible forests, inhabited by numerous tribes of savages, it was natural that a disposition to superstition should rather gain than lose ground, and that to other dangers and horrors with which they were surrounded, the colonists should have added fears of the devil, not merely as the Evil Principle tempting human nature to sin, and thus endangering our salvation, but as combined with sorcerers and witches to inflict death and torture upon children and others.

The first case which I observe was that of four children of a person called John Goodwin, a mason. The eldest, a girl, had quarrelled with the laundress of the family about some linen which was amissing. The mother of the laundress, an ignorant, testy, and choleric old Irishwoman, scolded the accuser ; and shortly after, the elder Goodwin, her sister and two brothers, were seized with such strange diseases that all their neighbours concluded they were bewitched. They conducted themselves as those supposed to suffer under maladies created by such influence were accustomed to do. They stiffened their necks so hard at one time that the joints could not be moved; at another time their necks were so flexible and supple that it seemed the bone was dissolved. They had violent convulsions, in which their jaws snapped with the force of a spring-trap set for vermin. Their limbs were curiously contorted, and to those who had a taste for the marvellous, seemed entirely dislocated and displaced. Amid these distortions, they cried out against the poor old woman, whose name was Glover, alleging that she was in presence with them adding to their torments. The miser-able Irishwoman, who hardly could speak the English language, repeated her Pater Noster and Ave Maria like a good Catholic ; but there were some words which she had forgotten. She was therefore supposed to be unable to pronounce the whole consistently and correctly, and condemned and executed accordingly.

But the children of Goodwin found the trade they were engaged in to be too profitable to be laid aside, and the eldest in particular continued all the external signs of witchcraft and possession. Some of these were excellently calculated to flatter the self-opinion and prejudices of the Calvinist ministers by whom she was attended, and accordingly bear in their very front the character of studied and voluntary imposture. The young woman, acting, as was supposed, under the influence of the devil, read a Quaker treatise with ease and apparent satisfaction ; but a book written against the poor inoffensive Friends the devil would not allow his victim to touch. She could look on a Church of England

Prayer-book, and read the portions of Scripture which it contains without difficulty or impediment ; but the spirit which possessed her threw her into fits if she attempted to read the same Scriptures from the Bible, as if the awe which it is supposed the fiends entertain for Holy Writ depended, not on the meaning of the words, but the arrangement of the page, and the type in which they were printed. This singular species of flattery was designed to captivate the clergyman through his professional opinions ; others were more strictly personal. The afflicted damsel seems to have been somewhat of the humour of the Inamorata of Messrs. Smack, Pluck, Catch, and Company, and had, like her, merry as well as melancholy fits. She often imagined that her attendant spirits brought her a handsome pony to ride off with them to their rendezvous. On such occasions she made a spring upwards, as if to mount her horse, and then, still seated on her chair, mimicked with dexterity and agility the motions of the animal pacing, trotting, and galloping, like a child on the nurse's knee ; but when she cantered in this manner upstairs, she affected inability to enter the clergyman's study, and when she was pulled into it by force, used to become quite well, and stand up as a rational being. " Reasons were given for this," says the simple minister, " that seem more kind than true." Shortly after this, she appears to have treated the poor divine with a species of sweetness and attention, which gave him greater embarrassment than her former violence. She used to break in upon him at his studies to importune him to come downstairs, and thus advantaged doubtless the kingdom of Satan by the interruption of his pursuits. At length the Goodwins were, or appeared to be, cured. But the example had been given and caught, and the blood of poor Dame Glover, which had been the introduction to this tale of a hobby-horse, was to be the forerunner of new atrocities and fearfully more general follies.

This scene opened by the illness of two girls, a daughter

and niece of Mr. Parvis, the minister of Salem, who fell under an affliction similar to that of the Goodwins. Their mouths were stopped, their throats choked, their limbs racked, thorns were stuck into their flesh, and pins were ejected from their stomachs. An Indian and his wife, servants of the family, endeavouring, by some spell of their own, to discover by whom the fatal charm had been imposed on their master's children, drew themselves under suspicion, and were hanged. The judges and juries persevered, encouraged by the discovery of these poor Indians' guilt, and hoping they might thus expel from the colony the authors of such practices. They acted, says Mather, the historian, under a conscientious wish to do justly; but the cases of witchcraft and possession increased as if they were transmitted by contagion, and the same sort of spectral evidence being received which had occasioned the condemnation of the Indian woman Titu, became generally fatal. The afflicted persons failed not to see the spectres, as they were termed, of the persons by whom they were tormented. Against this species of evidence no *alibi* could be offered, because it was admitted, as we have said elsewhere, that the real persons of the accused were not there present; and everything rested upon the assumption that the afflicted persons were telling the truth, since their evidence could not be redargued. These spectres were generally represented as offering their victims a book, on signing which they would be freed from their torments. Sometimes the devil appeared in person, and added his own eloquence to move the afflicted persons to consent.

At first, as seems natural enough, the poor and miserable alone were involved; but presently, when such evidence was admitted as incontrovertible, the afflicted began to see the spectral appearances of persons of higher condition and of irreproachable lives, some of whom were arrested, some made their escape, while several were executed. The more that suffered the greater became the number of afflicted persons, and the wider and the more numerous were the denunciations against supposed witches. The accused were of all ages. A child of five years old was indicted by some of the afflicted, who imagined they saw this juvenile wizard active in tormenting them, and appealed to the mark of little teeth on their bodies, where they stated it had bitten them. A poor dog was also hanged as having been alleged to be busy in this infernal persecution. These gross insults on common reason occasioned a revulsion in public feeling, but not till many lives had been sacrificed. By this means nineteen men and women were executed, besides a stout-hearted man named Cory, who refused to plead, and was accordingly pressed to death according to the old law. On this horrible occasion a circumstance took place disgusting to humanity, which must yet be told, to show how superstition can steel the heart of a man against the misery of his fellow-creature. The dying man, in the mortal agony, thrust out his tongue, which the sheriff crammed with his cane back again into his mouth. Eight persons were condemned besides those who had actually suffered, and no less than two hundred were in prison and under examination.

Men began then to ask whether the devil might not artfully deceive the afflicted into the accusation of good and innocent persons by presenting witches and fiends in the resemblance of blameless persons, as engaged in the tormenting of their diseased country-folk. This argument was by no means inconsistent with the belief in witchcraft, and was the more readily listened to on that account. Besides, men found that no rank or condition could save them from the danger of this horrible accusation if they continued to encourage the witnesses in such an unlimited course as had hitherto been granted to them. Influenced by these reflections, the settlers awoke as from a dream, and the voice of the public, which had so lately demanded vengeance on all who were suspected of sorcery, began now, on the other hand, to lament the effusion of blood, under the strong suspicion that part of it at least had been innocently and unjustly sacrificed. In Mather's own language, which we use as that of a man deeply convinced of the reality of the crime, " experience showed that the more were apprehended the more were still afflicted by Satan, and the number of confessions increasing did but increase the number of the accused, and the execution of some made way to the apprehension of others. For still the afflicted complained of being tormented by new objects as the former were removed, so that some of those that were concerned grew amazed at the number and condition of those that were accused, and feared that Satan, by his wiles, had enwrapped innocent persons under the imputation of that crime ; and at last, as was evidently seen, there must be a stop put, or the generation of the kingdom of God would fall under condemnation."*

The prosecutions were therefore suddenly stopped, the prisoners dismissed, the condemned pardoned, and even those who had confessed, the number of whom was very extraordinary, were pardoned amongst others ; and the author we have just quoted thus records the result :— " When this prosecution ceased, the Lord so chained up Satan that the afflicted grew presently well. The accused were generally quiet, and for five years there was no such molestation among us."

To this it must be added that the congregation of Salem compelled Mr. Parvis, in whose family the disturbance had begun, and who, they alleged, was the person by whom it was most fiercely driven on in the commencement, to leave his settlement amongst them. Such of the accused as had

---

* Mather's "Magnalia," book vi. chap. lxxxii. The zealous author, however, regrets the general gaol-delivery on the score of sorcery and thinks, had the times been calm, the case might have required a farther investigation, and that, on the whole, the matter was ended too abruptly But, the temper of the times considered, he admits candidly that it is better to act moderately in matters capital, and to let the guilty escape, than run the risk of destroying the innocent.

confessed the acts of witchcraft imputed to them generally denied and retracted their confessions, asserting them to have been made under fear of torture, influence of persuasion, or other circumstances exclusive of their free will. Several of the judges and jurors concerned in the sentence of those who were executed published their penitence for their rashness in convicting these unfortunate persons ; and one of the judges, a man of the most importance in the colony, observed, during the rest of his life, the anniversary of the first execution as a day of solemn fast and humiliation for his own share in the transaction. Even the barbarous Indians were struck with wonder at the infatuation of the English colonists on this occasion, and drew disadvantageous comparisons between them and the French, among whom, as they remarked, " the Great Spirit sends no witches."

The system of witchcraft, as believed in Scotland, must next claim our attention, as it is different in some respects from that of England, and subsisted to a later period, and was prosecuted with much more severity.

LETTER IX.

Scottish Trials—Earl of Mar—Lady Glammis—William Barton—
Witches of Auldearne—Their Rites and Charms—Their Trans-
formation into Hares — Satan's Severity towards them — Their
Crimes—Sir George Mackenzie's Opinion of Witchcraft—Instances
of Confessions made by the Accused, in despair, and to avoid
future annoyance and persecution—Examination by Pricking—The
Mode of Judicial Procedure against Witches, and nature of the
Evidence admissible, opened a door to Accusers, and left the
Accused no chance of escape—The Superstition of the Scottish
Clergy in King James VI.'s time led them, like their Sovereign, to
encourage Witch-Prosecutions—Case of Bessie Graham—Supposed
Conspiracy to Shipwreck James in his Voyage to Denmark—
Meetings of the Witches, and Rites performed to accomplish their
purpose—Trial of Margaret Barclay in 1618—Case of Major Weir
—Sir John Clerk among the first who declined acting as Com-
missioner on the Trial of a Witch—Paisley and Pittenweem Witches
—A Prosecution in Caithness prevented by the Interference of the
King's Advocate in 1718—The Last Sentence of Death for Witch-
craft pronounced in Scotland in 1722—Remains of the Witch
Superstition — Case of supposed Witchcraft, related from the
Author's own knowledge, which took place so late as 1800.

FOR many years the Scottish nation had been remarkable for
a credulous belief in witchcraft, and repeated examples were
supplied by the annals of sanguinary executions on this sad
accusation.   Our acquaintance with the slender foundation
on which Boetius and Buchanan reared the early part of
their histories may greatly incline us to doubt whether a
king named Duffus ever reigned in Scotland, and, still more,
whether he died by the agency of a gang of witches, who
inflicted torments upon an image made in his name, for the
sake of compassing his death.   In the tale of Macbeth,
which is another early instance of Demonology in Scottish
history, the weird-sisters, who were the original prophetesses,

appeared to the usurper in a dream, and are described as *volæ*, or sibyls, rather than as witches, though Shakspeare has stamped the latter character indelibly upon them.

One of the earliest real cases of importance founded upon witchcraft was, like those of the Duchess of Gloucester and others in the sister country, mingled with an accusation of a political nature, which, rather than the sorcery, brought the culprits to their fate.   The Earl of Mar, brother of James III. of Scotland, fell under the king's suspicion for consulting with witches and sorcerers how to shorten the king's days.   On such a charge, very inexplicitly stated, the unhappy Mar was bled to death in his own lodgings without either trial or conviction ; immediately after which catastrophe twelve women of obscure rank and three or four wizards, or warlocks, as they were termed, were burnt at Edinburgh, to give a colour to the Earl's guilt.

In the year 1537 a noble matron fell a victim to a similar charge.   This was Janet Douglas, Lady Glammis, who, with her son, her second husband, and several others, stood accused of attempting James's life by poison, with a view to the restoration of the Douglas family, of which Lady Glammis's brother, the Earl of Angus, was the head.   She died much pitied by the people, who seem to have thought the articles against her forged for the purpose of taking her life, her kindred and very name being so obnoxious to the King.

Previous to this lady's execution there would appear to have been but few prosecuted to death on the score of witchcraft, although the want of the justiciary records of that period leaves us in uncertainty.   But in the end of the fifteenth and beginning of the sixteenth centuries, when such charges grew general over Europe, cases of the kind occurred very often in Scotland, and, as we have already noticed, were sometimes of a peculiar character.   There is, indeed, a certain monotony in most tales of the kind.   The vassals are usually induced to sell themselves at a small price to the

Author of Ill, who, having commonly to do with women, drives a very hard bargain. On the contrary, when he was pleased to enact the female on a similar occasion, he brought his gallant, one William Barton, a fortune of no less than fifteen pounds, which, even supposing it to have been the Scottish denomination of coin, was a very liberal endowment compared with his niggardly conduct towards the fair sex on such an occasion. Neither did he pass false coin on this occasion, but, on the contrary, generously gave Burton a merk, to keep the fifteen pounds whole. In observing on Satan's conduct in this matter, Master George Sinclair observes that it is fortunate the Enemy is but seldom permitted to bribe so high (as £15 Scots); for were this the case, he might find few men or women capable of resisting his munificence. I look upon this as one of the most severe reflections on our forefathers' poverty which is extant.

In many of the Scottish witches' trials, as to the description of Satan's Domdaniel, and the Sabbath which he there celebrates, the northern superstition agrees with that of England. But some of the confessions depart from the monotony of repetition, and add some more fanciful circumstances than occur in the general case. Isobel Gowdie's confession, already mentioned, is extremely minute, and some part of it at least may be quoted, as there are other passages not very edifying. The witches of Auldearne, according to this penitent, were so numerous, that they were told off into squads, or *covines*, as they were termed, to each of which were appointed two officers. One of these was called the Maiden of the Covine, and was usually, like Tam o' Shanter's Nannie, a girl of personal attractions, whom Satan placed beside himself, and treated with particular attention, which greatly provoked the spite of the old hags, who felt themselves insulted by the preference.* When assembled, they dug up graves, and possessed themselves of the carcases

---

* This word Covine seems to signify a subdivision or squad. The

(of unchristened infants in particular), whose joints and members they used in their magic unguents and salves. When they desired to secure for their own use the crop of some neighbour, they made a pretence of ploughing it with a yoke of paddocks. These foul creatures drew the plough, which was held by the devil himself. The plough-harness and soams were of quicken grass, the sock and coulter were made out of a riglen's horn, and the covine attended on the operation, praying the devil to transfer to them the fruit of the ground so traversed, and leave the proprietors nothing but thistles and briars. The witches' sports, with their elfin archery, I have already noticed (page 136). They entered the house of the Earl of Murray himself, and such other mansions as were not fenced against them by vigil and prayer, and feasted on the provisions they found there.

As these witches were the countrywomen of the weird sisters in Macbeth, the reader may be desirous to hear some of their spells, and of the poetry by which they were accompanied and enforced. They used to hash the flesh of an unchristened child, mixed with that of dogs and sheep, and place it in the house of those whom they devoted to destruction in body or goods, saying or singing—

> " We put this intill this hame,
> In our lord the Devil's name ;
> The first hands that handle thee,
> Burn'd and scalded may they be !
> We will destroy houses and hald,
> With the sheep and nolt into the fauld ;
> And little sall come to the fore,
> Of all the rest of the little store !"

Metamorphoses were, according to Isobel, very common among them, and the forms of crows, cats, hares, and other

tree near the front of an ancient castle was called the *Covine tree*, probably because the lord received his company there.

> " He is lord of the hunting horn,
> And king of the Covine tree ;
> He's well loo'd in the western waters,
> But best of his ain minnie."

animals, were on such occasions assumed. In the hare shape Isobel herself had a bad adventure. She had been sent by the devil to Auldearne in that favourite disguise, with some message to her neighbours, but had the misfortune to meet Peter Papley of Killhill's servants going to labour, having his hounds with them. The hounds sprung on the disguised witch, "and I," says Isobel, "run a very long time, but being hard pressed, was forced to take to my own house, the door being open, and there took refuge behind a chest." But the hounds came in and took the other side of the chest, so that Isobel only escaped by getting into another house, and gaining time to say the disenchanting rhyme :—

> " Hare, hare, God send thee care !
> I am in a hare's likeness now ;
> But I shall be a woman even now—
> Hare, hare, God send thee care !"

Such accidents, she said, were not uncommon, and the witches were sometimes bitten by the dogs, of which the marks remained after their restoration to human shape. But none had been killed on such occasions.

The ceremonial of the Sabbath meetings was very strict. The Foul Fiend was very rigid in exacting the most ceremonious attention from his votaries, and the title of Lord when addressed by them. Sometimes, however, the weird sisters, when whispering amongst themselves, irreverently spoke of their sovereign by the name of Black John ; upon such occasions the Fiend rushed on them like a schoolmaster who surprises his pupils in delict, and beat and buffeted them without mercy or discretion, saying, "I ken weel enough what you are saying of me." Then might be seen the various tempers of those whom he commanded. Alexander Elder, in Earlseat, often fell under his lord's displeasure for neglect of duty, and, being weak and simple, could never defend himself save with tears, cries, and entreaties for mercy ; but some of the women, according to

Isobel Gowdie's confession, had more of the spirit which animated the old dame of Kellyburn Braes. Margaret Wilson, in Auldearne, would " defend herself finely," and make her hands save her head, after the old Scottish manner. Bessie Wilson could also speak very crustily with her tongue, and " belled the cat" with the devil stoutly. The others chiefly took refuge in crying " Pity ! mercy !' and such like, while Satan kept beating them with wool cards and other sharp scourges, without attending to their entreaties or complaints. There were attendant devils and imps, who served the witches. They were usually distinguished by their liveries, which were sad-dun, grass-green, sea-green, and yellow. The witches were taught to call these imps by names, some of which might belong to humanity, while others had a diabolical sound. These were Robert the Jakis, Saunders the Red Reaver, Thomas the Feary, Swein, an old Scandinavian Duerg probably ; the Roaring Lion, Thief of Hell, Wait-upon-Herself, MacKeeler, Robert the Rule, Hendrie Craig, and Rorie. These names, odd and uncouth enough, are better imagined at least than those which Hopkins contrived for the imps which he discovered —such as Pyewacket, Peck-in-the-Crown, Sack-and-Sugar, News, Vinegar-Tom, and Grizell Greedigut, the broad vulgarity of which epithets shows what a flat imagination he brought to support his impudent fictions.

The devil, who commanded the fair sisterhood, being fond of mimicking the forms of the Christian church, used to rebaptize the witches with their blood, and in his own great name. The proud-stomached Margaret Wilson, who scorned to take a blow unrepaid, even from Satan himself, was called Pickle-nearest-the-Wind ; her compeer, Bessie Wilson, was Throw-the-Cornyard ; Elspet Nishe's was Bessie Bald ; Bessie Hay's nickname was Able-and-Stout; and Jane Mairten, the Maiden of the Covine, was called Ower-the-Dike-with-it.

Isobel took upon herself, and imputed to her sisters, as

already mentioned, the death of sundry persons shot with elf-arrows, because they had omitted to bless themselves as the aerial flight of the hags swept past them.* She had herself the temerity to shoot at the Laird of Park as he was riding through a ford, but missed him through the influence of the running stream, perhaps, for which she thanks God in her confession; and adds, that at the time she received a great cuff from Bessie Hay for her awkwardness. They devoted the male children of this gentleman (of the well-known family of Gordon of Park, I presume) to wasting illness, by the following lines, placing at the same time in the fire figures composed of clay mixed with paste, to repre-sent the object :—

> " We put this water amongst this meal,
>   For long dwining† and ill heal ;
>   We put it in into the fire,
>   To burn them up stook and stour.‡
>   That they be burned with our will,
>   Like any stikkle§ in a kiln."

Such was the singular confession of Isobel Gowdie, made voluntarily, it would seem, and without compulsion of any kind, judicially authenticated by the subscription of the notary, clergymen, and gentlemen present ; adhered to after their separate *diets*, as they are called, of examination, and containing no variety or contradiction in its details. Whatever might be her state of mind in other respects, she seems to have been perfectly conscious of the perilous consequence of her disclosures to her own person. "I do not deserve," says she, " to be seated here at ease and unharmed, but rather to be stretched on an iron rack : nor can my crimes be atoned for, were I to be drawn asunder by wild horses."

It only remains to suppose that this wretched creature was under the dominion of some peculiar species of lunacy,

---

* See p. 136.
‡ We should read perhaps, "limb and lire."

† Pining.
§ Stubble.

to which a full perusal of her confession might perhaps guide a medical person of judgment and experience. Her case is interesting, as throwing upon the rites and ceremonies of the Scottish witches a light which we seek in vain elsewhere.

Other unfortunate persons were betrayed to their own reproof by other means than the derangement of mind which seems to have operated on Isobel Gowdie. Some, as we have seen, endeavoured to escape from the charge of witchcraft by admitting an intercourse with the fairy people ; an excuse which was never admitted as relevant. Others were subjected to cruel tortures, by which our ancestors thought the guilty might be brought to confession, but which far more frequently compelled the innocent to bear evidence against themselves. On this subject the celebrated Sir George Mackenzie, "that noble wit of Scotland," as he is termed by Dryden, has some most judicious reflections, which we shall endeavour to abstract as the result of the experience of one who, in his capacity of Lord Advocate, had often occasion to conduct witch-trials, and who, not doubting the existence of the crime, was of opinion that, on account of its very horror, it required the clearest and most strict probation.

He first insists on the great improbability of the fiend, without riches to bestow, and avowedly subjected to a higher power, being able to enlist such numbers of recruits, and the little advantage which he himself would gain by doing so. But, 2dly, says Mackenzie, " the persons ordinarily accused of this crime are poor ignorant men, or else women, who understand not the nature of what they are accused of ; and many mistake their own fears and apprehensions for witchcraft, of which I shall give two instances. One, of a poor weaver who, after he had confessed witchcraft, being asked how he saw the devil, made answer, ' Like flies dancing about the candle.' Another, of a woman, who asked seriously, when she was accused, if a woman might be a witch and not know it? And it is dangerous that persons, of all others the most simple, should be tried for a crime of all others the most mysterious. 3rdly, These poor creatures, when they are defamed, become so confounded with fear and the close prison in which they are kept, and so starved for want of meat and drink, either of which wants is enough to disarm the strongest reason, that hardly wiser and more serious people than they would escape distraction; and when men are confounded with fear and apprehension, they will imagine things the most ridiculous and absurd" of which instances are given. 4thly, " Most of these poor creatures are tortured by their keepers, who, being persuaded they do God good service, think it their duty to vex and torment poor prisoners delivered up to them as rebels to heaven and enemies to men; and I know" (continues Sir George), "*ex certissima scientia,* that most of all that ever were taken were tormented in this manner, and this usage was the ground of all their confession; and albeit the poor miscreants cannot prove this usage, the actors being the only witnesses, yet the judge should be jealous of it, as that which did at first elicit the confession, and for fear of which they dare not retract it." 5thly, This learned author gives us an instance how these unfortunate creatures might be reduced to confession by the very infamy which the accusation cast upon them, and which was sure to follow, condemning them for life to a state of necessity, misery, and suspicion, such as any person of reputation would willingly exchange for a short death, however painful.

" I went when I was a justice-deput to examine some women who had confessed judicially, and one of them, who was a silly creature, told me under secresie, that she had not confest because she was guilty, but being a poor creature who wrought for her meat, and being defamed for a witch, she knew she would starve, for no person thereafter would either give her meat or lodging, and that all men would

beat her and hound dogs at her, and that therefore she
desired to be out of the world; whereupon she wept most
bitterly, and upon her knees called God to witness to what
she said. Another told me that she was afraid the devil
would challenge a right to her, after she was said to be his
servant, and would haunt her, as the minister said, when he
was desiring her to confess, and therefore she desired to
die. And really ministers are oft times indiscreet in their
zeal to have poor creatures to confess in this; and I recommend to judges that the wisest ministers should be sent to
them, and those who are sent should be cautious in this
particular."*

As a corollary to this affecting story, I may quote the case
of a woman in Lauder jail, who lay there with other females
on a charge of witchcraft. Her companions in prison were
adjudged to die, and she too had, by a confession as full as
theirs, given herself up as guilty. She therefore sent for
the minister of the town, and entreated to be put to death
with the others who had been appointed to suffer upon the
next Monday. The clergyman, however, as well as others,
had adopted a strong persuasion that this confession was
made up in the pride of her heart, for the destruction of her
own life, and had no foundation in truth. We give the
result in the minister's words :—

" Therefore much pains was taken on her by ministers
and others on Saturday, Sunday, and Monday morning, that
she might resile from that confession which was suspected
to be but a temptation of the devil, to destroy both her
soul and body; yea, it was charged home upon her by the
ministers, that there was just ground of jealousy that her
confession was not sincere, and she was charged before the
Lord to declare the truth, and not to take her blood upon
her own head. Yet she stiffly adhered to what she had
said, and cried always to be put away with the rest. Whereupon, on Monday morning, being called before the judges,

* Mackenzie's "Criminal Law," p. 45.

and confessing before them what she had said, she was found guilty and condemned to die with the rest that same day. Being carried forth to the place of execution, she remained silent during the first, second, and third prayer, and then perceiving that there remained no more but to rise and go to the stake, she lifted up her body, and with a loud voice cried out, 'Now all you that see me this day, know that I am now to die as a witch by my own confession, and I free all men, especially the ministers and magistrates, of the guilt of my blood. I take it wholly upon myself—my blood be upon my own head ; and as I must make answer to the God of Heaven presently, I declare I am as free of witchcraft as any child ; but being delated by a malicious woman, and put in prison under the name of a witch, disowned by my husband and friends, and seeing no ground of hope of my coming out of prison, or ever coming in credit again, through the temptation of the devil I made up that confession on purpose to destroy my own life, being weary of it, and choosing rather to die than live ;'—and so died. Which lamentable story, as it did then astonish all the spectators, none of which could restrain themselves from tears ; so it may be to all a demonstration of Satan's subtlety, whose design is still to destroy all, partly by tempting many to presumption, and some others to despair. These things to be of truth, are attested by an eye and ear witness who is yet alive, a faithful minister of the gospel."* It is strange the inference does not seem to have been deduced, that as one woman out of very despair renounced her own life, the same might have been the case in many other instances, wherein the confessions of the accused constituted the principal if not sole evidence of the guilt.

One celebrated mode of detecting witches and torturing them at the same time, to draw forth confession, was by running pins into their body, on pretence of discovering the

* Sinclair's " Satan's Invisible World Discovered," p. 43.

devil's stigma, or mark, which was said to be inflicted by him upon all his vassals, and to be insensible to pain. This species of search, the practice of the infamous Hopkins, was in Scotland reduced to a trade; and the young witchfinder was allowed to torture the accused party, as if in exercise of a lawful calling, although Sir George Mackenzie stigmatises it as a horrid imposture. I observe in the Collections of Mr. Pitcairn, that at the trial of Janet Peaston of Dalkeith the magistrates and ministers of that market town caused John Kincaid of Tranent, the common pricker, to exercise his craft upon her, "who found two marks of what he called the devil's making, and which appeared indeed to be so, for she could not feel the pin when it was put into either of the said marks, nor did they (the marks) bleed when they were taken out again; and when she was asked where she thought the pins were put in, she pointed to a part of her body distant from the real place. They were pins of three inches in length."

Besides the fact that the persons of old people especially sometimes contain spots void of sensibility, there is also room to believe that the professed prickers used a pin the point or lower part of which was, on being pressed down, sheathed in the upper, which was hollow for the purpose, and that which appeared to enter the body did not pierce it at all. But, were it worth while to dwell on a subject so ridiculous, we might recollect that in so terrible an agony of shame as is likely to convulse a human being under such a trial, and such personal insults, the blood is apt to return to the heart, and a slight wound, as with a pin, may be inflicted without being followed by blood. In the latter end of the seventeenth century this childish, indecent, and brutal practice began to be called by its right name. Fountainhall has recorded that in 1678 the Privy Council received the complaint of a poor woman who had been abused by a country magistrate and one of those impostors called prickers. They expressed high displeasure against the presumption of the parties complained against, and treated the pricker as a common cheat.*

From this and other instances it appears that the predominance of the superstition of witchcraft, and the proneness to persecute those accused of such practices in Scotland, were increased by the too great readiness of subordinate judges to interfere in matters which were, in fact, beyond their jurisdiction. The Supreme Court of Justiciary was that in which the cause properly and exclusively ought to have been tried. But, in practice, each inferior judge in the country, the pettiest bailie in the most trifling burgh, the smallest and most ignorant baron of a rude territory, took it on him to arrest, imprison, and examine, in which examinations, as we have already seen, the accused suffered the grossest injustice. The copies of these examinations, made up of extorted confessions, or the evidence of inhabile witnesses, were all that were transmitted to the Privy Council, who were to direct the future mode of procedure. Thus no creature was secure against the malice or folly of some defamatory accusation, if there was a timid or superstitious judge, though of the meanest denomination, to be found within the district.

But, secondly, it was the course of the Privy Council to appoint commissions of the gentlemen of the country, and particularly of the clergymen, though not likely, from their education, to be freed from general prejudice, and peculiarly liable to be affected by the clamour of the neighbourhood against the delinquent. Now, as it is well known that such a commission could not be granted in a case of murder in the county where the crime was charged, there seems no good reason why the trial of witches, so liable to excite the passions, should not have been uniformly tried by a court whose rank and condition secured them from the suspicion of partiality. But our ancestors arranged it otherwise, and it was the consequence that such commissioners

* Fountainhall's "Decisions," vol. i. p. 15.

very seldom, by acquitting the persons brought before them,
lost an opportunity of destroying a witch.

Neither must it be forgotten that the proof led in
support of the prosecution was of a kind very unusual in
jurisprudence.   The lawyers admitted as evidence what
they called *damnum minatum, et malum secutum* — some
mischief, that is to say, following close upon a threat, or
wish of revenge, uttered by the supposed witch, which,
though it might be attributed to the most natural course
of events, was supposed necessarily to be in consequence
of the menaces of the accused.

Sometimes this vague species of evidence was still more
loosely adduced, and allegations of danger threatened and
mischief ensuing were admitted, though the menaces had
not come from the accused party herself.   On 10th June,
1661, as John Stewart, one of a party of stout burghers of
Dalkeith appointed to guard an old woman called Christian
Wilson from that town to Niddrie, was cleaning his gun,
he was slyly questioned by Janet Cocke, another confessing
witch, who probably saw his courage was not entirely constant, "What would you think if the devil raise a whirlwind,
and take her from you on the road to-morrow?"   Sure
enough, on their journey to Niddrie the party actually
were assailed by a sudden gust of wind (not a very uncommon event in that climate), which scarce permitted
the valiant guard to keep their feet, while the miserable
prisoner was blown into a pool of water, and with difficulty
raised again.   There is some ground to hope that this extraordinary evidence was not admitted upon the trial.

There is a story told of an old wizard, whose real name
was Alexander Hunter, though he was more generally known
by the nickname of Hatteraick, which it had pleased the
devil to confer upon him.   The man had for some time
adopted the credit of being a conjurer, and curing the diseases of man and beast by spells and charms.   One
summer's day, on a green hill-side, the devil appeared to

him in shape of a grave " Mediciner," addressing him thus roundly, " Sandie, you have too long followed my trade without acknowledging me for a master. You must now enlist with me and become my servant, and I will teach you your trade better." Hatteraick consented to the proposal, and we shall let the Rev. Mr. George Sinclair tell the rest of the tale.

"After this he grew very famous through the country for his charming and curing of diseases in men and beasts, and turned a vagrant fellow like a jockie,* gaining meal, and flesh, and money by his charms, such was the ignorance of many at that time. Whatever house he came to none durst refuse Hatteraick an alms, rather for his ill than his good. One day he came to the yait (gate) of Samuelston, when some friends after dinner were going to horse. A young gentleman, brother to the lady, seeing him, switcht him about the ears, saying—'You warlock carle, what have you to do here?' Whereupon the fellow goes away grumbling, and was overheard to say, 'You shall dear buy this ere it be long.' This was *damnum minatum.* The young gentleman conveyed his friends a far way off, and came home that way again, where he supped. After supper, taking his horse and crossing Tyne water to go home, he rides through a shady piece of a haugh, commonly called Allers, and the evening being somewhat dark, he met with some persons there that begat a dreadful consternation in him, which for the most part he would never reveal. This was *malum secutum.* When he came home the servants observed terror and fear in his countenance. The next day he became distracted, and was bound for several days. His sister, the Lady Samuelston, hearing of it, was heard say, 'Surely that knave Hatteraick is the cause of his trouble; call for him in all haste.' When he had come to her, 'Sandie,' says she, 'what is this you have done to my brother William?' 'I told him,' says he, 'I should make

* Or Scottish wandering beggar.

him repent of his striking me at the yait lately.' She, giving the rogue fair words, and promising him his pockful of meal, with beef and cheese, persuaded the fellow to cure him again. He undertook the business. ' But I must first,' says he, ' have one of his sarks' (shirts), which was soon gotten. What pranks he played with it cannot be known, but within a short while the gentleman recovered his health. When Hatteraick came to receive his wages he told the lady, ' Your brother William shall quickly go off the country, but shall never return.' She, knowing the fellow's prophecies to hold true, caused the brother to make a disposition to her of all his patrimony, to the defrauding of his younger brother, George. After that this warlock had abused the country for a long time, he was at last apprehended at Dunbar, and brought into Edinburgh, and burnt upon the Castle-hill."*

Now, if Hatteraick was really put to death on such evidence, it is worth while to consider what was its real amount. A hot-tempered swaggering young gentleman horsewhips a beggar of ill fame for loitering about the gate of his sister's house. The beggar grumbles, as any man would. The young man, riding in the night, and probably in liquor, through a dark shady place, is frightened by, he would not, and probably could not, tell what, and has a fever fit. His sister employs the wizard to take off the spell according to his profession ; and here is *damnum minatum, et malum secutum*, and all legal cause for burning a man to ashes ! The vagrant Hatteraick probably knew something of the wild young man which might soon oblige him to leave the country ; and the selfish Lady Samuelston, learning the probability of his departure, committed a fraud which ought to have rendered her evidence inadmissible.

Besides these particular disadvantages, to which the parties accused of this crime in Scotland were necessarily exposed, both in relation to the judicature by which they

* Sinclair's "Satan's Invisible World Discovered," p. 98.

were tried and the evidence upon which they were convicted, their situation was rendered intolerable by the detes-
tation in which they were held by all ranks. The gentry
hated them because the diseases and death of their relations
and children were often imputed to them; the grossly superstitious vulgar abhorred them with still more perfect dread
and loathing. And amongst those natural feelings, others
of a less pardonable description found means to shelter
themselves. In one case, we are informed by Mackenzie, a
poor girl was to die for witchcraft, of whom the real crime
was that she had attracted too great a share, in the lady's
opinion, of the attention of the laird.

Having thus given some reasons why the prosecutions for
witchcraft in Scotland were so numerous and fatal, we return
to the general history of the trials recorded from the reign of
James V. to the union of the kingdoms. Through the reign
of Queen Mary these trials for sorcery became numerous,
and the crime was subjected to heavier punishment by the
73rd Act of her 9th Parliament. But when James VI. approached to years of discretion, the extreme anxiety which
he displayed to penetrate more deeply into mysteries which
others had regarded as a very millstone of obscurity, drew
still larger attention to the subject. The sovereign had
exhausted his talents of investigation on the subject of witchcraft, and credit was given to all who acted in defence of the
opinions of the reigning prince. This natural tendency to
comply with the opinions of the sovereign was much augmented by the disposition of the Kirk to the same sentiments. We have already said that these venerable persons
entertained, with good faith, the general erroneous belief
respecting witchcraft—regarding it indeed as a crime which
affected their own order more nearly than others in the
state, since, especially called to the service of heaven, they
were peculiarly bound to oppose the incursions of Satan.
The works which remain behind them show, among better
things, an unhesitating belief in what were called by them

"special providences;" and this was equalled, at least, by their credulity as to the actual interference of evil spirits in the affairs of this world. They applied these principles of belief to the meanest causes. A horse falling lame was a snare of the devil to keep the good clergyman from preaching; the arrival of a skilful farrier was accounted a special providence to defeat the purpose of Satan. This was, doubtless, in a general sense true, since nothing can happen without the foreknowledge and will of Heaven; but we are authorized to believe that the period of supernatural interference has long passed away, and that the great Creator is content to execute his purposes by the operation of those laws which influence the general course of nature. Our ancient Scottish divines thought otherwise. Surrounded, as they conceived themselves, by the snares and temptations of hell, and relying on the aid of Heaven, they entered into war with the kingdom of Satan, as the crusaders of old invaded the land of Palestine, with the same confidence in the justice of their cause and similar indifference concerning the feelings of those whom they accounted the enemies of God and man. We have already seen that even the conviction that a woman was innocent of the crime of witchcraft did not induce a worthy clergyman to use any effort to withdraw her from the stake; and in the same collection* there occur some observable passages of God's providence to a godly minister in giving him "full clearness" concerning Bessie Grahame, suspected of witchcraft. The whole detail is a curious illustration of the spirit of credulity which well-disposed men brought with them to such investigations, and how easily the gravest doubts were removed rather than a witch should be left undetected.

Bessie Grahame had been committed, it would seem, under suspicions of no great weight, since the minister,

---

* "Satan's Invisible World," by Mr. George Sinclair. The author was Professor of Moral Philosophy in the University of Glasgow, and afterwards minister of Eastwood, in Renfrewshire.

after various conferences, found her defence so successful,
that he actually pitied her hard usage, and wished for her
delivery from prison, especially as he doubted whether a
civil court would send her to an assize, or whether an assize
would be disposed to convict her. While the minister was
in this doubt, a fellow named Begg was employed as a skilful pricker ; by whose authority it is not said, he thrust a
great brass pin up to the head in a wart on the woman's
back, which he affirmed to be the devil's mark. A commission was granted for trial ; but still the chief gentlemen in
the county refused to act, and the clergyman's own doubts
were far from being removed. This put the worthy man
upon a solemn prayer to God, "that if he would find out a
way for giving the minister full clearness of her guilt, he
would acknowledge it as a singular favour and mercy."
This, according to his idea, was accomplished in the following manner, which he regarded as an answer to his prayer.
One evening the clergyman, with Alexander Simpson, the
kirk-officer, and his own servant, had visited Bessie in her
cell, to urge her to confession, but in vain. As they
stood on the stair-head behind the door, they heard the
prisoner, whom they had left alone in her place of confinement, discoursing with another person, who used a low and
ghostly tone, which the minister instantly recognised as the
Foul Fiend's voice. But for this discovery we should have
been of opinion that Bessie Grahame talked to herself, as
melancholy and despairing wretches are in the habit of
doing. But as Alexander Simpson pretended to understand
the sense of what was said within the cell, and the minister
himself was pretty sure he heard two voices at the same
time, he regarded the overhearing this conversation as the
answer of the Deity to his petition, and thenceforth was
troubled with no doubts either as to the reasonableness and
propriety of his prayer, or the guilt of Bessie Grahame,
though she died obstinate, and would not confess ; nay,
made a most decent and Christian end, acquitting her

judges and jury of her blood, in respect of the strong delusion under which they laboured.

Although the ministers, whose opinions were but two
strongly on this head in correspondence with the prevailing
superstitions of the people, nourished in the early system of
church government a considerable desire to secure their
own immunities and privileges as a national church, which
failed not at last to be brought into contact with the king's
prerogative ; yet in the earlier part of his reign, James, when
freed from the influence of such a favourite as the profligate
Stuart, Earl of Arran, was in his personal qualities rather
acceptable to the clergy of his kingdom and period.   At
his departing from Scotland on his romantic expedition to
bring home a consort from Denmark, he very politically
recommended to the clergy to contribute all that lay in their
power to assist the civil magistrates, and preserve the public
peace of the kingdom.   The king after his return acknowledged with many thanks the care which the clergy had
bestowed in this particular.   Nor were they slack in assuming the merit to themselves, for they often reminded him in
their future discords that his kingdom had never been so
quiet as during his voyage to Denmark, when the clergy
were in a great measure intrusted with the charge of the
public government.

During the halcyon period of union between kirk and
king their hearty agreement on the subject of witchcraft
failed not to heat the fires against the persons suspected of
such iniquity.   The clergy considered that the Roman
Catholics, their principal enemies, were equally devoted to
the devil, the mass, and the witches, which in their opinion
were mutually associated together, and natural allies in the
great cause of mischief.   On the other hand, the pedantic
sovereign having exercised his learning and ingenuity in
the Demonologia, considered the execution of every witch
who was burnt as a necessary conclusion of his own royal
syllogisms.   The juries were also afraid of the consequences

of acquittal to themselves, being liable to suffer under an assize of error should they be thought to have been unjustly merciful; and as the witches tried were personally as insignificant as the charge itself was odious, there was no restraint whatever upon those in whose hands their fate lay, and there seldom wanted some such confession as we have often mentioned, or such evidence as that collected by the minister who overheard the dialogue between the witch and her master, to salve their consciences and reconcile them to bring in a verdict of guilty.

The execution of witches became for these reasons very common in Scotland, where the king seemed in some measure to have made himself a party in the cause, and the clergy esteemed themselves such from the very nature of their profession. But the general spite of Satan and his adherents was supposed to be especially directed against James, on account of his match with Anne of Denmark—the union of a Protestant princess with a Protestant prince, the King of Scotland and heir of England being, it could not be doubted, an event which struck the whole kingdom of darkness with alarm. James was self-gratified by the unusual spirit which he had displayed on his voyage in quest of his bride, and well disposed to fancy that he had performed it in positive opposition, not only to the indirect policy of Elizabeth, but to the malevolent purpose of hell itself. His fleet had been tempest-tost, and he very naturally believed that the prince of the power of the air had been personally active on the occasion.

The principal person implicated in these heretical and treasonable undertakings was one Agnes Simpson, or Samson, called the Wise Wife of Keith, and described by Archbishop Spottiswood, not as one of the base or ignorant class of ordinary witches, but a grave matron, composed and deliberate in her answers, which were all to some purpose. This grave dame, from the terms of her indictment, seems to have been a kind of white witch, affecting to cure diseases by words and charms, a dangerous profession considering the times in which she lived. Neither did she always keep the right and sheltered side of the law in such delicate operations. One article of her indictment proves this, and at the same time establishes that the Wise Woman of Keith knew how to turn her profession to account; for, being consulted in the illness of Isobel Hamilton, she gave her opinion that nothing could amend her unless the devil was raised ; and the sick woman's husband, startling at the proposal, and being indifferent perhaps about the issue, would not bestow the necessary expenses, whereupon the Wise Wife refused to raise the devil, and the patient died. This woman was principally engaged in an extensive conspiracy to destroy the fleet of the queen by raising a tempest ; and to take the king's life by anointing his linen with poisonous materials, and by constructing figures of clay, to be wasted and tormented after the usual fashion of necromancy.

Amongst her associates was an unhappy lady of much higher degree. This was Dame Euphane MacCalzean, the widow of a Senator of the College of Justice, and a person infinitely above the rank of the obscure witches with whom she was joined in her crime. Mr. Pitcairn supposes that this connexion may have arisen from her devotion to the Catholic faith and her friendship for the Earl of Bothwell.

The third person in this singular league of sorcerers was Doctor John Fian, otherwise Cunninghame, who was schoolmaster at Tranent, and enjoyed much hazardous reputation as a warlock. This man was made the hero of the whole tale of necromancy, in an account of it published at London, and entitled, " News from Scotland," which has been lately reprinted by the Roxburghe Club. It is remarkable that the Scottish witchcrafts were not thought sufficiently horrible by the editor of this tract, without adding to them the story of a philtre being applied to a cow's hair instead of that of the young woman for whom it was designed, and telling how the animal came lowing after the sorcerer to his schoolroom door, like a second Pasiphaë, the original of which charm occurs in the story of Apuleius.*

Besides these persons, there was one Barbara Napier, alias Douglas, a person of some rank; Geillis Duncan, a very active witch; and about thirty other poor creatures of the lowest condition—among the rest, and doorkeeper to the conclave, a silly old ploughman, called as his nickname Graymeal, who was cuffed by the devil for saying simply, " God bless the king !"

When the monarch of Scotland sprung this strong covey of his favourite game, they afforded the Privy Council and him sport for the greatest part of the remaining winter. He attended on the examinations himself, and by one means or or other, they were indifferently well dressed to his palate.

Agnes Sampson, the grave matron before mentioned, after being an hour tortured by the twisting of a cord around her head, according to the custom of the Buccaneers, confessed that she had consulted with one Richard Grahame concerning the probable length of the king's life, and the means of shortening it. But Satan, to whom they at length resorted for advice, told them in French respecting King James, *Il est un homme de Dieu.* The poor woman also acknowledged that she had held a meeting with those of her sisterhood, who had charmed a cat by certain spells, having four joints of men knit to its feet, which they threw into the sea to excite a tempest. Another frolic they had when, like the weird sisters in Macbeth, they embarked in sieves with much mirth and jollity, the Fiend rolling himself before them upon the waves, dimly seen, and resembling a huge haystack in size and appearance. They went on board of a foreign ship richly laded with wines, where, invisible to the crew, they feasted till the sport grew tiresome, and then Satan sunk the vessel and all on board.

* " Lucii Apuleii Metamorphoses," lib. iii.

Fian, or Cunninghame, was also visited by the sharpest tortures, ordinary and extraordinary. The nails were torn from his fingers with smith's pincers; pins were driven into the places which the nails usually defended; his knees were crushed in *the boots,* his finger bones were splintered in the pilniewinks. At length his constancy, hitherto sustained, as the bystanders supposed, by the help of the devil, was fairly overcome, and he gave an account of a great witch-meeting at North Berwick, where they paced round the church *withershinns,* that is, in reverse of the motion of the sun. Fian then blew into the lock of the church-door, whereupon the bolts gave way, the unhallowed crew entered, and their master the devil appeared to his servants in the shape of a black man occupying the pulpit. He was saluted with an "Hail, Master!" but the company were dissatisfied with his not having brought a picture of the king, repeatedly promised, which was to place his majesty at the mercy of this infernal crew. The devil was particularly upbraided on this subject by divers respectable-looking females—no question, Euphane MacCalzean, Barbara Napier, Agnes Sampson, and some other amateur witch above those of the ordinary profession. The devil on this memorable occasion forgot himself, and called Fian by his own name, instead of the demoniacal *sobriquet* of Rob the Rowar, which had been assigned to him as Master of the Rows or Rolls. This was considered as bad taste, and the rule is still observed at every rendezvous of forgers, smugglers, or the like, where it is accounted very indifferent manners to name an individual by his own name, in case of affording ground of evidence which may upon a day of trial be brought against him. Satan, something disconcerted, concluded the evening with a divertisement and a dance after his own manner. The former consisted in disinterring a new-buried corpse, and dividing it in fragments among the company, and the ball was maintained by well-nigh two hundred persons, who danced a ring dance, singing this chant—

" Cummer, gang ye before ; Cummer gang ye.
 Gif ye will not gang before, Cummers, let me."

After this choral exhibition, the music seems to have been rather imperfect, the number of dancers considered. Geillis Duncan was the only instrumental performer, and she played on a Jew's harp, called in Scotland a *trump*. Dr. Fian, muffled, led the ring, and was highly honoured, generally acting as clerk or recorder, as above mentioned.

King James was deeply interested in those mysterious meetings, and took great delight to be present at the examinations of the accused. He sent for Geillis Duncan, and caused her to play before him the same tune to which Satan and his companions led the brawl in North Berwick churchyard.* His ears were gratified in another way, for at this meeting it was said the witches demanded of the devil why he did bear such enmity against the king? who returned the flattering answer that the king was the greatest enemy whom he had in the world.

Almost all these poor wretches were executed, nor did Euphane MacCalzean's station in life save her from the common doom, which was strangling to death, and burning to ashes thereafter. The majority of the jury which tried Barbara Napier having acquitted her of attendance at the North Berwick meeting, were themselves threatened with a trial for wilful error upon an assize, and could only escape from severe censure and punishment by pleading guilty, and submitting themselves to the king's pleasure. This rigorous and iniquitous conduct shows a sufficient reason why there should be so few acquittals from a charge of witchcraft where the juries were so much at the mercy of the crown.

It would be disgusting to follow the numerous cases

---

* The music of this witch tune is unhappily lost. But that of another, believed to have been popular on such occasions, is preserved.
" The silly bit chicken, gar cast her a pickle,
 And she will grow mickle,
 And she will do good."

in which the same uniform credulity, the same extorted confessions, the same prejudiced and exaggerated evidence, concluded in the same tragedy at the stake and the pile. The alterations and trenching which lately took place for the purpose of improving the Castlehill of Edinburgh displayed the ashes of the numbers who had perished in this manner, of whom a large proportion must have been executed between 1590, when the great discovery was made concerning Euphane MacCalzean and the Wise Wife of Keith and their accomplices, and the union of the crowns.

Nor did King James's removal to England soften this horrible persecution. In Sir Thomas Hamilton's Minutes of Proceedings in the Privy Council, there occurs a singular entry, evincing plainly that the Earl of Mar, and others of James's Council, were becoming fully sensible of the desperate iniquity and inhumanity of these proceedings. I have modernized the spelling that this appalling record may be legible to all my readers.

" 1608, December 1. The Earl of Mar declared to the Council that some women were taken in Broughton as witches, and being put to an assize and convicted, albeit they persevered constant in their denial to the end, yet they were burned quick [*alive*], after such a cruel manner that some of them died in despair, renouncing and blaspheming [God] ; and others, half burned, brak out of the fire,* and were cast quick in it again, till they were burned to the death."

This singular document shows that even in the reign of James, so soon as his own august person was removed from Edinburgh, his dutiful Privy Council began to think that they had supt full with horrors, and were satiated with the

---

* I am obliged to the kindness of Mr. Pitcairn for this singular extract. The southern reader must be informed that the jurisdiction or regality of Broughton embraced Holyrood, Canongate, Leith, and other suburban parts of Edinburgh, and bore the same relation to that city as the borough of Southwark to London.

excess of cruelty which dashed half-consumed wretches back into the flames from which they were striving to escape.

But the picture, however much it may have been disgusting and terrifying to the Council at the time, and though the intention of the entry upon the records was obviously for the purpose of preventing such horrid cruelties in future, had no lasting effect on the course of justice, as the severities against witches were most unhappily still considered necessary. Through the whole of the sixteenth, and the greater part of the seventeenth century, little abatement in the persecution of this metaphysical crime of witchcraft can be traced in the kingdom. Even while the Independents held the reins of government, Cromwell himself, and his major-generals and substitutes, were obliged to please the common people of Scotland by abandoning the victims accused of witchcraft to the power of the law, though the journals of the time express the horror and disgust with which the English sectarians beheld a practice so inconsistent with their own humane principle of universal toleration.

Instead of plunging into a history of these events which, generally speaking, are in detail as monotonous as they are melancholy, it may amuse the reader to confine the narrative to a single trial, having in the course of it some peculiar and romantic events. It is the tale of a sailor's wife, more tragic in its event than that of the chestnut-muncher in Macbeth.*

Margaret Barclay, wife of Archibald Dein, burgess of Irvine, had been slandered by her sister-in-law, Janet Lyal, the spouse of John Dein, brother of Archibald, and by John Dein himself, as guilty of some act of theft. Upon this provocation Margaret Barclay raised an action of slander before the church court, which prosecution, after some procedure, the kirk-session discharged by directing a recon-

---

* A copy of the record of the trial, which took place in Ayrshire, was sent to me by a friend who withheld his name, so that I can only thank him in this general acknowledgment.

ciliation between the parties. Nevertheless, although the two women shook hands before the court, yet the said Margaret Barclay declared that she gave her hand only in obedience to the kirk-session, but that she still retained her hatred and ill-will against John Dein and his wife, Janet Lyal. About this time the bark of John Dein was about to sail for France, and Andrew Train, or Tran, provost of the burgh of Irvine, who was an owner of the vessel, went with him to superintend the commercial part of the voyage. Two other merchants of some consequence went in the same vessel, with a sufficient number of mariners. Margaret Barclay, the revengeful person already mentioned, was heard to imprecate curses upon the provost's argosy, praying to God that sea nor salt-water might never bear the ship, and that *partans* (crabs) might eat the crew at the bottom of the sea.

When, under these auspices, the ship was absent on her voyage, a vagabond fellow, named John Stewart, pretending to have knowledge of jugglery, and to possess the power of a spaeman, came to the residence of Tran, the provost, and dropped explicit hints that the ship was lost, and that the good woman of the house was a widow. The sad truth was afterwards learned on more certain information. Two of the seamen, after a space of doubt and anxiety, arrived, with the melancholy tidings that the bark, of which John Dein was skipper and Provost Tran part owner, had been wrecked on the coast of England, near Padstow, when all on board had been lost, except the two sailors who brought the notice. Suspicion of sorcery, in those days easily awakened, was fixed on Margaret Barclay, who had imprecated curses on the ship, and on John Stewart, the juggler, who had seemed to know of the evil fate of the voyage before he could have become acquainted with it by natural means.

Stewart, who was first apprehended, acknowledged that Margaret Barclay, the other suspected person, had applied to him to teach her some magic arts, "in order that she might get gear, kye's milk, love of man, her heart's desire on such persons as had done her wrong, and, finally, that she might obtain the fruit of sea and land." Stewart declared that he denied to Margaret that he possessed the said arts himself, or had the power of communicating them. So far was well; but, true or false, he added a string of circumstances, whether voluntarily declared or extracted by torture, which tended to fix the cause of the loss of the bark on Margaret Barclay. He had come, he said, to this woman's house in Irvine, shortly after the ship set sail from harbour. He went to Margaret's house by night, and found her engaged, with other two women, in making clay figures; one of the figures was made handsome, with fair hair, supposed to represent Provost Tran. They then proceeded to mould a figure of a ship in clay, and during this labour the devil appeared to the company in the shape of a handsome black lap-dog, such as ladies use to keep.* He added that the whole party left the house together, and went into an empty waste-house nearer the seaport, which house he pointed out to the city magistrates. From this house they went to the sea-side, followed by the black lap-dog aforesaid, and cast in the figures of clay representing the ship and the men; after which the sea raged, roared, and became red like the juice of madder in a dyer's cauldron.

This confession having been extorted from the unfortunate juggler, the female acquaintances of Margaret Barclay were next convened, that he might point out her associates in forming the charm, when he pitched upon a woman called Isobel Insh, or Taylor, who resolutely denied having ever seen him before. She was imprisoned, however, in the belfry of the church. An addition to the evidence against the poor old woman Insh was then procured from her own daughter, Margaret Tailzeour, *a child of eight years old*, who lived as servant with Margaret Barclay, the person principally accused. This child, who was keeper of a baby belonging to Margaret Barclay, either from terror or the innate love of

* This may remind the reader of Cazotte's "Diable Amoureux."

falsehood which we have observed as proper to childhood, declared that she was present when the fatal models of clay were formed, and that, in plunging them in the sea, Margaret Barclay her mistress, and her mother Isobel Insh, were assisted by another woman, and a girl of fourteen years old, who dwelt at the town-head. Legally considered, the evidence of this child was contradictory and inconsistent with the confession of the juggler, for it assigned other particulars and *dramatis personæ* in many respects different. But all was accounted sufficiently regular, especially since the girl failed not to swear to the presence of the black dog, to whose appearance she also added the additional terrors of that of a black man. The dog also, according to her account, emitted flashes from its jaws and nostrils to illuminate the witches during the performance of the spell. The child maintained this story even to her mother's face, only alleging that Isobel Insh remained behind in the waste-house, and was not present when the images were put into the sea. For her own countenance and presence on the occasion, and to ensure her secrecy, her mistress promised her a pair of new shoes.

John Stewart, being re-examined and confronted with the child, was easily compelled to allow that the "little smatchet" was there, and to give that marvellous account of his correspondence with Elfland which we have noticed elsewhere.

The conspiracy thus far, as they conceived, disclosed, the magistrates and ministers wrought hard with Isobel Insh to prevail upon her to tell the truth ; and she at length acknowledged her presence at the time when the models of the ship and mariners were destroyed, but endeavoured so to modify her declaration as to deny all personal accession to the guilt. This poor creature almost admitted the supernatural powers imputed to her, promising Bailie Dunlop (also a mariner), by whom she was imprisoned, that, if he would dismiss her, he should never make a bad voyage, but have success in all his dealings by sea and land. She was finally brought to promise that she would fully confess the whole that she knew of the affair on the morrow.

But finding herself in so hard a strait, the unfortunate woman made use of the darkness to attempt an escape. With this view she got out by a back window of the belfry, although, says the report, there were "iron bolts, locks, and fetters on her," and attained the roof of the church, where, losing her footing, she sustained a severe fall and was greatly bruised. Being apprehended, Bailie Dunlop again urged her to confess; but the poor woman was determined to appeal to a more merciful tribunal, and maintained her innocence to the last minute of her life, denying all that she had formerly admitted, and dying five days after her fall from the roof of the church. The inhabitants of Irvine attributed her death to poison.

The scene began to thicken, for a commission was granted for the trial of the two remaining persons accused, namely, Stewart, the juggler, and Margaret Barclay. The day of trial being arrived, the following singular events took place, which we give as stated in the record :—

" My Lord and Earl of Eglintoune (who dwells within the space of one mile to the said burgh) having come to the said burgh at the earnest request of the said justices, for giving to them of his lordship's countenance, concurrence and assistance, in trying of the foresaid devilish practices, conform to the tenor of the foresaid commission, the said John Stewart, for his better preserving to the day of the assize, was put in a sure lockfast booth, where no manner of person might have access to him till the downsitting of the Justice Court, and for avoiding of putting violent hands on himself, he was very strictly guarded and fettered by the arms, as use is. And upon that same day of the assize, about half an hour before the downsitting of the Justice Court, Mr. David Dickson, minister at Irvine, and Mr. George Dunbar, minister of Air, having gone to

him to exhort him to call on his God for mercy for his bygone wicked and evil life, and that God would of his infinite
mercy loose him out of the bonds of the devil, whom he
had served these many years bygone, he acquiesced in their
prayer and godly exhortation, and uttered these words :—
" I am so straitly guarded that it lies not in my power to
get my hand to take off my bonnet, nor to get bread to my
mouth.' And immediately after the departing of the two
ministers from him, the juggler being sent for at the desire
of my Lord of Eglintoune, to be confronted with a woman
of the burgh of Air, called Janet Bous, who was apprehended
by the magistrates of the burgh of Air for witchcraft, and
sent to the burgh of Irvine purposely for that affair, he was
found by the burgh officers who went about him, strangled
and hanged by the cruik of the door, with a *tait* of hemp,
or a string made of hemp, supposed to have been his garter,
or string of his bonnet, not above the length of two span
long, his knees not being from the ground half a span, and
was brought out of the house, his life not being totally
expelled.   But notwithstanding of whatsoever means used
in the contrary for remeid of his life, he revived not, but so
ended his life miserably, by the help of the devil his
master.

" And because there was then only in life the said Margaret Barclay, and that the persons summoned to pass upon
her assize and upon the assize of the juggler who, by the
help of the devil his master, had put violent hands on himself, were all present within the said burgh ; therefore, and
for eschewing of the like in the person of the said Margaret,
our sovereign lord's justices in that part particularly above-
named, constituted by commission after solemn delibera-
tion and advice of the said noble lord, whose concurrence
and advice was chiefly required and taken in this matter,
concluded with all possible diligence before the downsitting
of the Justice Court to put the said Margaret in torture ; in
respect the devil, by God's permission, had made her asso-

ciates who were the lights of the cause, to be their own *burrioes* (slayers). They used the torture underwritten as being most safe and gentle (as the said noble lord assured the said justices), by putting of her two bare legs in a pair of stocks, and thereafter by onlaying of certain iron gauds (bars) severally one by one, and then eiking and augmenting the weight by laying on more gauds, and in easing of her by offtaking of the iron gauds one or more as occasion offered, which iron gauds were but little short gauds, and broke not the skin of her legs, &c.

"After using of the which kind of *gentle torture*, the said Margaret began, according to the increase of the pain, to cry and crave for God's cause to take off her shins the foresaid irons, and she should declare truly the whole matter. Which being removed, she began at her former denial; and being of new essayed in torture as of befoir, she then uttered these words : ' Take off, take off, and before God I shall show you the whole form !'

" And the said irons being of new, upon her faithfull promise, removed, she then desired my Lord of Eglintoune, the said four justices, and the said Mr. David Dickson, minister of the burgh, Mr. George Dunbar, minister of Ayr, and Mr. Mitchell Wallace, minister of Kilmarnock, and Mr. John Cunninghame, minister of Dalry, and Hugh Kennedy, provost of Ayr, to come by themselves and to remove all others, and she should declare truly, as she should answer to God the whole matter. Whose desire in that being fulfilled she made her confession in this manner, but (*i.e.*, without) any kind of demand, freely, without interrogation ; God's name by earnest prayer being called upon for opening of her lips, and easing of her heart, that she, by rendering of the truth, might glorify and magnify his holy name, and disappoint the enemy of her salvation."—*Trial of Margaret Barclay, &c.*, 1618.

Margaret Barclay, who was a young and lively person, had hitherto conducted herself like a passionate and high-

tempered woman innocently accused, and the only appearance of conviction obtained against her was, that she carried
about her rowan-tree and coloured thread, to make, as she
said, her cow give milk, when it began to fail. But the
gentle torture—a strange junction of words—recommended
as an anodyne by the good Lord Eglinton—the placing,
namely, her legs in the stocks, and loading her bare shins
with bars of iron, overcame her resolution ; when, at her
screams and declarations that she was willing to tell all, the
weights were removed. She then told a story of destroying
the ship of John Dein, affirming that it was with the purpose
of killing only her brother-in-law and Provost Tran, and
saving the rest of the crew. She at the same time involved
in the guilt Isobel Crawford. This poor woman was also
apprehended, and in great terror confessed the imputed
crime, retorting the principal blame on Margaret Barclay
herself. The trial was then appointed to proceed, when
Alexander Dein, the husband of Margaret Barclay, appeared
in court with a lawyer to act in his wife's behalf. Apparently,
the sight of her husband awakened some hope and desire of
life, for when the prisoner was asked by the lawyer whether
she wished to be defended ? she answered, " As you please·
But all I have confest was in agony of torture ; and, before
God, all I have spoken is false and untrue." To which she
pathetically added, " Ye have been too long in coming."

The jury, unmoved by these affecting circumstances, proceeded upon the principle that the confession of the accused
could not be considered as made under the influence of
torture, since the bars were not actually upon her limbs at
the time it was delivered, although they were placed at her
elbow ready to be again laid on her bare shins, if she was less
explicit in her declaration than her auditors wished. On this
nice distinction they in one voice found Margaret Barclay
guilty. It is singular that she should have again returned to
her confession after sentence, and died affirming it ; the explanation of which, however, might be either that she had

really in her ignorance and folly tampered with some idle spells, or that an apparent penitence for her offence, however imaginary, was the only mode in which she could obtain any share of public sympathy at her death, or a portion of the prayers of the clergy and congregation, which, in her circumstances, she might be willing to purchase, even by confession of what all believed respecting her. It is remarkable that she earnestly entreated the magistrates that no harm should be done to Isobel Crawford, the woman whom she had herself accused. This unfortunate young creature was strangled at the stake, and her body burnt to ashes, having died with many expressions of religion and penitence.

It was one fatal consequence of these cruel persecutions, that one pile was usually lighted at the embers of another. Accordingly in the present case, three victims having already perished by this accusation, the magistrates, incensed at the nature of the crime, so perilous as it seemed to men of a maritime life, and at the loss of several friends of their own, one of whom had been their principal magistrate, did not forbear to insist against Isobel Crawford, inculpated by Margaret Barclay's confession. A new commission was granted for her trial, and after the assistant minister of Irvine, Mr. David Dickson, had made earnest prayers to God for opening her obdurate and closed heart, she was subjected to the torture of iron bars laid upon her bare shins, her feet being in the stocks, as in the case of Margaret Barclay.

She endured this torture with incredible firmness, since she did "admirably, without any kind of din or exclamation, suffer above thirty stone of iron to be laid on her legs, never shrinking thereat in any sort, but remaining, as it were, steady." But in shifting the situation of the iron bars, and removing them to another part of her shins, her constancy gave way; she broke out into horrible cries (though not more than three bars were then actually on her person) of —" Tak aff—tak aff!" On being relieved from the torture,

she made the usual confession of all that she was charged
with, and of a connexion with the devil which had subsisted
for several years. Sentence was given against her accordingly. After this had been denounced, she openly denied
all her former confessions, and died without any sign of repentance, offering repeated interruption to the minister in his
prayer, and absolutely refusing to pardon the executioner.

This tragedy happened in the year 1613, and recorded, as
it is, very particularly and at considerable length, forms the
most detailed specimen I have met with of a Scottish trial
for witchcraft—illustrating, in particular, how poor wretches,
abandoned, as they conceived, by God and the world,
deprived of all human sympathy, and exposed to personal
tortures of an acute description, became disposed to throw
away the lives that were rendered bitter to them by a
voluntary confession of guilt, rather than struggle hopelessly
against so many evils. Four persons here lost their lives,
merely because the throwing some clay models into the sea,
a fact told differently by the witnesses who spoke of it,
corresponded with the season, for no day was fixed in which
a particular vessel was lost. It is scarce possible that, after
reading such a story, a man of sense can listen for an
instant to the evidence founded on confessions thus obtained, which has been almost the sole reason by which a
few individuals, even in modern times, have endeavoured to
justify a belief in the existence of witchcraft.

The result of the judicial examination of a criminal,
when extorted by such means, is the most suspicious of all
evidence, and even when voluntarily given, is scarce admissible without the corroboration of other testimony.

We might here take leave of our Scottish history of
witchcraft by barely mentioning that many hundreds, nay
perhaps thousands, lost their lives during two centuries on
such charges and such evidence as proved the death of
those persons in the trial of the Irvine witches. One case,
however, is so much distinguished by fame among the

numerous instances which occurred in Scottish history, that we are under the necessity of bestowing a few words upon those celebrated persons, Major Weir and his sister.

The case of this notorious wizard was remarkable chiefly from his being a man of some condition (the son of a gentleman, and his mother a lady of family in Clydesdale), which was seldom the case with those that fell under similar accusations. It was also remarkable in his case that he had been a Covenanter, and peculiarly attached to that cause. In the years of the Commonwealth this man was trusted and employed by those who were then at the head of affairs, and was in 1649 commander of the City-Guard of Edinburgh, which procured him his title of Major. In this capacity he was understood, as was indeed implied in the duties of that officer at the period, to be very strict in executing severity upon such Royalists as fell under his military charge. It appears that the Major, with a maiden sister who had kept his house, was subject to fits of melancholic lunacy, an infirmity easily reconcilable with the formal pretences which he made to a high show of religious zeal. He was peculiar in his gift of prayer, and, as was the custom of the period, was often called to exercise his talent by the bedside of sick persons, until it came to be observed that, by some association, which it is more easy to conceive than to explain, he could not pray with the same warmth and fluency of expression unless when he had in his hand a stick of peculiar shape and appearance, which he generally walked with. It was noticed, in short, that when this stick was taken from him, his wit and talent appeared to forsake him. This Major Weir was seized by the magistrates on a strange whisper that became current respecting vile practices, which he seems to have admitted without either shame or contrition. The disgusting profligacies which he confessed were of such a character that it may be charitably hoped most of them were the fruits of a depraved imagination, though he appears to have been in many respects a wicked and criminal hypocrite. When he had completed his confession, he avowed solemnly that he had not confessed the hundredth part of the crimes which he had committed. From this time he would answer no interrogatory, nor would he have recourse to prayer, arguing that, as he had no hope whatever of escaping Satan, there was no need of incensing him by vain efforts at repentance. His witchcraft seems to have been taken for granted on his own confession, as his indictment was chiefly founded on the same document, in which he alleged he had never seen the devil, but any feeling he had of him was in the dark. He received sentence of death, which he suffered 12th April, 1670, at the Gallow-hill, between Leith and Edinburgh. He died so stupidly sullen and impenitent as to justify the opinion that he was oppressed with a kind of melancholy frenzy, the consequence perhaps of remorse, but such as urged him not to repent, but to despair. It seems probable that he was burnt alive. His sister, with whom he was supposed to have had an incestuous connexion, was condemned also to death, leaving a stronger and more explicit testimony of their mutual sins than could be extracted from the Major. She gave, as usual, some account of her connexion with the queen of the fairies, and acknowledged the assistance she received from that sovereign in spinning an unusual quantity of yarn. Of her brother she said that one day a friend called upon them at noonday with a fiery chariot, and invited them to visit a friend at Dalkeith, and that while there her brother received information of the event of the battle of Worcester. No one saw the style of their equipage except themselves. On the scaffold this woman, determining, as she said, to die "with the greatest shame possible," was with difficulty prevented from throwing off her clothes before the people, and with scarce less trouble was she flung from the ladder by the executioner. Her last words were in the tone of the sect to which

her brother had so long affected to belong: "Many,"
she said, "weep and lament for a poor old wretch like me;
but alas! few are weeping for a broken Covenant."

The Scottish prelatists, upon whom the Covenanters used
to throw many aspersions respecting their receiving proof
against shot from the devil, and other infernal practices,
rejoiced to have an opportunity, in their turn, to retort on
their adversaries the charge of sorcery. Dr. Hickes, the
author of "Thesaurus Septentrionalis," published on the
subject of Major Weir, and the case of Mitchell, who fired
at the Archbishop of St. Andrews his book called "Ravaillac
Redivivus," written with the unjust purpose of attaching to
the religious sect to which the wizard and assassin belonged
the charge of having fostered and encouraged the crimes
they committed or attempted.

It is certain that no story of witchcraft or necromancy, so
many of which occurred near and in Edinburgh, made such
a lasting impression on the public mind as that of Major
Weir. The remains of the house in which he and his sister
lived are still shown at the head of the West Bow, which
has a gloomy aspect, well suited for a necromancer. It was
at different times a brazier's shop and a magazine for lint,
and in my younger days was employed for the latter use;
but no family would inhabit the haunted walls as a residence;
and bold was the urchin from the High School who dared
approach the gloomy ruin at the risk of seeing the Major's
enchanted staff parading through the old apartments, or
hearing the hum of the necromantic wheel, which procured
for his sister such a character as a spinner. At the time I
am writing this last fortress of superstitious renown is in
the course of being destroyed, in order to the modern im-
provements now carrying on in a quarter long thought
unimprovable.

As knowledge and learning began to increase, the
gentlemen and clergy of Scotland became ashamed of the
credulity of their ancestors, and witch trials, although not

discontinued, more seldom disgrace our records of criminal jurisprudence.

Sir John Clerk, a scholar and an antiquary, the grandfather of the late celebrated John Clerk of Eldin, had the honour to be amongst the first to decline acting as a commissioner on the trial of a witch, to which he was appointed so early as 1678,* alleging, drily, that he did not feel himself warlock (that is, conjurer) sufficient to be a judge upon such an inquisition. Allan Ramsay, his friend, and who must be supposed to speak the sense of his many respectable patrons, had delivered his opinion on the subject in the "Gentle Shepherd," where Mause's imaginary witchcraft constitutes the machinery of the poem.

Yet these dawnings of sense and humanity were obscured by the clouds of the ancient superstition on more than one distinguished occasion. In 1676, Sir George Maxwell, of Pollock, apparently a man of melancholic and valetudinary habits, believed himself bewitched to death by six witches, one man and five women, who were leagued for the purpose of tormenting a clay image in his likeness. The chief evidence on the subject was a vagabond girl, pretending to be deaf and dumb. But as her imposture was afterwards discovered and herself punished, it is reasonably to be concluded that she had herself formed the picture or image of Sir George, and had hid it where it was afterwards found in consequence of her own information. In the meantime, five of the accused were executed, and the sixth only escaped on account of extreme youth.

A still more remarkable case occurred at Paisley in 1697, where a young girl, about eleven years of age, daughter of John Shaw, of Bargarran, was the principal evidence. This unlucky damsel, beginning her practices out of a quarrel with a maid-servant, continued to imitate a case of possession so accurately that no less than twenty persons were condemned upon her evidence, of whom five were executed, besides one

* See Fountainhall's "Decisions," vol. i. p. 15.

John Reed, who hanged himself in prison, or, as was charitably said, was strangled by the devil in person, lest he
should make disclosures to the detriment of the service.
But even those who believed in witchcraft were now beginning to open their eyes to the dangers in the present mode
of prosecution. "I own," says the Rev. Mr. Bell in his
MS. "Treatise on Witchcraft," "there has been much harm
done to worthy and innocent persons in the common way
of finding out witches, and in the means made use of for
promoting the discovery of such wretches and bringing them
to justice ; so that oftentimes old age, poverty, features, and
ill-fame, with such like grounds not worthy to be represented
to a magistrate, have yet moved many to suspect and defame their neighbours, to the unspeakable prejudice of
Christian charity ; a late instance whereof we had in the
west, in the business of the sorceries exercised upon the
Laird of Bargarran's daughter, anno 1697—a time when
persons of more goodness and esteem than most of their
calumniators were defamed for witches, and which was occasioned mostly by the forwardness and absurd credulity of
diverse otherwise worthy ministers of the gospel, and some
topping professors in and about the city of Glasgow."*

Those who doubted of the sense of the law or reasonableness of the practice in such cases, began to take courage
and state their objections boldly. In the year 1704 a
frightful instance of popular bigotry occurred at Pittenweem.
A strolling vagabond, who affected fits, laid an accusation of
witchcraft against two women, who were accordingly seized
on, and imprisoned with the usual severities. One of the
unhappy creatures, Janet Cornfoot by name, escaped from
prison, but was unhappily caught, and brought back to
Pittenweem, where she fell into the hands of a ferocious
mob, consisting of rude seamen and fishers. The magistrates made no attempts for her rescue, and the crowd

* Law's "Memorialls," edited by C. K. Sharpe, Esq. : Prefatory
Notice, p. 93.

exercised their brutal pleasure on the poor old woman, pelted her with stones, swung her suspended on a rope betwixt a ship and the shore, and finally ended her miserable existence by throwing a door over her as she lay exhausted on the beach, and heaping stones upon it till she was pressed to death. As even the existing laws against witchcraft were transgressed by this brutal riot, a warm attack was made upon the magistrates and ministers of the town by those who were shocked at a tragedy of such a horrible cast. There were answers published, in which the parties assailed were zealously defended. The superior authorities were expected to take up the affair, but it so happened, during the general distraction of the country concerning the Union, that the murder went without the investigation which a crime so horrid demanded. Still, however, it was something gained that the cruelty was exposed to the public. The voice of general opinion was now appealed to, and in the long run the sentiments which it advocates are commonly those of good sense and humanity.

The officers in the higher branches of the law dared now assert their official authority and reserve for their own decision cases of supposed witchcraft which the fear of public clamour had induced them formerly to leave in the hands of inferior judges, operated upon by all the prejudices of the country and the populace.

In 1718, the celebrated lawyer, Robert Dundas of Arniston, then King's Advocate, wrote a severe letter of censure to the Sheriff-depute of Caithness, in the first place, as having neglected to communicate officially certain precognitions which he had led respecting some recent practices of witchcraft in his county. The Advocate reminded this local judge that the duty of inferior magistrates, in such cases, was to advise with the King's Counsel, first, whether they should be made subject of a trial or not; and if so, before what court, and in what manner, it should take place. He also called the magistrate's attention to a report, that he, the Sheriff-depute, intended to judge in the case himself; "a thing of too great difficulty to be tried without very deliberate advice, and beyond the jurisdiction of an inferior court." The Sheriff-depute sends, with his apology, the *precognition** of the affair, which is one of the most nonsensical in this nonsensical department of the law. A certain carpenter, named William Montgomery, was so infested with cats, which, as his servant-maid reported, "spoke among themselves," that he fell in a rage upon a party of these animals which had assembled in his house at irregular hours, and betwixt his Highland arms of knife, dirk, and broadsword, and his professional weapon of an axe, he made such a dispersion that they were quiet for the night. In consequence of his blows, two witches were said to have died. The case of a third, named Nin-Gilbert, was still more remarkable. Her leg being broken, the injured limb withered, pined, and finally fell off; on which the hag was enclosed in prison, where she also died; and the question which remained was, whether any process should be directed against persons whom, in her compelled confession, she had, as usual, informed against. The Lord Advocate, as may be supposed, quashed all further procedure.

In 1720, an unlucky boy, the third son of James, Lord Torphichen, took it into his head, under instructions, it is said, from a knavish governor, to play the possessed and bewitched person, laying the cause of his distress on certain old witches in Calder, near to which village his father had his mansion. The women were imprisoned, and one or two of them died; but the Crown counsel would not proceed to trial. The noble family also began to see through the cheat. The boy was sent to sea, and though he is said at one time to have been disposed to try his fits while on

---

* The *precognition* is the record of the preliminary evidence on which the public officers charged in Scotland with duties entrusted to a grand jury in England, incur the responsibility of sending an accused person to trial.

board, when the discipline of the navy proved too severe
for his cunning, in process of time he became a good sailor,
assisted gallantly in defence of the vessel against the pirates
of Angria, and finally was drowned in a storm.

In the year 1722, a Sheriff-depute of Sutherland, Captain
David Ross of Littledean, took it upon him, in flagrant
violation of the then established rules of jurisdiction, to
pronounce the last sentence of death for witchcraft which
was ever passed in Scotland. The victim was an insane
old woman belonging to the parish of Loth, who had so
little idea of her situation as to rejoice at the sight of the
fire which was destined to consume her. She had a daughter
lame both of hands and feet, a circumstance attributed to
the witch's having been used to transform her into a pony,
and get her shod by the devil. It does not appear that any
punishment was inflicted for this cruel abuse of the law on
the person of a creature so helpless ; but the son of the
lame daughter, he himself distinguished by the same misfortune, was living so lately as to receive the charity of the
present Marchioness of Stafford, Countess of Sutherland in
her own right, to whom the poor of her extensive country
are as well known as those of the higher order.

Since this deplorable action there has been no judicial
interference in Scotland on account of witchcraft, unless to
prevent explosions of popular enmity against people suspected of such a crime, of which some instances could be
produced. The remains of the superstition sometimes
occur ; there can be no doubt that the vulgar are still
addicted to the custom of scoring above the breath* (as it
is termed), and other counter-spells, evincing that the belief
in witchcraft is only asleep, and might in remote corners be
again awakened to deeds of blood. An instance or two
may be quoted chiefly as facts known to the author himself.

---

* Drawing blood, that is, by two cuts in the form of a cross on the
witch's forehead, confided in all throughout Scotland as the most
powerful counter charm.

In a remote part of the Highlands, an ignorant and malignant woman seems really to have meditated the destruction of her neighbour's property, by placing in a cow-house, or byre as we call it, a pot of baked clay containing locks of hair, parings of nails, and other trumpery. This precious spell was discovered, the design conjectured, and the witch would have been torn to pieces had not a high-spirited and excellent lady in the neighbourhood gathered some of her people (though these were not very fond of the service), and by main force taken the unfortunate creature out of the hands of the populace. The formidable spell is now in my possession.

About two years since, as they were taking down the walls of a building formerly used as a feeding-house for cattle, in the town of Dalkeith, there was found below the threshold-stone the withered heart of some animal stuck full of many scores of pins—a counter-charm, according to tradition, against the operations of witchcraft on the cattle which are kept within. Among the almost innumerable droves of bullocks which come down every year from the Highlands for the south, there is scarce one but has a curious knot upon his tail, which is also a precaution lest an evil eye or an evil spell may do the animal harm.

The last Scottish story with which I will trouble you happened in or shortly after the year 1800, and the whole circumstances are well known to me. The dearth of the years in the end of the eighteenth and beginning of this century was inconvenient to all, but distressing to the poor. A solitary old woman, in a wild and lonely district, subsisted chiefly by rearing chickens, an operation requiring so much care and attention that the gentry, and even the farmers' wives, often find it better to buy poultry at a certain age than to undertake the trouble of bringing them up. As the old woman in the present instance fought her way through life better than her neighbours, envy stigmatized her as having some unlawful mode of increasing the gains of her

little trade, and apparently she did not take much alarm at
the accusation. But she felt, like others, the dearth of the
years alluded to, and chiefly because the farmers were unwilling to sell grain in the very moderate quantities which
she was able to purchase, and without which her little stock
of poultry must have been inevitably starved. In distress on
this account, the dame went to a neighbouring farmer, a very
good-natured, sensible, honest man, and requested him as
a favour to sell her a peck of oats at any price. "Good
neighbour," he said, " I am sorry to be obliged to refuse you,
but my corn is measured out for Dalkeith market ; my carts
are loaded to set out, and to open these sacks again, and
for so small a quantity, would cast my accounts loose, and
create much trouble and disadvantage ; I dare say you will
get all you want at such a place, or such a place." On
receiving this answer, the old woman's temper gave way.
She scolded the wealthy farmer, and wished evil to his
property, which was just setting off for the market. They
parted, after some angry language on both sides ; and sure
enough, as the carts crossed the ford of the river beneath
the farm-house, off came the wheel from one of them, and
five or six sacks of corn were damaged by the water. The
good farmer hardly knew what to think of this ; there were
the two circumstances deemed of old essential and sufficient
to the crime of witchcraft—*Damnum minatum, et malum
secutum.* Scarce knowing what to believe, he hastened to
consult the sheriff of the county, as a friend rather than a
magistrate, upon a case so extraordinary. The official
person showed him that the laws against witchcraft were
abrogated, and had little difficulty to bring him to regard the
matter in its true light of an accident.

It is strange, but true, that the accused herself was not to
be reconciled to the sheriff's doctrine so easily. He reminded her that, if she used her tongue with so much
license, she must expose herself to suspicions, and that
should coincidences happen to irritate her neighbours, she

might suffer harm at a time when there was no one to protect her. He therefore requested her to be more cautious in her language for her own sake, professing, at the same time, his belief that her words and intentions were perfectly harmless, and that he had no apprehension of being hurt by her, let her wish her worst to him. She was rather more angry than pleased at the well-meaning sheriff's scepticism. "I would be laith to wish ony ill either to you or yours, sir," she said; "for I kenna how it is, but something aye comes after my words when I am ill-guided and speak ower fast." In short, she was obstinate in claiming an influence over the destiny of others by words and wishes, which might have in other times conveyed her to the stake, for which her expressions, their consequences, and her disposition to insist upon their efficacy, would certainly of old have made her a fit victim. At present the story is scarcely worth mentioning, but as it contains material resembling those out of which many tragic incidents have arisen.

So low, in short, is now the belief in witchcraft, that perhaps it is only received by those half-crazy individuals who feel a species of consequence derived from accidental coincidences, which, were they received by the community in general, would go near, as on former occasions, to cost the lives of those who make their boast of them. At least one hypochondriac patient is known to the author, who believes himself the victim of a gang of witches, and ascribes his illness to their charms, so that he wants nothing but an indulgent judge to awake again the old ideas of sorcery.

LETTER X.

Other Mystic Arts independent of Witchcraft—Astrology—Its Influence during the 16th and 17th Centuries—Base Ignorance of those who practised it—Lilly's History of his Life and Times—Astrologer's Society—Dr. Lamb—Dr. Forman—Establishment of the Royal Society—Partridge—Connexion of Astrologers with Elementary Spirits—Dr. Dun—Irish Superstition of the Banshie—Similar Superstition in the Highlands — Brownie — Ghosts—Belief of Ancient Philosophers on that Subject—Inquiry into the respect due to such Tales in Modern Times—Evidence of a Ghost against a Murderer—Ghost of Sir George Villiers—Story of Earl St. Vincent —Of a British General Officer—Of an Apparition in France—Of the Second Lord Lyttelton—Of Bill Jones—Of Jarvis Matcham— Trial of two Highlanders for the Murder of Sergeant Davis, discovered by a Ghost—Disturbances at Woodstock, anno 1649—Imposture called the Stockwell Ghost—Similar Case in Scotland— Ghost appearing to an Exciseman—Story of a Disturbed House discovered by the firmness of the Proprietor—Apparition at Plymouth—A Club of Philosophers—Ghost Adventure of a Farmer— Trick upon a Veteran Soldier—Ghost Stories recommended by the Skill of the Authors who compose them—Mrs. Veal's Ghost— Dunton's Apparition Evidence—Effect of Appropriate Scenery to Encourage a Tendency to Superstition—Differs at distant Periods of Life—Night at Glammis Castle about 1791—Visit to Dunvegan in 1814.

WHILE the vulgar endeavoured to obtain a glance into the darkness of futurity by consulting the witch or fortune-teller, the great were supposed to have a royal path of their own, commanding a view from a loftier quarter of the same *terra incognita*. This was represented as accessible by several routes. Physiognomy, chiromancy, and other fantastic arts of prediction afforded each its mystical assistance and guidance. But the road most flattering to human vanity, while it was at the same time most seductive to human credulity, was that of astrology, the queen of mystic sciences, who flattered those who confided in her that the planets and stars in their spheres figure forth and influence the fate of the creatures of mortality, and that a sage acquainted with her lore could predict, with some approach to certainty, the events of any man's career, his chance of success in life or in marriage, his advance in favour of the great, or answer any other horary questions, as they were termed, which he might be anxious to propound, provided always he could supply the exact moment of his birth.   This, in the sixteenth and greater part of the seventeenth centuries, was all that was necessary to enable the astrologer to erect a scheme of the position of the heavenly bodies, which should disclose the life of the interrogator, or Native, as he was called, with all its changes, past, present, and to come.

Imagination was dazzled by a prospect so splendid ; and we find that in the sixteenth century the cultivation of this fantastic science was the serious object of men whose under-standings and acquirements admit of no question.   Bacon himself allowed the truth which might be found in a well-regulated astrology, making thus a distinction betwixt the art as commonly practised and the manner in which it might, as he conceived, be made a proper use of.   But a grave or sober use of this science, if even Bacon could have taught such moderation, would not have suited the temper of those who, inflamed by hopes of temporal aggrandizement, pre-tended to understand and explain to others the language of the stars.   Almost all the other paths of mystic knowledge led to poverty ; even the alchemist, though talking loud and high of the endless treasures his art was to produce, lived from day to day and from year to year upon hopes as un-substantial as the smoke of his furnace.   But the pursuits of the astrologer were such as called for instant remuneration. He became rich by the eager hopes and fond credulity of those who consulted him, and that artist lived by duping others, instead of starving, like others, by duping himself. The wisest men have been cheated by the idea that some supernatural influence upheld and guided them; and from the time of Wallenstein to that of Buonaparte, ambition and success have placed confidence in the species of fatalism inspired by a belief of the influence of their own star. Such being the case, the science was little pursued by those who, faithful in their remarks and reports, must soon have discovered its delusive vanity through the splendour of its professions; and the place of such calm and disinterested pursuers of truth was occupied by a set of men sometimes ingenious, always forward and assuming, whose knowledge was imposition, whose responses were, like the oracles of yore, grounded on the desire of deceit, and who, if sometimes they were elevated into rank and fortune, were more frequently found classed with rogues and vagabonds. This was the more apt to be the case that a sufficient stock of impudence, and some knowledge by rote of the terms of art, were all the store of information necessary for establishing a conjurer. The natural consequence of the degraded character of the professors was the degradation of the art itself. Lilly, who wrote the history of his own life and times, notices in that curious volume the most distinguished persons of his day, who made pretensions to astrology, and almost without exception describes them as profligate, worthless, sharking cheats, abandoned to vice, and imposing, by the grossest frauds, upon the silly fools who consulted them. From what we learn of his own history, Lilly himself, a low-born ignorant man, with some gloomy shades of fanaticism in his temperament, was sufficiently fitted to dupe others, and perhaps cheated himself merely by perusing, at an advanced period of life, some of the astrological tracts devised by men of less cunning, though perhaps more pretence to science, than he himself might boast. Yet the public still continue to swallow these gross impositions, though coming from such unworthy authority. The astrologers embraced different sides of the Civil War, and the king on one side, with the Parliamentary leaders on the other, were both equally curious to know, and eager to believe, what Lilly, Wharton, or Gadbury had discovered from the heavens touching the fortune of the strife. Lilly was a prudent person, contriving with some address to shift the sails of his prophetic bark so as to suit the current of the time, and the gale of fortune. No person could better discover from various omens the course of Charles's misfortunes, so soon as they had come to pass. In the time of the Commonwealth he foresaw the perpetual destruction of the monarchy, and in 1660 this did not prevent his foreseeing the restoration of Charles II. He maintained some credit even among the better classes, for Aubrey and Ashmole both called themselves his friends, being persons extremely credulous, doubtless, respecting the mystic arts. Once a year, too, the astrologers had a public dinner or feast, where the knaves were patronised by the company of such fools as claimed the title of Philomaths—that is, lovers of the mathematics, by which name were still distinguished those who encouraged the pursuit of mystical prescience, the most opposite possible to exact science. Elias Ashmole, the "most honourable Esquire," to whom Lilly's life is dedicated, seldom failed to attend; nay, several men of sense and knowledge honoured this rendezvous. Congreve's picture of a man like Foresight, the dupe of astrology and its sister arts, was then common in society. But the astrologers of the 17th century did not confine themselves to the stars. There was no province of fraud which they did not practise; they were scandalous as panders, and as quacks sold potions for the most unworthy purposes. For such reasons the common people detested the astrologers of the great as cordially as they did the more vulgar witches of their own sphere.

Dr. Lamb, patronised by the Duke of Buckingham, who, like other overgrown favourites, was inclined to cherish astrology, was in 1640 pulled to pieces in the city of London by the enraged populace, and his maid-servant, thirteen years afterwards, hanged as a witch at Salisbury. In the villanous transaction of the poisoning of Sir Thomas Overbury, in King James's time, much mention was made of the art and skill of Dr. Forman, another professor of the same sort with Lamb, who was consulted by the Countess of Essex on the best mode of conducting her guilty intrigue with the Earl of Somerset. He was dead before the affair broke out, which might otherwise have cost him the gibbet, as it did all others concerned, with the exception only of the principal parties, the atrocious authors of the crime. When the cause was tried, some little puppets were produced in court, which were viewed by one party with horror, as representing the most horrid spells. It was even said that the devil was about to pull down the court-house on their being discovered. Others of the audience only saw in them the baby figures on which the dressmakers then, as now, were accustomed to expose new fashions.

The erection of the Royal Society, dedicated to far different purposes than the pursuits of astrology, had a natural operation in bringing the latter into discredit; and although the credulity of the ignorant and uninformed continued to support some pretenders to that science, the name of Philomath, assumed by these persons and their clients, began to sink under ridicule and contempt. When Sir Richard Steele set up the paper called the *Guardian*, he chose, under the title of Nestor Ironside, to assume the character of an astrologer, and issued predictions accordingly, one of which, announcing the death of a person called Partridge, once a shoemaker, but at the time the conductor of an Astrological Almanack, led to a controversy, which was supported with great humour by Swift and other wags. I believe you will find that this, with Swift's Elegy on the same person, is one of the last occasions in which astrology has afforded even a jest to the good people of England.

This dishonoured science has some right to be mentioned in a " Treatise on Demonology," because the earlier astro-

logers, though denying the use of all necromancy—that is-
unlawful or black magic—pretended always to a correspond,
ence with the various spirits of the elements, on the principles of the Rosicrucian philosophy. They affirmed they
could bind to their service, and imprison in a ring, a mirror,
or a stone, some fairy, sylph, or salamander, and compel it
to appear when called, and render answers to such questions as the viewer should propose. It is remarkable that
the sage himself did not pretend to see the spirit ; but the
task of viewer, or reader, was entrusted to a third party, a
boy or girl usually under the years of puberty. Dr. Dee, an
excellent mathematician, had a stone of this kind, and is
said to have been imposed upon concerning the spirits
attached to it, their actions and answers, by the report of
one Kelly who acted as his viewer. The unfortunate Dee
was ruined by his associates both in fortune and reputation.
His show-stone or mirror is still preserved among other
curiosities in the British Museum. Some superstition of the
same kind was introduced by the celebrated Count Cagli-
ostro, during the course of the intrigue respecting the diamond
necklace in which the late Marie Antoinette was so unfortunately implicated.

Dismissing this general class of impostors, who are now
seldom heard of, we come now briefly to mention some
leading superstitions once, perhaps, common to all the
countries of Europe, but now restricted to those which continue to be inhabited by an undisturbed and native race.
Of these, one of the most beautiful is the Irish fiction which
assigns to certain families of ancient descent and distinguished rank the privilege of a Banshie, as she is called, or
household fairy, whose office it is to appear, seemingly
mourning, while she announces the approaching death of
some one of the destined race. The subject has been so
lately and beautifully investigated and illustrated by Mr.
Crofton Croker and others, that I may dispense with being
very particular regarding it. If I am rightly informed, the

distinction of a banshie is only allowed to families of the
pure Milesian stock, and is never ascribed to any descendant of the proudest Norman or boldest Saxon who followed the banner of Earl Strongbow, much less to adven-
turers of later date who have obtained settlements in the
Green Isle.

Several families of the Highlands of Scotland anciently
laid claim to the distinction of an attendant spirit who performed the office of the Irish banshie. Amongst them, however, the functions of this attendant genius, whose form and
appearance differed in different cases, were not limited to
announcing the dissolution of those whose days were num-
bered. The Highlanders contrived to exact from them
other points of service, sometimes as warding off dangers of
battle; at others, as guarding and protecting the infant heir
through the dangers of childhood ; and sometimes as con-
descending to interfere even in the sports of the chieftain,
and point out the fittest move to be made at chess, or the
best card to be played at any other game. Among those
spirits who have deigned to vouch their existence by appearance of late years, is that of an ancestor of the family of
MacLean of Lochbuy. Before the death of any of his race
the phantom-chief gallops along the sea-beach near to the
castle, announcing the event by cries and lamentations.
The spectre is said to have rode his rounds and uttered his
death-cries within these few years, in consequence of which
the family and clan, though much shocked, were in no
way surprised to hear by next accounts that their gallant
chief was dead at Lisbon, where he served under Lord
Wellington.

Of a meaner origin and occupation was the Scottish
Brownie, already mentioned as somewhat resembling
Robin Goodfellow in the frolicsome days of Old England.
This spirit was easily banished, or, as it was styled, hired
away, by the offer of clothes or food ; but many of the simple
inhabitants could little see the prudence of parting with

such a useful domestic drudge, who served faithfully, without fee and reward, food or raiment. Neither was it all times safe to reject Brownie's assistance. Thus, we are informed by Brand, that a young man in the Orkneys " used to brew, and sometimes read upon his Bible ; to whom an old woman in the house said, that Brownie was displeased with that book he read upon, which, if he continued to do, they would get no more service of Brownie ; but he, being better instructed from that book, which was Brownie's eyesore and the object of his wrath, when he brewed, would not suffer any sacrifice to be given to Brownie; whereupon the first and second brewings were spoilt, and for no use ; for though the wort wrought well, yet in a little time it left off working, and grew cold ; but of the third broust, or brewing, he had ale very good, though he would not give any sacrifice to Brownie, with whom afterwards they were no more troubled." Another story of the same kind is told of a lady in Uist, who refused, on religious grounds, the usual sacrifice to this domestic spirit. The first and second brewings failed, but the third succeeded; and thus, when Brownie lost the perquisite to which he had been so long accustomed, he abandoned the inhospitable house, where his services had so long been faithfully rendered. The last place in the south of Scotland supposed to have been honoured, or benefited, by the residence of a Brownie, was Bodsbeck in Moffatdale, which has been the subject of an entertaining tale by Mr. James Hogg, the self-instructed genius of Ettrick Forest.

These particular superstitions, however, are too limited, and too much obliterated from recollection, to call for special discussion. The general faith in fairies has already undergone our consideration; but something remains to be said upon another species of superstition, so general that it may be called proper to mankind in every climate ; so deeply rooted also in human belief, that it is found to survive in states of society during which all other fictions of the same order are entirely dismissed from influence. Mr. Crabbe, with his usual felicity, has called the belief in ghosts "the last lingering fiction of the brain."

Nothing appears more simple at the first view of the subject, than that human memory should recall and bring back to the eye of the imagination, in perfect similitude, even the very form and features of a person with whom we have been long conversant, or which have been imprinted in our minds with indelible strength by some striking circumstances touching our meeting in life. The son does not easily forget the aspect of an affectionate father; and, for reasons opposite but equally powerful, the countenance of a murdered person is engraved upon the recollection of his slayer. A thousand additional circumstances, far too obvious to require recapitulation, render the supposed apparition of the dead the most ordinary spectral phenomenon which is ever believed to occur among the living. All that we have formerly said respecting supernatural appearances in general, applies with peculiar force to the belief of ghosts; for whether the cause of delusion exists in an excited imagination or a disordered organic system, it is in this way that it commonly exhibits itself. Hence Lucretius himself, the most absolute of sceptics, considers the existence of ghosts, and their frequent apparition, as facts so undeniable that he endeavours to account for them at the expense of assenting to a class of phenomena very irreconcilable to his general system. As he will not allow of the existence of the human soul, and at the same time cannot venture to question the phenomena supposed to haunt the repositories of the dead, he is obliged to adopt the belief that the body consists of several coats like those of an onion, and that the outmost and thinnest, being detached by death, continues to wander near the place of sepulture, in the exact resemblance of the person while alive.

We have said there are many ghost stories which we do not feel at liberty to challenge as impostures, because we are confident that those who relate them on their own authority actually believe what they assert, and may have good reason for doing so, though there is no real phantom after all. We are far, therefore, from averring that such tales are necessarily false. It is easy to suppose the visionary has been imposed upon by a lively dream, a waking reverie, the excitation of a powerful imagination, or the misrepresentation of a diseased organ of sight; and in one or other of these causes, to say nothing of a system of deception which may in many instances be probable, we apprehend a solution will be found for all cases of what are called real ghost stories.

In truth, the evidence with respect to such apparitions is very seldom accurately or distinctly questioned. A supernatural tale is in most cases received as an agreeable mode of amusing society, and he would be rather accounted a sturdy moralist than an entertaining companion who should employ himself in assailing its credibility. It would indeed be a solecism in manners, something like that of impeaching the genuine value of the antiquities exhibited by a good-natured collector for the gratification of his guests. This difficulty will appear greater should a company have the rare good fortune to meet the person who himself witnessed the wonders which he tells; a well-bred or prudent man will, under such circumstances, abstain from using the rules of cross-examination practised in a court of justice; and if in any case he presumes to do so, he is in danger of receiving answers, even from the most candid and honourable persons, which are rather fitted to support the credit of the story which they stand committed to maintain, than to the pure service of unadorned truth. The narrator is asked, for example, some unimportant question with respect to the apparition; he answers it on the hasty suggestion of his own imagination, tinged as it is with belief of the general fact, and by doing so often gives a feature of minute evidence which was before wanting, and this with perfect unconsciousness on his own part. It is a rare occurrence, indeed, to find an opportunity of dealing with an actual ghost-seer; such instances, however, I have certainly myself met with, and that in the case of able, wise, candid, and resolute persons, of whose veracity I had every reason to be confident. But in such instances shades of mental aberration have afterwards occurred, which sufficiently accounted for the supposed apparitions, and will incline me always to feel alarmed in behalf of the continued health of a friend who should conceive himself to have witnessed such a visitation.

The nearest approximation which can be generally made to exact evidence in this case, is the word of some individual who has had the story, it may be, from the person to whom it has happened, but most likely from his family, or some friend of the family. Far more commonly the narrator possesses no better means of knowledge than that of dwelling in the country where the thing happened, or being well acquainted with the outside of the mansion in the inside of which the ghost appeared.

In every point the evidence of such a second-hand retailer of the mystic story must fall under the adjudged case in an English court. The judge stopped a witness who was about to give an account of the murder upon trial, as it was narrated to him by the ghost of the murdered person. "Hold, sir," said his lordship; "the ghost is an excellent witness, and his evidence the best possible; but he cannot be heard by proxy in this court. Summon him hither, and I'll hear him in person; but your communication is mere hearsay, which my office compels me to reject." Yet it is upon the credit of one man, who pledges it upon that of three or four persons, who have told it successively to each other, that we are often expected to believe an incident inconsistent with the laws of Nature, however agreeable to our love of the wonderful and the horrible.

In estimating the truth or falsehood of such stories it is evident we can derive no proofs from that period of society when men affirmed boldly, and believed stoutly, all the wonders which could be coined or fancied. That such stories are believed and told by grave historians, only shows that the wisest men cannot rise in all things above the general ignorance of their age. Upon the evidence of such historians we might as well believe the portents of ancient or the miracles of modern Rome. For example, we read in Clarendon of the apparition of the ghost of Sir George Villiers to an ancient dependant. This is no doubt a story told by a grave author, at a time when such stories were believed by all the world ; but does it follow that our reason must acquiesce in a statement so positively contradicted by the voice of Nature through all her works ? The miracle of raising a dead man was positively refused by our Saviour to the Jews, who demanded it as a proof of his mission, because they had already sufficient grounds of conviction ; and, as they believed them not, it was irresistibly argued by the Divine Person whom they tempted, that neither would they believe if one arose from the dead. Shall we suppose that a miracle refused for the conversion of God's chosen people was sent on a vain errand to save the life of a profligate spendthrift ? I lay aside, you observe, entirely the not unreasonable supposition that Towers, or whatever was the ghost-seer's name, desirous to make an impression upon Buckingham, as an old servant of his house, might be tempted to give him his advice, of which we are not told the import, in the character of his father's spirit, and authenticate the tale by the mention of some token known to him as a former retainer of the family. The Duke was superstitious, and the ready dupe of astrologers and soothsayers. The manner in which he had provoked the fury of the people must have warned every reflecting person of his approaching fate ; and, the age considered, it was not unnatural that a faithful friend should take this mode of calling his attention to his perilous situation. Or, if we suppose that the incident was not a mere pretext to obtain access to the Duke's ear, the messenger may have been impressed upon by an idle dream—in a word, numberless conjectures might be formed for accounting for the event in a natural way, the most extravagant of which is more probable than that the laws of Nature were broken through in order to give a vain and fruitless warning to an ambitious minion.

It is the same with all those that are called accredited ghost stories usually told at the fireside. They want evidence. It is true that the general wish to believe, rather than power of believing, has given some such stories a certain currency in society. I may mention, as one of the class of tales I mean, that of the late Earl St. Vincent, who watched, with a friend, it is said, a whole night, in order to detect the cause of certain nocturnal disturbances which took place in a certain mansion. The house was under lease to Mrs. Ricketts, his sister. The result of his lordship's vigil is said to have been that he heard the noises without being able to detect the causes, and insisted on his sister giving up the house. This is told as a real story, with a thousand different circumstances. But who has heard or seen an authentic account from Earl St. Vincent, or from his " companion of the watch," or from his lordship's sister? And as in any other case such sure species of direct evidence would be necessary to prove the facts, it seems unreasonable to believe such a story on slighter terms. When the particulars are precisely fixed and known, it might be time to enquire whether Lord St. Vincent, amid the other eminent qualities of a first-rate seaman, might not be in some degree tinged with their tendency to superstition ; and still farther, whether, having ascertained the existence of disturbances not immediately or easily detected, his lordship might not advise his sister rather to remove than to remain in a house so haunted, though he might believe that poachers or smugglers were the worst ghosts by whom it was disturbed.

The story of two highly respectable officers in the British

army, who are supposed to have seen the spectre of the brother of one of them in a hut, or barrack, in America, is also one of those accredited ghost tales, which attain a sort of brevet rank as true, from the mention of respectable names as the parties who witnessed the vision. But we are left without a glimpse when, how, and in what terms, this story obtained its currency; as also by whom, and in what manner, it was first circulated; and among the numbers by whom it has been quoted, although all agree in the general event, scarcely two, even of those who pretend to the best information, tell the story in the same way.

Another such story, in which the name of a lady of condition is made use of as having seen an apparition in a country-seat in France, is so far better borne out than those I have mentioned, that I have seen a narrative of the circumstances attested by the party principally concerned. That the house was disturbed seems to be certain, but the circumstances (though very remarkable) did not, in my mind, by any means exclude the probability that the disturbance and appearances were occasioned by the dexterous management of some mischievously-disposed persons.

The remarkable circumstance of Thomas, the second Lord Lyttelton, prophesying his own death within a few minutes, upon the information of an apparition, has been always quoted as a true story. But of late it has been said and published, that the unfortunate nobleman had previously determined to take poison, and of course had it in his own power to ascertain the execution of the prediction. It was no doubt singular that a man, who meditated his exit from the world, should have chosen to play such a trick on his friends. But it is still more credible that a whimsical man should do so wild a thing, than that a messenger should be sent from the dead to tell a libertine at what precise hour he should expire.

To this list other stories of the same class might be added. But it is sufficient to show that such stories as these, having gained a certain degree of currency in the world, and bearing creditable names on their front, walk through society unchallenged, like bills through a bank when they bear respectable indorsations, although, it may be, the signatures are forged after all. There is, indeed, an unwillingness very closely to examine such subjects, for the secret fund of superstition in every man's bosom is gratified by believing them to be true, or at least induces him to abstain from challenging them as false. And no doubt it must happen that the transpiring of incidents, in which men have actually seen, or conceived that they saw, apparitions which were invisible to others, contributes to the increase of such stories—which do accordingly sometimes meet us in a shape of veracity difficult to question.

The following story was narrated to me by my friend, Mr. William Clerk, chief clerk to the Jury Court, Edinburgh, when he first learned it, now nearly thirty years ago, from a passenger in the mail-coach. With Mr. Clerk's consent, I gave the story at that time to poor Mat Lewis, who published it with a ghost-ballad which he adjusted on the same theme. From the minuteness of the original detail, however, the narrative is better calculated for prose than verse ; and more especially as the friend to whom it was originally communicated is one of the most accurate, intelligent, and acute persons whom I have known in the course of my life, I am willing to preserve the precise story in this place.

It was about the eventful year 1800, when the Emperor Paul laid his ill-judged embargo on British trade, that my friend Mr. William Clerk, on a journey to London, found himself in company, in the mail-coach, with a seafaring man of middle age and respectable appearance, who announced himself as master of a vessel in the Baltic trade, and a sufferer by the embargo. In the course of the desultory conversation which takes place on such occasions the seaman observed, in compliance with a common superstition, "I wish we may have good luck on our journey—there is a magpie." "And why should that be unlucky?" said my

friend. " I cannot tell you that," replied the sailor ; " but
all the world agrees that one magpie bodes bad luck—two
are not so bad, but three are the devil.   I never saw three
magpies but twice, and once I had near lost my vessel, and
the second I fell from a horse, and was hurt." This conversation led Mr. Clerk to observe that he supposed he
believed also in ghosts, since he credited such auguries.
" And if I do," said the sailor, " I may have my own reasons
for doing so ;" and he spoke this in a deep and serious
manner, implying that he felt deeply what he was saying.
On being further urged, he confessed that, if he could believe
his own eyes, there was one ghost at least which he had seen
repeatedly.   He then told his story as I now relate it.

Our mariner had in his youth gone mate of a slave
vessel from Liverpool, of which town he seemed to be a
native.   The captain of the vessel was a man of a variable
temper, sometimes kind and courteous to his men, but
subject to fits of humour, dislike, and passion, during which
he was very violent, tyrannical, and cruel.   He took a particular dislike at one sailor aboard, an elderly man, called
Bill Jones, or some such name.   He seldom spoke to this
person without threats and abuse, which the old man, with
the license which sailors take on merchant vessels, was very
apt to return.   On one occasion Bill Jones appeared slow
in getting out on the yard to hand a sail.   The captain,
according to custom, abused the seaman as a lubberly rascal,
who got fat by leaving his duty to other people.   The man
made a saucy answer, almost amounting to mutiny, on which,
in a towering passion, the captain ran down to his cabin, and
returned with a blunderbuss loaded with slugs, with which
he took deliberate aim at the supposed mutineer, fired, and
mortally wounded him. The man was handed down from the
yard, and stretched on the deck, evidently dying.   He fixed
his eyes on the captain, and said, " Sir, you have done for
me, but *I will never leave you.*"   The captain, in return,
swore at him for a fat lubber, and said he would have him

thrown into the slave-kettle, where they made food for the negroes, and see how much fat he had got. The man died. His body was actually thrown into the slave-kettle, and the narrator observed, with a *naïveté* which confirmed the extent of his own belief in the truth of what he told, " There was not much fat about him after all."

The captain told the crew they must keep absolute silence on the subject of what had passed ; and as the mate was not willing to give an explicit and absolute promise, he ordered him to be confined below. After a day or two he came to the mate, and demanded if he had an intention to deliver him up for trial when the vessel got home. The mate, who was tired of close confinement in that sultry climate, spoke his commander fair, and obtained his liberty. When he mingled among the crew once more he found them impressed with the idea, not unnatural in their situation, that the ghost of the dead man appeared among them when they had a spell of duty, especially if a sail was to be handed, on which occasion the spectre was sure to be out upon the yard before any of the crew. The narrator had seen this apparition himself repeatedly—he believed the captain saw it also, but he took no notice of it for some time, and the crew, terrified at the violent temper of the man, dared not call his attention to it. Thus they held on their course homeward with great fear and anxiety.

At length the captain invited the mate, who was now in a sort of favour, to go down to the cabin and take a glass of grog with him. In this interview he assumed a very grave and anxious aspect. " I need not tell you, Jack," he said, " what sort of hand we have got on board with us. He told me he would never leave me, and he has kept his word. You only see him now and then, but he is always by my side, and never out of my sight. At this very moment I see him—I am determined to bear it no longer, and I have resolved to leave you."

The mate replied that his leaving the vessel while out of

the sight of any land was impossible. He advised, that if the captain apprehended any bad consequences from what had happened, he should run for the west of France or Ireland, and there go ashore, and leave him, the mate, to carry the vessel into Liverpool. The captain only shook his head gloomily, and reiterated his determination to leave the ship. At this moment the mate was called to the deck for some purpose or other, and the instant he got up the companion-ladder he heard a splash in the water, and looking over the ship's side, saw that the captain had thrown himself into the sea from the quarter-gallery, and was running astern at the rate of six knots an hour. When just about to sink he seemed to make a last exertion, sprung half out of the water, and clasped his hands towards the mate, calling, "By ——, Bill is with me now !" and then sunk, to be seen no more.

After hearing this singular story Mr. Clerk asked some questions about the captain, and whether his companion considered him as at all times rational. The sailor seemed struck with the question, and answered, after a moment's delay, that in general *he conversationed well enough.*

It would have been desirable to have been able to ascertain how far this extraordinary tale was founded on fact; but want of time and other circumstances prevented Mr. Clerk from learning the names and dates, that might to a certain degree have verified the events. Granting the murder to have taken place, and the tale to have been truly told, there was nothing more likely to arise among the ship's company than the belief in the apparition; as the captain was a man of a passionate and irritable disposition, it was nowise improbable that he, the victim of remorse, should participate in the horrible visions of those less concerned, especially as he was compelled to avoid communicating his sentiments with any one else; and the catastrophe would in such a case be but the natural consequence of that superstitious remorse which has conducted so many criminals to suicide or the gallows. If the fellow-traveller of Mr. Clerk be not allowed this degree of credit, he must at least be admitted to have displayed a singular talent for the composition of the horrible in fiction. The tale, properly detailed, might have made the fortune of a romancer.

I cannot forbear giving you, as congenial to this story, another instance of a guilt-formed phantom, which made considerable noise about twenty years ago or more. I am, I think, tolerably correct in the details, though I have lost the account of the trial. Jarvis Matcham—such, if I am not mistaken, was the name of my hero—was pay-sergeant in a regiment, where he was so highly esteemed as a steady and accurate man that he was permitted opportunity to embezzle a considerable part of the money lodged in his hands for pay of soldiers, bounty of recruits (then a large sum), and other charges which fell within his duty. He was summoned to join his regiment from a town where he had been on the recruiting service, and this perhaps under some shade of suspicion. Matcham perceived discovery was at hand, and would have deserted had it not been for the presence of a little drummer lad, who was the only one of his party appointed to attend him. In the desperation of his crime he resolved to murder the poor boy, and avail himself of some balance of money to make his escape. He meditated this wickedness the more readily that the drummer, he thought, had been put as a spy on him. He perpetrated his crime, and changing his dress after the deed was done, made a long walk across the country to an inn on the Portsmouth road, where he halted and went to bed, desiring to be called when the first Portsmouth coach came. The waiter summoned him accordingly, but long after remembered that, when he shook the guest by the shoulder, his first words as he awoke were: "My God! I did not kill him."

Matcham went to the seaport by the coach, and instantly entered as an able-bodied landsman or marine, I know not which. His sobriety and attention to duty gained him the

same good opinion of the officers in his new service which he had enjoyed in the army. He was afloat for several years, and behaved remarkably well in some actions. At length the vessel came into Plymouth, was paid off, and some of the crew, amongst whom was Jarvis Matcham, were dismissed as too old for service. He and another seaman resolved to walk to town, and took the route by Salisbury. It was when within two or three miles of this celebrated city that they were overtaken by a tempest so sudden, and accompanied with such vivid lightning and thunder so dreadfully loud, that the obdurate conscience of the old sinner began to be awakened. He expressed more terror than seemed natural for one who was familiar with the war of elements, and began to look and talk so wildly that his companion became aware that something more than usual was the matter. At length Matcham complained to his companion that the stones rose from the road and flew after him. He desired the man to walk on the other side of the highway to see if they would follow him when he was alone. The sailor complied, and Jarvis Matcham complained that the stones still flew after him and did not pursue the other. " But what is worse," he added, coming up to his companion, and whispering, with a tone of mystery and fear, " who is that little drummer-boy, and what business has he to follow us so closely ?" " I can see no one," answered the seaman, infected by the superstition of his associate. " What! not see that little boy with the bloody pantaloons !" exclaimed the secret murderer, so much to the terror of his comrade that he conjured him, if he had anything on his mind, to make a clear conscience as far as confession could do it. The criminal fetched a deep groan, and declared that he was unable longer to endure the life which he had led for years. He then confessed the murder of the drummer, and added that, as a considerable reward had been offered, he wished his comrade to deliver him up to the magistrates of Salisbury, as he would desire a shipmate to profit by his fate, which he was now convinced was inevitable. Having overcome his friend's objections to this mode of proceeding, Jarvis Matcham was surrendered to justice accordingly, and made a full confession of his guilt. But before the trial the love of life returned The prisoner denied his confession, and pleaded Not Guilty. By this time, however, full evidence had been procured from other quarters. Witnesses appeared from his former regiment to prove his identity with the murderer and deserter, and the waiter remembered the ominous words which he had spoken when he awoke him to join the Portsmouth coach. Jarvis Matcham was found guilty and executed. When his last chance of life was over he returned to his confession, and with his dying breath averred, and truly, as he thought, the truth of the vision on Salisbury Plain. Similar stories might be produced, showing plainly that, under the direction of Heaven, the influence of superstitious fear may be the appointed means of bringing the criminal to repentance for his own sake, and to punishment for the advantage of society.

Cases of this kind are numerous and easily imagined, so I shall dwell on them no further; but rather advert to at least an equally abundant class of ghost stories, in which the apparition is pleased not to torment the actual murderer, but proceeds in a very circuitous manner, acquainting some stranger or ignorant old woman with the particulars of his fate, who, though perhaps unacquainted with all the parties, is directed by a phantom to lay the facts before a magistrate. In this respect we must certainly allow that ghosts have, as we are informed by the facetious Captain Grose, forms and customs peculiar to themselves.

There would be no edification and little amusement in treating of clumsy deceptions of this kind, where the grossness of the imposture detects itself. But occasionally cases occur like the following, with respect to which it is more difficult, to use James Boswell's phrase, "to know what to think."

Upon the 10th of June, 1754, Duncan Terig, *alias* Clark,

and Alexander Bain MacDonald, two Highlanders, were tried before the Court of Justiciary, Edinburgh, for the murder of Arthur Davis, sergeant in Guise's regiment, on the 28th September, 1749. The accident happened not long after the civil war, the embers of which were still reeking, so there existed too many reasons on account of which an English soldier, straggling far from assistance, might be privately cut off by the inhabitants of these wilds. It appears that Sergeant Davis was missing for years, without any certainty as to his fate. At length, an account of the murder appeared from the evidence of one Alexander MacPherson (a Highlander, speaking no language but Gaelic, and sworn by an interpreter), who gave the following extraordinary account of his cause of knowledge : — He was, he said, in bed in his cottage, when an apparition came to his bedside and commanded him to rise and follow him out of doors. Believing his visitor to be one Farquharson, a neighbour and friend, the witness did as he was bid ; and when they were without the cottage, the appearance told the witness he was the ghost of Sergeant Davis, and requested him to go and bury his mortal remains, which lay concealed in a place he pointed out in a moorland tract called the Hill of Christie. He desired him to take Farquharson with him as an assistant. Next day the witness went to the place specified, and there found the bones of a human body much decayed. The witness did not at that time bury the bones so found, in consequence of which negligence the sergeant's ghost again appeared to him, upbraiding him with his breach of promise. On this occasion the witness asked the ghost who were the murderers, and received for answer that he had been slain by the prisoners at the bar. The witness, after this second visitation, called the assistance of Farquharson, and buried the body.

Farquharson was brought in evidence to prove that the preceding witness, MacPherson, had called him to the burial of the bones, and told him the same story which he repeated in court. Isabel MacHardie, a person who slept in one of the beds which run along the wall in an ordinary Highland hut, declared that upon the night when MacPherson said he saw the ghost, she saw a naked man enter the house and go towards MacPherson's bed.

Yet though the supernatural incident was thus fortified, and although there were other strong presumptions against the prisoners, the story of the apparition threw an air of ridicule on the whole evidence for the prosecution. It was followed up by the counsel for the prisoners asking, in the cross-examination of MacPherson, "What language did the ghost speak in?" The witness, who was himself ignorant cf English, replied, "As good Gaelic as I ever heard in Lochaber." "Pretty well for the ghost of an English sergeant," answered the counsel. The inference was rather smart and plausible than sound, for, the apparition of the ghost being admitted, we know too little of the other world to judge whether all languages may not be alike familiar to those who belonged to it. It imposed, however, on the jury, who found the accused parties not guilty, although their counsel and solicitor and most of the court were satisfied of their having committed the murder. In this case the interference of the ghost seems to have rather impeded the vengeance which it was doubtless the murdered sergeant's desire to obtain. Yet there may be various modes of explaining this mysterious story, of which the following conjecture may pass for one.

The reader may suppose that MacPherson was privy to the fact of the murder, perhaps as an accomplice or otherwise, and may also suppose that, from motives of remorse for the action, or of enmity to those who had committed it, he entertained a wish to bring them to justice. But through the whole Highlands there is no character more detestable than that of an informer, or one who takes what is called Tascal-money, or reward for discovery of crimes. To have informed against Terig and MacDonald might have cost MacPherson his life; and it is far from being impossible that he had recourse to the story of the ghost, knowing well that his superstitious countrymen would pardon his communicating the commission entrusted to him by a being from the other world, although he might probably have been murdered if his delation of the crime had been supposed voluntary. This explanation, in exact conformity with the sentiments of the Highlanders on such subjects, would reduce the whole story to a stroke of address on the part of the witness.

It is therefore of the last consequence, in considering the truth of stories of ghosts and apparitions, to consider the possibility of wilful deception, whether on the part of those who are agents in the supposed disturbances, or the author of the legend. We shall separately notice an instance or two of either kind.

The most celebrated instance in which human agency was used to copy the disturbances imputed to supernatural beings refers to the ancient palace of Woodstock, when the Commissioners of the Long Parliament came down to dispark what had been lately a royal residence. The Commissioners arrived at Woodstock, 13th October, 1649, determined to wipe away the memory of all that connected itself with the recollection of monarchy in England. But in the course of their progress they were encountered by obstacles which apparently came from the next world. Their bed-chambers were infested with visits of a thing resembling a dog, but which came and passed as mere earthly dogs cannot do. Logs of wood, the remains of a very large tree called the King's Oak, which they had splintered into billets for burning, were tossed through the house, and the chairs displaced and shuffled about. While they were in bed the feet of their couches were lifted higher than their heads, and then dropped with violence. Trenchers "without a wish" flew at their heads of free will. Thunder and lightning came next, which were set down to the same cause. Spectres made their appearance, as they thought, in different shapes, and one of the party saw the apparition of a hoof, which kicked a candlestick and lighted candle into the middle of the room, and then politely scratched on the red snuff to extinguish it. Other and worse tricks were practised on the astonished Commissioners who, considering that all the fiends of hell were let loose upon them, retreated from Woodstock without completing an errand which was, in their opinion, impeded by infernal powers, though the opposition offered was rather of a playful and malicious than of a dangerous cast.

The whole matter was, after the Restoration, discovered to be the trick of one of their own party, who had attended the Commissioners as a clerk, under the name of Giles Sharp. This man, whose real name was Joseph Collins of Oxford, called *Funny Joe*, was a concealed loyalist, and well acquainted with the old mansion of Woodstock, where he had been brought up before the Civil War. Being a bold, active spirited man, Joe availed himself of his local knowledge of trap-doors and private passages so as to favour the tricks which he played off upon his masters by aid of his fellow-domestics. The Commissioners' personal reliance on him made his task the more easy, and it was all along remarked that trusty Giles Sharp saw the most extraordinary sights and visions among the whole party. The unearthly terrors experienced by the Commissioners are detailed with due gravity by Sinclair, and also, I think, by Dr. Plott. But although the detection or explanation of the real history of the Woodstock demons has also been published, and I have myself seen it, I have at this time forgotten whether it exists in a separate collection, or where it is to be looked for.

Similar disturbances have been often experienced while it was the custom to believe in and dread such frolics of the invisible world, and under circumstances which induce us to wonder, both at the extreme trouble taken by the agents in these impostures, and the slight motives from which they have been induced to do much wanton mischief. Still greater is our modern surprise at the apparently simple means by which terror has been excited to so general an extent, that even the wisest and most prudent have not escaped its contagious influence.

On the first point I am afraid there can be no better reason assigned than the conscious pride of superiority, which induces the human being in all cases to enjoy and practise every means of employing an influence over his fellow-mortals; to which we may safely add that general love of tormenting, as common to our race as to that noble mimick of humanity, the monkey. To this is owing the delight with which every school-boy anticipates the effects of throwing a stone into a glass shop; and to this we must also ascribe the otherwise unaccountable pleasure which individuals have taken in practising the tricksy pranks of a goblin, and filling a household or neighbourhood with anxiety and dismay, with little gratification to themselves besides the consciousness of dexterity if they remain undiscovered, and with the risk of loss of character and punishment should the imposture be found out.

In the year 1772, a train of transactions, commencing upon Twelfth Day, threw the utmost consternation into the village of Stockwell, near London, and impressed upon some of its inhabitants the inevitable belief that they were produced by invisible agents. The plates, dishes, china, and glass-ware and small movables of every kind, contained in the house of Mrs. Golding, an elderly lady, seemed suddenly to become animated, shifted their places, flew through the room, and were broken to pieces. The particulars of this commotion were as curious as the loss and damage occasioned in this extraordinary manner were alarming and intolerable. Amidst this combustion, a young woman, Mrs. Golding's maid, named Anne Robinson, was walking backwards and forwards, nor could she be prevailed on to sit down for a moment excepting while the family were at prayers, during which time no disturbance happened. This Anne Robinson had been but a few days in the old lady's service, and it was remarkable that she endured with great composure the extraordinary display which others beheld with terror, and coolly advised her mistress not to be alarmed or uneasy, as these things could not be helped. This excited an idea that she had some reason for being so composed, not inconsistent with a degree of connexion with what was going forward. The afflicted Mrs. Golding, as she might be well termed, considering such a commotion and demolition among her goods and chattels, invited neighbours to stay in her house, but they soon became unable to bear the sight of these supernatural proceedings, which went so far that not above two cups and saucers remained out of a valuable set of china. She next abandoned her dwelling, and took refuge with a neighbour, but, finding his movables were seized with the same sort of St. Vitus's dance, her landlord reluctantly refused to shelter any longer a woman who seemed to be persecuted by so strange a subject of vexation. Mrs. Golding's suspicions against Anne Robinson now gaining ground, she dismissed her maid, and the hubbub among her movables ceased at once and for ever.

This circumstance of itself indicates that Anne Robinson was the cause of these extraordinary disturbances, as has been since more completely ascertained by a Mr. Brayfield, who persuaded Anne, long after the events had happened, to make him her confidant. There was a love story connected with the case, in which the only magic was the dexterity of Anne Robinson and the simplicity of the spectators. She had fixed long horse hairs to some of the crockery, and placed wires under others, by which she could throw them down without touching them. Other things she dexterously threw about, which the spectators, who did not watch her motions, imputed to invisible agency. At times, when the family were absent, she loosened the hold of the strings by which the hams, bacon, and similar articles were suspended, so that they fell on the slightest motion. She employed some simple chemical secrets, and, delighted with the success of her pranks, pushed them farther than she at first intended. Such was the solution of the whole mystery, which, known by the name of the Stock-well ghost, terrified many well-meaning persons, and had been nearly as famous as that of Cock Lane, which may be hinted at as another imposture of the same kind. So many and wonderful are the appearances described, that when I first met with the original publication I was strongly im-pressed with the belief that the narrative was like some of Swift's advertisements, a jocular experiment upon the credu-lity of the public. But it was certainly published *bona fide*, and Mr. Hone, on the authority of Mr. Brayfield, has since fully explained the wonder.*

Many such impositions have been detected, and many others have been successfully concealed; but to know what has been discovered in many instances gives us the assur-ance of the ruling cause in all. I remember a scene of the kind attempted to be got up near Edinburgh, but detected at once by a sheriff's officer, a sort of persons whose habits of incredulity and suspicious observation render them very dangerous spectators on such occasions. The late excellent Mr. Walker, minister at Dunottar, in the Mearns, gave me a curious account of an imposture of this kind, practised by a young country girl, who was surprisingly quick at throwing stones, turf, and other missiles, with such dexterity that it was for a long time impossible to ascertain her agency in the disturbances of which she was the sole cause.

The belief of the spectators that such scenes of disturb-ance arise from invisible beings will appear less surprising if we consider the common feats of jugglers, or professors of legerdemain, and recollect that it is only the frequent exhi-bition of such powers which reconciles us to them as matters of course, although they are wonders at which in our fathers' time men would have cried out either sorcery or miracles. The spectator also, who has been himself duped, makes no very respectable appearance when convicted of his error ; and thence, if too candid to add to the evidence of super-natural agency, is yet unwilling to stand convicted by

* See Hone's "Every-Day Book," p. 62.

cross-examination, of having been imposed on, and unconsciously becomes disposed rather to colour more highly than the truth, than acquiesce in an explanation resting on his having been too hasty a believer. Very often, too, the detection depends upon the combination of certain circumstances, which, apprehended, necessarily explain the whole story.

For example, I once heard a sensible and intelligent friend in company express himself convinced of the truth of a wonderful story, told him by an intelligent and bold man, about an apparition. The scene lay in an ancient castle on the coast of Morven or the Isle of Mull, where the ghost-seer chanced to be resident. He was given to understand by the family, when betaking himself to rest, that the chamber in which he slept was occasionally disquieted by supernatural appearances. Being at that time no believer in such stories, he attended little to this hint, until the witching hour of night, when he was awakened from a dead sleep by the pressure of a human hand on his body. He looked up at the figure of a tall Highlander, in the antique and picturesque dress of his country, only that his brows were bound with a bloody bandage. Struck with sudden and extreme fear, he was willing to have sprung from bed, but the spectre stood before him in the bright moonlight, its one arm extended so as to master him if he attempted to rise ; the other hand held up in a warning and grave posture, as menacing the Lowlander if he should attempt to quit his recumbent position. Thus he lay in mortal agony for more than an hour, after which it pleased the spectre of ancient days to leave him to more sound repose. So singular a story had on its side the usual number of votes from the company, till, upon cross-examination, it was explained that the principal person concerned was an exciseman. After which *eclaircissement* the same explanation struck all present, viz., the Highlanders of the mansion had chosen to detain the exciseman by the apparition of an ancient heroic ghost, in order to disguise from his vigilance the removal of certain modern enough spirits, which his duty might have called upon him to seize. Here a single circumstance explained the whole ghost story.

At other times it happens that the meanness and trifling nature of a cause not very obvious to observation has occasioned it to be entirely overlooked, even on account of that very meanness, since no one is willing to acknowledge that he has been alarmed by a cause of little consequence, and which he would be ashamed of mentioning. An incident of this sort happened to a gentleman of birth and distinction, who is well known in the political world, and was detected by the precision of his observation. Shortly after he succeeded to his estate and title, there was a rumour among his servants concerning a strange noise heard in the family mansion at night, the cause of which they had found it impossible to trace. The gentleman resolved to watch himself, with a domestic who had grown old in the family, and who had begun to murmur strange things concerning the knocking having followed so close upon the death of his old master. They watched until the noise was heard, which they listened to with that strange uncertainty attending midnight sounds which prevents the hearers from immediately tracing them to the spot where they arise, while the silence of the night generally occasions the imputing to them more than the due importance which they would receive if mingled with the usual noises of daylight. At length the gentleman and his servant traced the sounds which they had repeatedly heard to a small store-room used as a place for keeping provisions of various kinds for the family, of which the old butler had the key. They entered this place, and remained there for some time without hearing the noises which they had traced thither ; at length the sound was heard, but much lower than it had formerly seemed to be, while acted upon at a distance by the imagination of the hearers. The cause was immediately discovered. A rat caught in an old-fashioned trap had occasioned this tumult by its efforts to escape, in which it was able to raise the trap-door of its prison to a certain

height, but was then obliged to drop it. The noise of the
fall, resounding through the house, had occasioned the disturbance which, but for the cool investigation of the proprietor, might easily have established an accredited ghost
story. The circumstance was told me by the gentleman to
whom it happened.

There are other occasions in which the ghost story is rendered credible by some remarkable combination of circumstances very unlikely to have happened, and which no one
could have supposed unless some particular fortune occasioned a discovery.

An apparition which took place at Plymouth is well known,
but it has been differently related ; and having some reason
to think the following edition correct, it is an incident so
much to my purpose that you must pardon its insertion.

A club of persons connected with science and literature
was formed at the great sea-town I have named. During
the summer months the society met in a cave by the sea-
shore ; during those of autumn and winter they convened
within the premises of a tavern, but, for the sake of privacy,
had their meetings in a summer-house situated in the
garden, at a distance from the main building. Some of the
members to whom the position of their own dwellings
rendered this convenient, had a pass-key to the garden-
door, by which they could enter the garden and reach the
summer-house without the publicity or trouble of passing
through the open tavern. It was the rule of this club that
its members presided alternately. On one occasion, in the
winter, the president of the evening chanced to be very ill;
indeed, was reported to be on his death-bed. The club met
as usual, and, from a sentiment of respect, left vacant the
chair which ought to have been occupied by him if in his
usual health ; for the same reason, the conversation turned
upon the absent gentleman's talents, and the loss expected
to the society by his death. While they were upon this
melancholy theme, the door suddenly opened, and the appearance of the president entered the room. He wore a

white wrapper, a nightcap round his brow, the appearance of which was that of death itself. He stalked into the room with unusual gravity, took the vacant place of ceremony, lifted the empty glass which stood before him, bowed around, and put it to his lips; then replaced it on the table, and stalked out of the room as silent as he had entered it. The company remained deeply appalled; at length, after many observations on the strangeness of what they had seen, they resolved to dispatch two of their number as ambassadors, to see how it fared with the president, who had thus strangely appeared among them. They went, and returned with the frightful intelligence that the friend after whom they had enquired was that evening deceased.

The astonished party then resolved that they would remain absolutely silent respecting the wonderful sight which they had seen. Their habits were too philosophical to permit them to believe that they had actually seen the ghost of their deceased brother, and at the same time they were too wise men to wish to confirm the superstition of the vulgar by what might seem indubitable evidence of a ghost. The affair was therefore kept a strict secret, although, as usual, some dubious rumours of the tale found their way to the public. Several years afterwards, an old woman who had long filled the place of a sick-nurse, was taken very ill, and on her death-bed was attended by a medical member of the philosophical club. To him, with many expressions of regret, she acknowledged that she had long before attended Mr. ——, naming the president whose appearance had surprised the club so strangely, and that she felt distress of conscience on account of the manner in which he died. She said that as his malady was attended by light-headedness, she had been directed to keep a close watch upon him during his illness. Unhappily she slept, and during her sleep the patient had awaked and left the apartment. When, on her own awaking, she found the bed empty and the patient gone, she forthwith hurried out of the house to seek him, and met him in the act of returning. She got him, she said, replaced in bed, but it was only to die there. She added, to convince her hearer of the truth of what she said, that immediately after the poor gentleman expired, a deputation of two members from the club came to enquire after their president's health, and received for answer that he was already dead. This confession explained the whole matter. The delirious patient had very naturally taken the road to the club, from some recollections of his duty of the night. In approaching and retiring from the apartment he had used one of the pass-keys already mentioned, which made his way shorter. On the other hand, the gentlemen sent to enquire after his health had reached his lodging by a more circuitous road ; and thus there had been time for him to return to what proved his death-bed, long before they reached his chamber. The philosophical witnesses of this strange scene were now as anxious to spread the story as they had formerly been to conceal it, since it showed in what a remarkable manner men's eyes might turn traitors to them, and impress them with ideas far different from the truth.

Another occurrence of the same kind, although scarcely so striking in its circumstances, was yet one which, had it remained unexplained, might have passed as an indubitable instance of a supernatural apparition.

A Teviotdale farmer was riding from a fair, at which he had indulged himself with John Barleycorn, but not to that extent of defying goblins which it inspired into the gallant Tam o' Shanter. He was pondering with some anxiety upon the dangers of travelling alone on a solitary road which passed the corner of a churchyard, now near at hand, when he saw before him in the moonlight a pale female form standing upon the very wall which surrounded the ceme- tery. The road was very narrow, with no opportunity of giving the apparent phantom what seamen call a wide berth. It was, however, the only path which led to the rider's home, who therefore resolved, at all risks, to pass the apparition. He accordingly approached, as slowly as possible, the spot where the spectre stood, while the figure remained, now perfectly still and silent, now brandishing its arms and gibbering to the moon. When the farmer came close to the spot he dashed in the spurs and set the horse off upon a gallop ; but the spectre did not miss its opportunity. As he passed the corner where she was perched, she contrived to drop behind the horseman and seize him round the waist, a manœuvre which greatly increased the speed of the horse and the terror of the rider ; for the hand of her who sat behind him, when pressed upon his, felt as cold as that of a corpse. At his own house at length he arrived, and bid the servants who came to attend him, " Tak aff the ghaist !" They took off accordingly a female in white, and the poor farmer himself was conveyed to bed, where he lay struggling for weeks with a strong nervous fever. The female was found to be a maniac, who had been left a widow very suddenly by an affectionate husband, and the nature and cause of her malady induced her, when she could make her escape, to wander to the churchyard, where she sometimes wildly wept over his grave, and sometimes, standing on the corner of the churchyard wall, looked out, and mistook every stranger on horseback for the husband she had lost. If this woman, which was very possible, had dropt from the horse unobserved by him whom she had made her involuntary companion, it would have been very hard to have convinced the honest farmer that he had not actually performed part of his journey with a ghost behind him.

There is also a large class of stories of this sort, where various secrets of chemistry, of acoustics, ventriloquism, or other arts, have been either employed to dupe the spectators, or have tended to do so through mere accident and coincidence. Of these it is scarce necessary to quote instances ; but the following may be told as a tale recounted by a foreign nobleman known to me nearly thirty years ago, whose life, lost in the service of his sovereign, proved too short for his friends and his native land.

At a certain old castle on the confines of Hungary, the lord to whom it belonged had determined upon giving an entertainment worthy of his own rank and of the magnificence of the antique mansion which he inhabited. The guests of course were numerous, and among them was a veteran officer of hussars, remarkable for his bravery. When the arrangements for the night were made this officer was informed that there would be difficulty in accommodating the company in the castle, large as was, unless some one would take the risk of sleeping in a room supposed to be haunted, and that, as he was known to be above such prejudices, the apartment was in the first place proposed for his occupation, as the person least likely to suffer a bad night's rest from such a cause. The major thankfully accepted the preference, and having shared the festivity of the evening, retired after midnight, having denounced vengeance against any one who should presume by any trick to disturb his repose ; a threat which his habits would, it was supposed, render him sufficiently ready to execute. Somewhat contrary to the custom in these cases, the major went to bed, having left his candle burning and laid his trusty pistols, carefully loaded, on the table by his bedside.

He had not slept an hour when he was awakened by a solemn strain of music. He looked out. Three ladies, fantastically dressed in green, were seen in the lower end of the apartment, who sung a solemn requiem. The major listened for some time with delight; at length he tired. "Ladies," he said, "this is very well, but somewhat monotonous—will you be so kind as to change the tune?" The ladies continued singing ; he expostulated, but the music was not interrupted. The major began to grow angry: "Ladies," he said, " I must consider this as a trick for the purpose of terrifying me, and as I regard it as an impertinence, I shall take a rough mode of stopping it." With that he began to handle his pistols. The ladies sung on. He then got seriously angry : " I will but wait five minutes," he said, "and then fire without hesitation." The song was uninterrupted—the five minutes were expired. " I still give you law, ladies," he said, " while I count twenty." This produced as little effect as his former threats. He counted one, two, three accordingly ; but on approaching the end of the number, and repeating more than once his determination to fire, the last numbers, seventeen—eighteen—nineteen, were pronounced with considerable pauses between, and an assurance that the pistols were cocked. The ladies sun on. As he pronounced the word twenty he fired both pistols against the musical damsels—but the ladies sung on ! The major was overcome by the unexpected inefficacy of his violence, and had an illness which lasted more than three weeks. The trick put upon him may be shortly described by the fact that the female choristers were placed in an adjoining room, and that he only fired at their reflection thrown forward into that in which he slept by the effect of a concave mirror.

Other stories of the same kind are numerous and well known. The apparition of the Brocken mountain, after having occasioned great admiration and some fear, is now ascertained by philosophers to be a gigantic reflection, which makes the traveller's shadow, represented upon the misty clouds, appear a colossal figure of almost immeasurable size. By a similar deception men have been induced, in Westmoreland and other mountainous countries, to imagine they saw troops of horse and armies marching and countermarching, which were in fact only the reflection of horses pasturing upon an opposite height, or of the forms of peaceful travellers.

A very curious case of this kind was communicated to me by the son of the lady principally concerned, and tends to show out of what mean materials a venerable apparition may be sometimes formed. In youth this lady resided with her father, a man of sense and resolution. Their house was situated in the principal street of a town of some size. The back part of the house ran at right angles to an Anabaptist chapel, divided from it by a small cabbage-garden. The young lady used sometimes to indulge the romantic love of solitude by sitting in her own apartment in the evening till twilight, and even darkness, was approaching. One evening, while she was thus placed, she was surprised to see a gleamy figure, as of some aerial being, hovering, as it were, against the arched window in the end of the Anabaptist chapel. Its head was surrounded by that halo which painters give to the Catholic saints ; and while the young lady's attention was fixed on an object so extraordinary, the figure bent gracefully towards her more than once, as if intimating a sense of her presence, and then disappeared. The seer of this striking vision descended to her family, so much discomposed as to call her father's attention. He obtained an account of the cause of her disturbance, and expressed his intention to watch in the apartment next night. He sat accordingly in his daughter's chamber, where she also attended him. Twilight came, and nothing appeared ; but as the gray light faded into darkness, the same female figure was seen hovering on the window ; the same shadowy form, the same pale light around the head, the same inclinations, as the evening before. "What do you think of this ?" said the daughter to the astonished father. "Anything, my dear," said the father, "rather than allow that we look upon what is supernatural." A strict research established a natural cause for the appearance on the window. It was the custom of an old woman, to whom the garden beneath was rented, to go out at night to gather cabbages. The lantern she carried in her hand threw up the refracted reflection of her form on the chapel window. As she stooped to gather her cabbages the reflection appeared to bend forward ; and that was the whole matter.

Another species of deception, affecting the credit of such supernatural communications, arises from the dexterity and skill of the authors who have made it their business to present such stories in the shape most likely to attract belief. Defoe—whose power in rendering credible that which was in itself very much the reverse was so peculiarly distinguished—has not failed to show his superiority in this species of composition. A bookseller of his acquaintance had, in the trade phrase, rather overprinted an edition of " Drelincourt on Death," and complained to Defoe of the loss which was likely to ensue. The experienced book-maker, with the purpose of recommending the edition, advised his friend to prefix the celebrated narrative of Mrs. Veal's ghost, which he wrote for the occasion, with such an air of truth, that although in fact it does not afford a single tittle of evidence properly so called, it nevertheless was swallowed so eagerly by the people that Drelincourt's work on death, which the supposed spirit recommended to the perusal of her friend Mrs. Bargrave, instead of sleeping on the editor's shelf, moved off by thousands at once ; the story, incredible in itself, and unsupported as it was by evidence or enquiry, was received as true, merely from the cunning of the narrator, and the addition of a number of adventitious circumstances, which no man alive could have conceived as having occurred to the mind of a person composing a fiction.

It did not require the talents of Defoe, though in that species of composition he must stand unrivalled, to fix the public attention on a ghost story. John Dunton, a man of scribbling celebrity at the time, succeeded to a great degree in imposing upon the public a tale which he calls the Apparition Evidence. The beginning of it, at least (for it is of great length), has something in it a little new. At Myne-head, in Somersetshire, lived an ancient gentlewoman named Mrs. Leckie, whose only son and duughter resided in family with her. The son traded to Ireland, and was supposed to be worth eight or ten thousand pounds. They had a child about five or six years old. This family was generally re-spected in Mynehead ; and especially Mrs. Leckie, the old lady, was so pleasant in society, that her friends used to say to her, and to each other, that it was a thousand pities such an excellent, good-humoured gentlewoman must, from her age, be soon lost to her friends. To which Mrs. Leckie often made the somewhat startling reply : " Forasmuch as you now seem to like me, I am afraid you will but little care to see or speak with me after my death, though I believe you may have that satisfaction." Die, however, she did, and after her funeral was repeatedly seen in her personal likeness, at home and abroad, by night and by noonday.

One story is told of a doctor of physic walking into the fields, who in his return met with this spectre, whom he at first accosted civilly, and paid her the courtesy of handing her over a stile. Observing, however, that she did not move her lips in speaking, or her eyes in looking round, he became suspicious of the condition of his companion, and showed some desire to be rid of her society. Offended at this, the hag at next stile planted herself upon it, and obstructed his passage. He got through at length with some difficulty, and not without a sound kick, and an admonition to pay more attention to the next aged gentlewoman whom he met. " But this," says John Dunton, " was a petty and inconsiderable prank to what she played in her son's house and elsewhere. She would at noonday appear upon the quay of Mynehead, and cry, ' A boat, a boat, ho ! a boat, a boat, ho ! ' If any boatmen or seamen were in sight, and did not come, they were sure to be cast away ; and if they did come, 'twas all one, they were cast away. It was equally dangerous to please and displease her. Her son had several ships sailing between Ireland and England ; no sooner did they make land, and come in sight of England, but this ghost would appear in the same garb and likeness as when she was alive, and, standing at the mainmast, would blow with a whistle, and though it were never so great a calm, yet immediately there would arise a most dreadful storm, that would break, wreck, and drown the ship and goods ; only the seamen would escape with their lives—the devil had no permission from God to take them away. Yet at this rate, by her frequent apparitions and disturbances, she had made a poor merchant

of her son, for his fair estate was all buried in the sea, and
he that was once worth thousands was reduced to a very
poor and low condition in the world ; for whether the ship
were his own or hired, or he had but goods on board
it to the value of twenty shillings, this troublesome ghost
would come as before, whistle in a calm at the mainmast at noonday, when they had descried land, and
then ship and goods went all out of hand to wreck ;
insomuch that he could at last get no ships wherein to
stow his goods, nor any mariner to sail in them ; for knowing what an uncomfortable, fatal, and losing voyage they
should make of it, they did all decline his service. In her
son's house she hath her constant haunts by day and night ;
but whether he did not, or would not own if he did, see her,
he always professed he never saw her. Sometimes when in
bed with his wife, she would cry out, ' Husband, look,
there's your mother !' And when he would turn to the
right side, then was she gone to the left ; and when to the
left side of the bed, then was she gone to the right ; only
one evening their only child, a girl of about five or six years
old, lying in a ruckle-bed under them, cries out, ' Oh, help
me, father ! help me, mother ! for grandmother will choke
me !' and before they could get to their child's assistance
she had murdered it ; they finding the poor girl dead, her
throat having been pinched by two fingers, which stopped
her breath and strangled her. This was the sorest of all
their afflictions ; their estate is gone, and now their child is
gone also ; you may guess at their grief and great sorrow.
One morning after the child's funeral, her husband being
abroad, about eleven in the forenoon, Mrs. Leckie the
younger goes up into her chamber to dress her head,
and as she was looking into the glass she spies her mother-
in-law, the old beldam, looking over her shoulder. This
cast her into a great horror ; but recollecting her affrighted
spirits, and recovering the exercise of her reason, faith, and
hope, having cast up a short and silent prayer to God, she
turns about, and bespeaks her : ' In the name of God,

mother, why do you trouble me?' 'Peace,' says the
spectrum; 'I will do thee no hurt.' 'What will you have
of me?' says the daughter," &c.* Dunton, the narrator and
probably the contriver of the story, proceeds to inform us at
length of a commission which the wife of Mr. Leckie
receives from the ghost to deliver to Atherton, Bishop of
Waterford, a guilty and unfortunate man, who afterwards
died by the hands of the executioner; but that part of the
subject is too disagreeable and tedious to enter upon.

So deep was the impression made by the story on the
inhabitants of Mynehead, that it is said the tradition of
Mrs. Leckie still remains in that port, and that mariners
belonging to it often, amid tempestuous weather, conceive
they hear the whistle-call of the implacable hag who was the
source of so much mischief to her own family. However,
already too desultory and too long, it would become in-
tolerably tedious were I to insist farther on the peculiar
sort of genius by which stories of this kind may be
embodied and prolonged.

I may, however, add, that the charm of the tale depends
much upon the age of the person to whom it is addressed;
and that the vivacity of fancy which engages us in youth to
pass over much that is absurd, in order to enjoy some single
trait of imagination, dies within us when we obtain the age
of manhood, and the sadder and graver regions which lie
beyond it. I am the more conscious of this, because I have
been myself at two periods of my life, distant from each
other, engaged in scenes favourable to that degree of
superstitious awe which my countrymen expressively call
being *eerie.*

On the first of these occasions I was only ninteeen or
twenty years old, when I happened to pass a night in the
magnificent old baronial castle of Glammis, the hereditary
seat of the Earls of Strathmore. The hoary pile contains
much in its appearance, and in the traditions connected
with it, impressive to the imagination. It was the scene of

* "Apparition Evidence."

the murder of a Scottish king of great antiquity ; not indeed the gracious Duncan, with whom the name naturally associates itself, but Malcolm the Second. It contains also a curious monument of the peril of feudal times, being a secret chamber, the entrance of which, by the law or custom of the family, must only be known to three persons at once, viz., the Earl of Strathmore, his heir apparent, and any third person whom they may take into their confidence. The extreme antiquity of the building is vouched by the immense thickness of the walls, and the wild and straggling arrangement of the accommodation within doors. As the late Earl of Strathmore seldom resided in that ancient mansion, it was, when I was there, but half-furnished, and that with movables of great antiquity, which, with the pieces of chivalric armour hanging upon the walls, greatly contributed to the general effect of the whole. After a very hospitable reception from the late Peter Proctor, Esq., then seneschal of the castle, in Lord Strathmore's absence, I was conducted to my apartment in a distant corner of the building. I must own, that as I heard door after door shut, after my conductor had retired, I began to consider myself too far from the living and somewhat too near the dead. We had passed through what is called "The King's Room," a vaulted apartment, garnished with stags' antlers and similar trophies of the chase, and said by tradition to be the spot of Malcolm's murder, and I had an idea of the vicinity of the castle chapel.

In spite of the truth of history, the whole night-scene in Macbeth's castle rushed at once upon my mind, and struck my imagination more forcibly than even when I have seen its terrors represented by the late John Kemble and his inimitable sister. In a word, I experienced sensations which, though not remarkable either for timidity or superstition, did not fail to affect me to the point of being disagreeable, while they were mingled at the same time with a strange and indescribable kind of pleasure, the recollection of which affords me gratification at this moment.

In the year 1814 accident placed me, then past middle life, in a situation somewhat similar to that which I have described.

I had been on a pleasure voyage with some friends around the north coast of Scotland, and in that course had arrived in the salt-water lake under the castle of Dunvegan, whose turrets, situated upon a frowning rock, rise immediately above the waves of the loch. As most of the party, and I myself in particular, chanced to be well known to the Laird of Macleod, we were welcomed to the castle with Highland hospitality, and glad to find ourselves in polished society, after a cruise of some duration. The most modern part of the castle was founded in the days of James VI. ; the more ancient is referred to a period " whose birth tradition notes not." Until the present Macleod connected by a drawbridge the site of the castle with the mainland of Skye, the access must have been extremely difficult. Indeed, so much greater was the regard paid to security than to convenience, that in former times the only access to the mansion arose through a vaulted cavern in a rock, up which a staircase ascended from the sea-shore, like the buildings we read of in the romances of Mrs. Radcliffe.

Such a castle, in the extremity of the Highlands, was of course furnished with many a tale of tradition, and many a superstitious legend, to fill occasional intervals in the music and song, as proper to the halls of Dunvegan as when Johnson commemorated them. We reviewed the arms and ancient valuables of this distinguished family—saw the dirk and broadsword of Rorie Mhor, and his horn, which would drench three chiefs of these degenerate days. The solemn drinking-cup of the Kings of Man must not be forgotten, nor the fairy banner given to Macleod by the Queen of Fairies ; that magic flag which has been victorious in two pitched fields, and will still float in the third, the bloodiest and the last, when the Elfin Sovereign shall, after the fight is ended, recall her banner, and carry off the standard-bearer.

Amid such tales of ancient tradition I had from Macleod

and his lady the courteous offer of the haunted apartment of the castle, about which, as a stranger, I might be supposed interested. Accordingly, I took possession of it about the witching hour. Except perhaps some tapestry hangings, and the extreme thickness of the walls, which argued great antiquity, nothing could have been more comfortable than the interior of the apartment; but if you looked from the windows the view was such as to correspond with the highest tone of superstition. An autumnal blast, sometimes driving mist before it, swept along the troubled billows of the lake, which it occasionally concealed, and by fits disclosed. The waves rushed in wild disorder on the shore, and covered with foam the steep piles of rock, which, rising from the sea in forms something resembling the human figure, have obtained the name of Macleod's Maidens, and in such a night seemed no bad representatives of the Norwegian goddesses called Choosers of the Slain, or Riders of the Storm. There was something of the dignity of danger in the scene; for on a platform beneath the windows lay an ancient battery of cannon, which had sometimes been used against privateers even of late years. The distant scene was a view of that part of the Quillan mountains which are called, from their form, Macleod's Dining-Tables. The voice of an angry cascade, termed the Nurse of Rorie Mhor, because that chief slept best in its vicinity, was heard from time to time mingling its notes with those of wind and wave. Such was the haunted room at Dunvegan, and as such it well deserved a less sleepy inhabitant. In the language of Dr. Johnson, who has stamped his memory on this remote place, " I looked around me, and wondered that I was not more affected ; but the mind is not at all times equally ready to be moved." In a word, it is necessary to confess that, of all I heard or saw, the most engaging spectacle was the comfortable bed, in which I hoped to make amends for some rough nights on ship-board, and where I slept accordingly without thinking of ghost or goblin till I was called by my servant in the morning.

From this I am taught to infer that tales of ghosts and demonology are out of date at forty years and upwards; that it is only in the morning of life that this feeling of superstition " comes o'er us like a summer cloud," affecting us with fear which is solemn and awful rather than painful; and I am tempted to think that, if I were to write on the subject at all, it should have been during a period of life when I could have treated it with more interesting vivacity, and might have been at least amusing if I could not be instructive. Even the present fashion of the world seems to be ill suited for studies of this fantastic nature; and the most ordinary mechanic has learning sufficient to laugh at the figments which in former times were believed by persons far advanced in the deepest knowledge of the age.

I cannot, however, in conscience carry my opinion of my countrymen's good sense so far as to exculpate them entirely from the charge of credulity. Those who are disposed to look for them may, without much trouble, see such manifest signs, both of superstition and the disposition to believe in its doctrines, as may render it no useless occupation to compare the follies of our fathers with our own. The sailors have a proverb that every man in his lifetime must eat a peck of impurity; and it seems yet more clear that every generation of the human race must swallow a certain measure of nonsense. There remains hope, however, that the grosser faults of our ancestors are now out of date; and that whatever follies the present race may be guilty of, the sense of humanity is too universally spread to permit them to think of tormenting wretches till they confess what is impossible, and then burning them for their pains.

THE END.

PRINTED BY BALLANTYNE, HANSON AND CO.
LONDON AND EDINBURGH

LETTERS ON DEMONOLOGY AND WITCHCRAFT

by
SIR WALTER SCOTT, BART.

EDITIONS

First Edition addressed to J. G. Lockhart, Esq. pp. ix. 402. John Murray: London, 1830. 12°.

Another Issue addressed to J. G. Lockhart, Esq. pp. ix. 402. 12 plates designed by George Cruikshank. John Murray: London, 1830. 12°.

American Edition addressed to J. G. Lockhart, Esq. pp. ix. 338. Harper & Bros: New York, 1845. 12°

Another Issue. In a series of letters addressed to J. G. Lockhart. Illustrated. pp. xi. 406. William Tegg: London, 1876. 8°.

Another Issue with an introduction by Henry Morley. pp. 320. George Routledge & Sons: London, 1884. 8°. *Histoire de la demonologie et de la sorcellerie.* Trans: A. Defauconpret. Paris: 1832.

Briefe über Dämonologie und Hexerei. Trans: G. N. Bärmann. Zwickau: 1833.

Other editions: American 1831, 1855. Italian 1839. Spanish 1876.

INDEX

Aberfoyle, parish of, 136
Academy of Science, French, 215
Adamson, Patrick, 130
Addison, Joseph (iii), 218
Adrian VI, Pope, 188
Advocates' Library, 101
Agrippa, Cornelius, 155, 157, 158
Alciatus, 169
Alexander III, King of Scots, 112
Ananias, 79
Angus, Earl of, 230
Apuleius, 86, 251
Arniston, Robert of, lawyer (See: Dundas, Robert)
Arthur, King, 104, 110-111, 145
Asmund, 90
Asiatics, 97, 103
Assueit, 90, 91, 92
Astrologers, 276ff
Athens, 84
Attila, 104
Aubrey, John, (vi), 45
Augustus, 161
Auldearne, witches of, 231, 234
Ayrshire, 123
Azrael, 48

Baal, 51, 52
Bacon, Francis, 160
Baird, James, 126
Balduinus, Franciscus, 168
Balquidder, parish of, 136
Barclay, Margaret, 134, 255-262
Barton, William, 231
Bedford, 219
Bedford, Duke of, 164
Beltane, 78, 82

Berlin, 25, 37. Royal Society of, 36, Philosophical Society of, 25
Blue Devils (malady), 22
Bodenham, Anne, (xix), (xx)
Bodin, Jean, (xii), 157
Boetius, Hector, historian, (xv), 229
Bordeaux, 170, 171
Borgia, Cardinal Steven, 71n
Boswell, James, 296
Bothwell, James Hepburn, Earl of, (viii), 84, 250
Bromley, Sir Edward, 202
Brown Dwarf, 98
Brown, William, 136
Brutus, 16, 17
Buchanan, George, historian, (xv), 229
Buckingham, Duke of, 184, 279
Butler, Samuel, (xv)
Burns, Robert, (vi), 44

Caesar, 16, 89
Calamy & Baxter, lawyers, 206, 209, 210
Callendar, Rose, witch, 213
Cambro-Briton (See: Obi Woman)
Camelot (Camlan), 111
Cameronians, 74
Canidia, sorceress, 85
Castillo, Don Bernal Dias de, (iv), 18
Castor and Pollux, (iii), 17
Celtic tribes, 78, 97, 98, 99, 100, 102, 105, 109, 110, 144, 145, 149
Ceres, (viii), 82
Charlemagne, 104
Charles II, King, 213
Chaucer, 144, 145, 148
Chorley, Forest, 147

[v]